WOMEN

AND

DISASTERS

WOMEN AND DISASTERS

From Theory To Practice

Edited by

Brenda D. Phillips and
Betty Hearn Morrow

Library of Congress Control Number: 2007909804
ISBN: Hardcover   978-1-4363-0880-9
                         Softcover   978-1-4363-0879-3

This book was printed in the United States of America.

This is the third book in the series on disaster published with the support of the International Reseach Committee on Disasters. The first two volumes were:

Quarantelli, E. L., ed. (1998) *What is a Disaster? Perspectives on the Question.* London: Routledge.

Stallings, Robert A., ed. (2002) *Methods of Disaster Research.* Philadelphia, PA: Xlibris.

Cover photo is provided courtesy of the Mennonite Disaster Service.

To order additional copies of this book, contact:
Xlibris Corporation
1-888-795-4274
www.Xlibris.com
Orders@Xlibris.com
24261

CONTENTS

LIST OF FIGURES

LIST OF TABLES

Dedicated with sincere appreciation to

Verta Taylor

and Mary Fran Myers

For making a difference to women who face disasters,
and to those who research disasters
and to those practice disaster management

CONTRIBUTORS

Cheryl Childers is associate professor of sociology at Washburn University in Topeka, Kansas, and is also Director of its Center for Diversity Studies. She currently serves as Book and Film Review Editor for the journal *International Journal of Mass Emergencies and Disasters*. She is one of the authors of *A Social Vulnerability Approach to Disasters*, which is part of FEMA's Higher Education Project. She teaches Sociology of Disasters, and speaks to professional and community groups about vulnerability to disasters. Her research interests include race/class/gender/age as contributing factors in the social construction of vulnerability to being in disaster and recovery after disaster. She also studies organizational behavior in disaster. She is currently Principal Investigator for a multi-site study examining the role of voluntary organizations in disaster relief and recovery.

Dr. Elaine Enarson is an American disaster sociologist currently teaching full-time in the Applied Disaster and Emergency Studies Department of Brandon University in Manitoba, Canada. The author of *Woods-Working Women: Sexual Integration in the U.S. Forest Service* (1984) and co-editor of the international reader *The Gendered Terrain of Disaster: Through Women's Eyes* (1998), her research and publications have addressed social vulnerability issues with particular emphasis on women and gender. Among these are studies of the impacts of Hurricane Andrew on women, response and preparedness in US and Canadian domestic violence agencies, women's paid and paid work in the Red River Valley flood, gender patterns in flood evacuation, women's human rights in disasters, the impacts of drought and earthquake on rural Indian women, gender, work and employment in disasters, and strategies for addressing high-risk social groups in local emergency management. Elaine has co-convened numerous workshops on gender and disaster risk reduction and collaborated with UN agencies on gender and disaster risk reduction initiatives. Before relocating to Canada, she was lead course developer of a FEMA course on social vulnerability, project manager of a grassroots risk assessment project with women in the Caribbean and director of the on-line Gender and Disaster Sourcebook initiative. In 2005, Elaine was the recipient of the Mary Fran Myers Gender and Disaster Award.

Maureen Fordham is a senior lecturer in disaster management at the University of Northumbria, Divisions of Geography and Environmental Management in Newcastle upon Tyne, United Kingdom. She served as the first woman Editor of *the International Journal of Mass Emergencies and Disasters* and serves as webmaster for the Gender and Disaster Network web site. Her research interests include sustainable hazard and disaster policy and management, vulnerable groups, community-based disaster/risk management, disaster and development linkages and research methods. Her interests in environmental management issues led her to serve as Rapporteur for the United Nations Expert Group Meeting on Environmental Management and the Mitigation of Natural Disasters: A gender Perspective. She has published many chapters and refereed papers including *Environmental Hazards*, the *Australian Journal of Disaster Management, Disasters, Disaster Prevention and Management* and others. In 2006, Maureen received the Mary Fran Myers Gender and Disaster Award.

Alice Fothergill is an assistant professor in the Sociology Department at the University of Vermont. Her areas of interest include family and childhood studies, disasters, gender, inequality, and qualitative methods. Her book, *Heads Above Water: Gender, Class, and Family in the Grand Forks Flood* (SUNY Press 2004), examines women's experiences in the 1997 flood in Grand Forks, North Dakota. Professor Fothergill has also conducted research on volunteerism in the aftermath of the September 11, 2001 terrorist attacks in New York City. Currently, she is conducting a research project on children and youth in Louisiana in the aftermath of Hurricane Katrina.

Richard Krajeski serves as a resource consultant for the Center for Hazards Assessment, Response and Technology at the University of New Orleans. His current readings and writings are social and ethical issues in development and resiliency especially as they relate to vulnerability. His academic background includes degrees in philosophy and theology. His doctoral studies were in the area of applied technology and ethics. He has an extensive background in psychology, organizational and grassroots community organizing and development, and volunteer management. Rev. Krajeski's disaster response experience includes addressing long-term emotional health issues, preparedness and mitigation efforts, local capacity building and sustainable development. He is a member of the Presbyterian Disaster Response Team, and served as a member of the national Presbyterian Disaster Response Advisory Committee. With his wife, Rev. Kristina J. Peterson, he has contributed significantly to the disaster response materials used by the religious community. He has been an invited presenter, keynote speaker and panel chair at the Natural Hazards Workshop in Boulder, Colorado. He has been a presenter at the International Society for Applied Anthropology and the Federal Emergency Management Agency Family and Community Preparedness Workshops on vulnerable populations. Rev. Krajeski was awarded the Disaster Response Meritorious Service Award by Church World Services in 1999 for "his outstanding work as an advocate with marginalized people and for being the conscience of Church World Service disaster response." He is a Fellow in the International Society for Applied Anthropology and is the parish associate at Bayou Blue Presbyterian Church.

William Lovekamp is an assistant professor of sociology at Eastern Illinois University. He holds a Ph.D. in Sociology from Southern Illinois University. His areas of specialization include sociology of disasters, environmental sociology, collective behavior, social movements, race and ethnic relations and gender. His dissertation research examined community level variations in disaster preparedness, risk and recovery in earthquake-stricken communities in California with a specific focus on gender, race, ethnicity, and social class. He is currently researching perceived tornado and earthquake risk and preparedness of college students and the capacity of Universities to integrate various elements of the FEMA Disaster Resistant University Initiative. He also serves as an advisory council member of and co-chair of the Disaster Action Team of his local American Red Cross office and faculty representative to the Illinois Homeland Security Education Alliance.

Betty Hearn Morrow is professor emeritus at Florida International University and former director of the Social and Behavioral Lab at the International Hurricane Center. Her work focuses on human and social factors contributing to the ability of individuals, families and communities to respond to hazards. A national panel she chaired recently at the Heinz Center for Science, Economics and the Environment resulted in the book, *Human Links to Coastal Disasters*. She co-edited a collection of women's experiences as disaster survivors and responders, *The Gendered Terrain of Disaster*. For the last decade, she has worked with a research team to analyze the effects of Hurricane Andrew on South Florida, funded by the National Science Foundation and resulting in the co-authored book, *Ethnicity, Gender and the Sociology of Disaster* as well as numerous related presentations and publications. She retired from academic in 2003, but continues an active research agenda as a consulting sociologist. In 2003, Berty received the Mary Fran Myers Gender and Disaster Award.

Jane Ollenburger is a professor at California State Polytechnic University Pomona in California. She holds her Ph.D. in Sociology from the University of Nebraska at Lincoln. Her current research interests include gender inequities in risk assessments for incarcerated women, and the effects of post-traumatic stress disorders on elderly victims of disasters. Recent publications include *Essential Statistics for the Social and Behavioral Sciences*, with Anthony Walsh; and *The Social Context of Law*, 2nd edition, with Sheryl J. Grana and Mark Nicholas. In her spare time, she and her husband publish science fiction for young adults.

Arthur Oyola-Yemaiel recently served as co-director of the Emergency Management Program at North Dakota State University. Previously, he was a researcher and planning consultant for the Florida Division of Emergency Management where he was responsible for the development of a research agenda for the Division in coordination and cooperation with higher education institutions and research centers in the state of Florida, and, as the Academic Liaison, he was responsible for integrating academic research with practical application. In addition, he was responsible for the coordination of the State Mitigation Strategy in accordance with Disaster Mitigation Act of 2000. His formal education is in meteorology, environmental sciences, economics and sociology/anthropology. His research and publications encompass the areas of disasters and emergency management including aspects of vulnerability, complex organizations, systems, development, social change, conflict resolution, and conservation/sustainability. His professional philosophy revolves around the integration of knowledge so that academic research and applied technologies will reduce hazard vulnerability thus creating disaster resistant/resilient communities. He has presented and published his work at national and international forums.

Kristina J. Peterson has been an advocate and activist in disaster vulnerability reduction since 1965. She is pursuing a doctoral degree in urban planning from University of New Orleans. Peterson is a research assistant at CHART, Center for Hazards Assessment, Response and Technology, working with a participatory collaboration model concerning resilience of coastal communities. Participatory vulnerability analysis and resiliency of community through community defined development is at the core of her work and studies. She has presented on collaborative justice, resiliency and mitigation which reflects parity in gender, race and class, at the Royal Geographical Society, University of Pittsburgh's Bio-terrorism Center, Oberlin College and Brandon University. She has used her extensive experience in participatory grassroots community organizing and development during the aftermath of Katrina and Rita. Kristina has been a disaster resource specialist for Church World Service and Presbyterian Disaster Response Team with special skills in long-term resource development and mitigation. She has contributed to the World Disaster Reports, and with her husband, Dick Krajeski she has been a major contributor to the literature on response to disaster for the religious sector. She is a regular presenter at the International Society for Applied Anthropology as well as the Natural Hazards Workshop. Peterson is Pastor of Bayou Blue Presbyterian Church and with her husband and cat, lives in a warehouse in Houma, LA.

Brenda D. Phillips is a full professor of emergency management at Oklahoma State University (OSU) and a Senior Researcher at OSU's Center for the Study of Disasters and Extreme Events. She previously directed the Women's Studies Program at Texas Woman's University. Dr. Phillips is past Secretary-Treasurer of the International Research Committee on Disasters. She has committed her professional work to reducing vulnerabilities of those impacted by socially structured and socially reproduced discrimination. She has researched, published and taught about the elderly, children, women, racial and ethnic minorities, persons with disabilities, low-income groups and others marginalized and made vulnerable to the impact of disasters. She teaches courses on populations at risk, research methods in disasters, and long-term, community-based recovery. Dr. Phillips has given invited presentations on vulnerability in The People's Republic of China, the United States, Costa Rica, Canada, New Zealand, Germany, India, and Australia. She has consulted and volunteered extensively throughout the United States on the topic of special needs and marginalized populations.

Graham Tobin is a professor of geography at the University of South Florida. He received his bachelor's degree from the University of Durham, doctorate from the University of Strathclyde, and was a Research Fellow at the University of Sheffield in Great Britain. He has been a faculty member at th University of Iowa, and at the University of Minnesota Duluth, before moving to Florida in 1996. His research interests encompass various aspects of natural hazards and water resources. His current research activities are concerned with evacuation planning and health problems associated with volcanic eruptions, environmental impacts of flooding, and pollution reduction strategies in urban areas.

Jennifer Wilson has worked in both the academic and practitioner sectors. Academically, she has contributed to development of doctoral studies in emergency management at North Dakota State University. Previously, she was in senior management at the Florida Division of Emergency Management where she helped develop long-range program plans and budget justifications for the Division, coordinated with the Federal Emergency Management Agency on state programmatic grants and capability assessments, and contributed to many special projects of the Director including producing written testimony for the Florida Governor. As the Accreditation Manager, she was responsible for the state accreditation process as well as agency policy and strategic management and planning. In addition, she provided expertise and coordination to developing, new, and existing emergency management degree programs at Florida universities and colleges as the Higher Education Coordinator. She received her doctorate degree in Sociology from Florida International University. Her areas of research interest include the professionalization of emergency management and social vulnerability to disasters. Dr. Wilson published the book entitled, *The State of Emergency Management 2000: The Process of Emergency Management Professionalization in the United States and Florida.*

FOREWARD

Joe Scanlon, Series Editor

In his study of the 1917 Halifax explosion—a study generally accepted as the first academic study of disaster—Samuel Henry Prince deliberately omitted references to the role of women though one of his main sources, a manuscript by his friend, Dwight Johnstone, contained a number of positive accounts about what women had done. By 1957, when the National Opinion Research Center began publishing its studies, women were no longer entirely ignored but their role was presented as generally passive though the authors did concede that women did take action when men failed to do so:

> . . . the general overall impression one gets from the interviews (is) that women, with notable exceptions, were rather passive in the post impact activities. However, there are a number of indications that this passivity may be a function of the social situation. Where no men were present to do what needed to be done, the women went ahead and did it. They did not wait around for others to come and assist them.

It is difficult to avoid concluding, as Joyce Neilsen does, that there may be a research bias. ". . . what researchers define as important activities (i.e. those worthy of research attention) are carried out primarily by those of one sex—men."

In recent years, this research bias has started to change for several reasons. First, more attention is being paid to what women do before, during and after disasters and especially to the special problems they encounter, including their ability to obtain assistance. Second, women are becoming more involved in many of the functions that were previously seen as significant and performed by males. For example, agencies such as police, fire and ambulance that were once completely male now have some, occasionally a great deal of female involvement. This latter change raises some interesting issues: when men were the only ones working outside the home, there was no question about which partner would leave the family in a disaster. Now it may be women who have the skills that are needed.

Yet there are still a good many issues to be dealt with. In the past, there were many extended families: when one family member left for emergency responsibilities, there were enough persons left to care for children. Second, most families had two parents: one could respond to emergency demands while the other took care of the family. Now, it is less common to find an extended family. It is more common to find a single parent family including one where that parent has emergency responsibilities. It is also more common to find families where both parents have emergency responsibilities. How are the demands of an emergency to be dealt with under such conditions? Who should stay and who should report to duty when one parent is a police officer and the other a physician? Who should stay and who should report to work when one spouse is a civil engineer—and there is widespread destruction—and the other is a firefighter—and there are no fires. What about an incident involving toxic spills when one has knowledge of hazardous chemicals and the other is a teacher (and an incident occurs while children are at school)? How must organizations deal with these realities in planning? As is often the case, once we start examining issues in a particular area, there are often more questions than answers.

The most important change in recent years is, however, the fact that scholars have started looking systematically at gender issues related to disasters. In the last decade and a half there has been a flood of gender related material coming out of Australia, the United Kingdom and the United States as well as from developing countries such as India and especially Bangladesh. Two of the scholars who have developed this field—Brenda Phillips and Betty Hearn Morrow—are the editors of this volume. It is now 13 years since Phillips described "Gender as a Variable in Emergency Response" in Robert Bolin's monograph on *The Loma Prieta Earthquake: Studies in Short-Term Impact*, nine years since Morrow and Elaine Enarson argued the case for gendered disaster research at the World Congress in Bielefeld, Germany, seven years since they wrote about "Hurricane Andrew Through Women's Eyes" and five years since they again teamed up to edit *The Gendered Terrain of Disaster*. The lengthy bibliography included in this volume makes it fair to say that thanks to the leadership of Phillips and Morrow and the efforts of them and many others research relating to gender and disaster is now firmly established.

In reading through this volume it becomes apparent that the authors have drawn on other fields in developing their ideas and their research. I think it is important—and this is something I have said before—that these other areas of scholarship start to draw on our work in the disaster area to further their research. I think it was Charles Fritz speaking at the World Congress in Toronto years ago who suggested two things that have stuck with me. One is disaster scholars have a special responsibility because they take advantage of the misery of others to do research that would not be possible in a labouratory. The second is that disasters—because of the strains they create on the social structure—often offer opportunities to expose things that are less obvious and therefore neglected at other times. The problems are universal but disaster research puts them in the spotlight.

This is the third volume in our current series on disaster. The first, *What is a Disaster? Perspectives on the Question*, edited by Henry Quarantelli, raised theoretical issues about the definition of disaster.

The second, *Methods of Disaster Research*, edited by Robert Stallings, covered methodologies used in disaster research. Although Stallings' book came out in 2002, just four years after *What is a Disaster?* was published, because of a series of publisher problems it actually took seven years to get it in print. Now that we have worked out a satisfactory relationship with Xlibris and gone on line, I think it is reasonable to expect that the books next in line with have fewer problems getting into print.

There is one other reason why I am optimistic about our publishing situation. During my last year as President of the International Research Committee on Disasters, Brenda Phillips took over the position of Secretary-Treasurer. Working with my successor as President, Ben Aguirre, she managed to solve a long troubling problem, our inability to get an appropriate tax status with the United States International Revenue Service, a situation that, among other things, made it difficult for us to acquire access to some funds that required such status. Now, thanks mainly to her, the IRCD is on firm financial footing and we have every reason to be confident this volume will be followed by many more.

Joseph Scanlon,
General Editor
International Research Committee on Disasters
Book Series

ACKNOWLEDGEMENTS

From the editors

The editors would like to recognize Verta Taylor who donated funds to pay for publishing this volume. We are also indebted to Robert Stallings, President of the International Research Committee on Disasters, who provided valuable guidance and to Joe Scanlon, Series Editor, who encouraged and nurtured this effort.

This work originally appeared in the *International Journal of Mass Emergencies and Disasters* in 1999 as a special issue on women and disasters. The chapters contained herein represent both updated and new material, all of which went through the peer review process again. For that, we wish to acknowledge both the original reviewers and those that most recently assisted in the review process.

The International Research Committee on Disasters (IRCD), established in India in 1982, recently celebrated 20 years in existence. The IRCD is a world-wide organization of researchers and practitioners interested in applying scientific research to real-world problems. We are indebted to the nearly 300 members, in over 30 nations, whose work continues to inform our own scholarship and practice

This volume would not have been possible without the support and contributions of the Gender and Disaster Network. For additional information, visit the Gender and Disaster Network, *www.gdnonline.*

org. We thank our colleagues and friends who have sustained interest and concern over women's experiences in disaster contexts; their work laid the foundation for this volume. In particular, we thank Maureen Fordham for her tireless efforts on behalf of scholarly research on gender and disasters. Finally, we thank our respective families for their contributions ranging from their general support of research to the daily efforts that make time for such work. Thank you, Dave Neal, Mary Jane Phillips and Bert Morrow.

Brenda Phillips and Betty Morrow

From the contributors, in order of their chapters

My thanks go to Dr. Kimberly Porter of the University of North Dakota Department of History and to Eliot Glassheim of the University of North Dakota Museum of Art for facilitating early access to resources. I also want to thank Alice Fothergill for sharing her work.

Elaine Enarson

I would like to acknowledge the contribution made by Anne-Michelle Ketteridge and Middlesex University Flood Hazard Research Centre in the earlier stages of the research, and by Anglia Polytechnic University for providing for some of the later fieldwork.

Maureen Fordham

I would like to thank Dr. Kathryn Ward at Southern Illinois University for her mentorship and advisement while working on this project. I would also like to thank Dr. Havidan Rodriguez for comments on an earlier version of this project presented at an American Sociological Association annual meeting and the anonymous reviewers for their insightful comments.

William Lovekamp

The authors would like to thank Dan Hoyt and Linda Hoyt at Iowa State University for their assistance with this project. This research has been undertaken with financial support from the Natural Hazards Research and Applications Information Center at the University of Colorado, Boulder, and a grant from the National Science Foundation (Grant NSF/SBR-9321930).

Jane Ollenburger and Graham Tobin

I would like to thank Joanne Belknap, Jennifer Lois, and Dana Johnson for their helpful comments on early drafts of this article, and the International Research Committee on Disasters for their support of my work. My research was supported in part by National Science Foundation Grant Number CMS-9312647 which is gratefully acknowledged. I also wish to thank Professors Kathy Tiemann and Cliff Staples at the University of North Dakota and the staff at the Community Violence Intervention Center in Grand Forks, North Dakota for their assistance.

Alice Fothergill

I gratefully acknowledge and thank Brenda Phillips, David Neal, Betty Hearn Morrow, and Jane Kushma for their professional assistance with this project; and Glenn Garcelon and Kathy Lowe of FEMA's National Teleregistration Center, who very graciously allowed me access to their data and their employees.

Cheryl Childers

We would like to acknowledge Dr. Betty Hearn Morrow, emeritus, Florida International University, Dr. Brenda D. Phillips, Oklahoma State University, and Elaine Enarson, Metropolitan State University, for their guidance and wisdom as pioneers in gender and disasters. Their contributions to this field will have long lasting impacts and has opened the way for others to advance the understanding of gender in this context. We would also like to recognize all researchers on gender and disasters as well as emergency management practitioners for their contributions to diminish disaster impacts on women.

Jennifer Wilson and Arthur Oyola-Yemaiel

We would like to thank the staff of Church World Service and Stan Hankins of Presbyterian Disaster Response for their support; our children and the churches we serve for putting up with "our comings and goings;" the many communities, survivors and local caregivers we have had the privilege to work with and learn from over the years; and friends from the research, academic and professional community who continually give encouragement and support.

Kris Peterson and Dick Krajeski

1

WHAT'S GENDER GOT TO DO WITH IT?

Brenda D. Phillips and Betty Hearn Morrow

In 1999, the *International Journal of Mass Emergencies and Disasters* published a special issue on women and disasters, which promptly sold out. This book brings back those materials in updated and expanded form along with new chapters. We begin this book by addressing some anticipated questions. What does gender have to do with disasters? Is it really that relevant to the work I do? Are men and women that different? But is gender really germane to the disaster-related work I do? How can the chapters in this book help me?

For those who might dismiss this volume as reflecting "political correctness," we offer an alternative view: the advocates, supporters, and contributors to this endeavor share a commitment to promoting a better understanding of vulnerabilities and capacities as they are affected by societies stratified by gender, age, disability, income, and race. Through our research, professional and community work, and activism, our goal is to influence the practice of emergency and disaster management in ways that result in safer and more humane communities—for everyone.

Disaster researchers are accumulating clear evidence that, as a group, women are likely to respond, experience, and be affected by disasters in ways that are qualitatively different. At the same time it is important to recognize and document women's diversity. Clearly, not all women experience disasters uniformly. The experience of a white, middle-class professional woman in a Texas town hit by a disaster will be vastly difference from that of a sub-Saharan woman in seclusion, or a disabled Brazilian elder. Privilege is relative to one's location in a given set of social, economic, political, and even religious circumstances, of which gender is only one factor, albeit a major one. Attending to the specific context in which a woman experiences a disaster (time, place, and circumstance) deepens explanations and provides routes for addressing the inequities cited in this volume. In other words, it's not simply the recognition of a male-female differential, but a deeper understanding of how gender relates to the complex interplay of power, resources, privilege, and stratification that will increase the effectiveness of the work we do.

A few examples of the effects of gender differences in disaster results should suffice. In a study of two Soviet earthquakes, Benin (1981: 143) reported that 18 percent of those who died were men, 47 percent were women, and 35 percent were children, giving the explanation that "women and children on their own find it more difficult to escape." Rivers (1982: 265) found that women experienced higher morbidity and mortality in famine situations, "the most important element of sex discrimination in [famine] disasters relates to the nutritional vulnerability of female children." Rivers (1982: 265), reporting on triage relief stratified by sex and age, provides this quote: "[S]top all this rubbish, it is we men who shall have the food, let the children die, we will make new children after the war." Using a rock concert tragedy as one example, Johnson (1987a; 1987b) draws a clear picture of the persistence of male advantage under desperate, life-threatening conditions. The context of any given disaster, including its nature and timing, will affect the gender-specific death rate, but the general pattern of discrimination and segregation of women and girls tends to place them at a disadvantage throughout the disaster response cycle. The tragic Indian Ocean Tsunami that claimed in excess of 300,000 lives across thirteen nations included an 80% mortality rate for women and children. The evidence is clear: this is not a tome generated by political correctness.

Any effort to achieve a true "culture of prevention" (*Stop Disasters* 1995) must address societal inequalities, whether related to gender, age, race, disability, or some other measure, and seek to engage all sectors of the community in mitigation efforts. Through our research and practice we are not likely to change fundamentally what is unjust in our societies, but we can recognize and address patterns of disadvantage which are likely to affect disaster resistance and response. At the same time, our work will benefit from the contributions of the previously disenfranchised. We offer this book as one step toward that goal.

It is our privilege to work with a growing cadre of disaster researchers and responders who are dedicated to documenting the experiences of women—their proactions and contributions, as well as reactions and needs. To this end we are pleased to serve as editors for this special collection on women and disaster as viewed from a variety of disciplines, professions, and perspectives that are theoretical, empirical, and practical.

GENDERED ROLES

Vulnerabilities and strengths

Cultures, communities, and families world-wide organize their social lives around gendered principles that influence disaster experiences as well as community and organizational responses. And while your community may seem to be "different"—to have women in positions of responsibility, for example—who are these women? How powerful are their voices? Do they reflect the diverse demographic make-up of your community? How pervasive are women in the emergency management sector? Are you fully utilizing the resources and talents of that "other half" of the population which is likely to know a great deal about what's going on in your community?

Throughout the world women bear disproportionate responsibility for raising children, caring for the ill, disabled, and elderly, and meeting the family's daily needs. These "female-identified" duties have not lessened appreciably as the economic responsibilities of women have increased in post-modern societies. For example, the average woman in the U.S spends about 20 hours in household tasks in addition to working full-time for remuneration (Robinson 1988; see Hochschild 1989 for further discussion). In developing nations, in conjunction with their household responsibilities, it has been estimated that women spend up to 16 hours daily in agricultural work. Through these daily tasks women acquire knowledge and skills which are at the center of disaster management. As one example:

> [W]omen play a vital role as both water suppliers and water managers. It is the women who have knowledge of the location, reliability and quality of the local water sources. They are responsible for collecting water and for controlling its use. (Rodda 1991: 51; see also Kabir 1995)

The salience to disaster work of women's family and household responsibilities forms a theme that runs through this collection. On the vulnerability side, as a result of their extensive involvement in, and strong identification with, the near environment, most women will be profoundly affected when their homes and neighborhoods are damaged or destroyed. On the resource side, this should place them at the center of effective disaster response.

We launch this book with a theoretical piece from Elaine Enarson and Brenda Phillips. Their work challenges us to rethink the ways in which we approach gendered disaster experiences. In particular, they highlight the myriad ways in which theory can produce new ways of understanding problems and visualizing solutions. Their work, both enlightening and provocative, is designed to "suggest theoretical and methodological resources . . . as a way of bringing the missing voice of women to social theory about disaster and hence to new forms of practice." From liberal feminist theory, they point out how social interaction generates gendered structures, socialization practices, and cultures that reproduce and institutionalize discrimination. Socialist feminism, with its emphasis on economic in/equality, compels the reader to examine how women's labor, productive and reproductive, marginalizes and endangers. Radical feminist theory seeks an understanding of subordination and self-domination as it relates to control of women's bodies. Multiracial and global feminist theory challenges not only mainstream theorizing, but feminist standpoints as well by asking "just who is the woman implicit in these theories?" Moving to feminist development theory, we see how women and men together face overwhelming odds as they battle global stratification, while simultaneously offering skills, networks, and local knowledge as resources for survival. Postmodern feminist theory is addressed as well, offering a new vantage point for not only theorizing but for data sources. Popular culture and disaster buffs should find postmodern feminism intriguing. Enarson and Phillips close by painting feminist political ecology as a "powerful and neglected force shaping environmental thinking and action." In an effort to link theory with practice, these authors provide a thorough listing of possible applications from each theoretical strand.

The next contribution is a report from Maureen Fordham on two qualitative studies of women's experiences during floods in Scotland in 1993 and 1994. The analysis focuses on the intersection of gender and social class, illustrating the particularly difficult conditions under which working-class women must continue caring for their families:

> They took us down to show us the rooms . . . it was filthy. The bedding, there was cigarette burns all over it, there was urine stains all over it . . . . There were cooking facilities but only at a certain time . . . . They wouldn't put the heating on. I asked the landlady if she could give us a wee towel, and she said no, they didn't supply towels because the tenants who'd been in were stealing them . . . . Nobody told us that you could go to certain places to get clothing, and things that you needed.

Fordham's work reminds us that, while some things can be generalized to women as a group, we need to document the often powerful ways in which other attributes, such as social class, race, ethnicity, and age, intersect with gender to accentuate the disaster-related problems of some groups, such as poor women.

Bill Lovekamp globalizes this volume even further, with a thorough examination of women's flood experiences in Bangladesh. He looks at how gender and disaster connect to the larger context by using a nine-stage disaster typology (Fothergill 1996). Bangladesh's extreme vulnerability to flooding, coupled with acute marginalization of women, reveals the dire problems disaster researchers and practitioners seek to alter. Lovekamp finds that "vulnerability to disasters is unequally distributed across classes, racial and ethnic groups and genders," most heavily impacting poor women and children in rural areas. In a good example of how socialist feminist theorizing can promote insight, he discovers that economic vulnerability, especially among single parents, hinders mitigation while heightening risk. The presumed solution, a micro-credit loan, can theoretically empower women but in reality "reinforce the cycle of poverty and debt and potentially increase women's vulnerability to future disasters." Women's responsibilities for preparedness (packing clothes, move household goods to the roof, feed the children) beleaguer their already-burdened daily routine—though compelling demonstrate what women could contribute in this phase. Women's lack of involvement in pre-disaster management, along with the influence of development schemes, increases risk and must change. Post-disaster, women's traditional roles prevent them from participating in recovery and mitigation efforts that might effectively alter existing structures and practices—while simultaneously exposing them to risk from contaminated water, diseases, and the hardships of travel to locate food and water. In these contexts, "mortality rates were consistently higher for women in virtually every age group . . . as compared to men." Psychological trauma under these conditions must be higher, though scant evidence exists to document this area of concern. Mitigating trauma can be enhanced through participating in post-disaster recovery—and women in Bangladesh do evidence such participation in both structural and non-structural efforts. Their contributions merit documentation for world-wide consideration and application. Lovekamp effectively points out the need for further research not only in Bangladesh, but in all developing nations and acutely juxtapositions vulnerability and capacity.

The relationship between disasters and psychological stress has been fairly well established, and the research focus has now moved toward a better understanding of the factors that influence it. Jane Ollenburger and Graham Tobin studied the psychological effects of a flood in Iowa (U.S.), examining its relationship to various health and social factors. Using a large control group, they found the anticipated gender differences, but, also as expected, all women were not equally affected. Their multivariate analysis revealed women's degree of stress to be associated with a "complex web of factors, including the presence of children, marital status, structure of household unit, age, socio-economic status, health, and the level of social attainment." These factors interact in a variety of ways to increase the vulnerability of certain women such as minority women in fair to poor health, young single mothers with children, and elderly women living alone.

Particularly germane to our argument here are the important ways in which the reproductive role of women renders them more vulnerable in times of crisis, pregnancy being the most obvious. Beyond pregnancy, the reproductive health and safety needs of women are important factors that they must take into consideration when making decisions about evacuation or about whether to remain in an isolated neighborhood after a disaster. While we cannot minimize the risk of women from sexual violence or their needs for birth control and other reproductive services, it is the act of mothering that renders them most vulnerable. Women responsible for the care of small children and other dependents are seriously burdened when it comes to disaster-related decisions and activities, returning us to the social creation of women's vulnerability.

Within households women may be doing most of the work, but they are likely to lack power and autonomy. While gender egalitarianism is increasingly professed as an ideal in many societies, the reality in most homes is that men and boys have greater freedom and autonomy and exert important control, not only over women and girls, but over household resources (such as cars and money) and over mobility. Gender stratification and norms can seriously limit the ability of women to make decisions about disaster preparation and evacuation and to access post-disaster resources. Impressionistic accounts from

Bangladesh indicate that women under Purdah seclusion norms did not seek aid or evacuate during seasonal floods (Kabir 1995: 5). Poverty further impacts women who are reluctant to abandon possessions to flood waters or theft. Post-flood epidemics impact women and children already made vulnerable through inadequate nutrition and poor health. Unfortunately, this power differential can lead to extreme dominance, even violence. There is growing evidence that incidents of violence against women increase in the period following a major disaster. Alice Fothergill presents case study evidence of the realities faced by some women:

> Things were very tense around the house . . . . Karen's husband became more and more angry—at the flood, at the city, at the Corps of Engineers, at his family, and, most of all, at his wife. "He likes things ordered and when things are out of order he doesn't like it. So the flood was a nightmare for him. It's not like his temperament completely changed with the flood, but I definitely do consider us to be a flood casualty. The flood did bring on his anger." Karen assumed that his anger would subside as time passed . . . . Instead, Greg's anger grew with each month following the flood. Indeed, a year after the flood his anger erupted into violence and he began beating Karen.

In another case Fothergill describes a disabled victim of domestic violence who was able to gain inner strength from having faced the loss of her home and property and survived on her own. Clearly, agencies which serve families, including shelters and services for battered women, need to be an integral part of community disaster planning.

Housing is of particular importance to women, both practically and emotionally. When homes are damaged or destroyed, women's domestic responsibilities not only continue but likely expand as they care for their families in shelters, damaged homes, and temporary housing, often under very difficult circumstances. In the second paper in this collection, Elaine Enarson uses examples from her work in two regions of the United States to suggest several key patterns or issues for further investigation. To paraphrase a few: conflict was reported between couples over priorities and decisions in household preparation, with women being less likely to delay taking action; government-assisted temporary housing decisions did not reflect the needs of women and children; some women, especially those living alone or heading a household, are at a disadvantage throughout the process, including encountering greater problems in locating affordable temporary or replacement housing; housing loss or disruption severely impacted women's ability to do everyday domestic and caregiving chores as well as many women's ability to continue home-based economic activities in the informal sector; and the lack of housing and safe space put some women at higher risk of violence. On the other hand some women took on non-traditional roles in the housing crisis, and some women organized politically to influence housing policy during the rebuilding phase. Enarson's bottom line is that women's "practical needs and long-range interests" in secure housing should be capitalized on by placing them at the center of emergency and disaster planning, indeed at community development in general.

One advantage enjoyed by women in modern societies is longevity. While the gap is decreasing somewhat, women can expect to live several years longer than men (and longer than their female counterparts in less developed nations). While inarguably a female advantage, the resulting demographics are an aged population that becomes increasingly female. Because of gender-specific economic differences, they also become increasingly poor, resulting in significant numbers of single or widowed elderly women without the physical or economic resources to deal with disasters effectively on their own. This implies that they will be targeted for government assistance, such as loans and grants. In fact, in her analysis of data from the tele-registration program of the U.S. Federal Emergency Management Agency (FEMA) after flooding in New Orleans, Louisiana, Cheryl Childers found that, while elderly single-female households were significantly more likely to apply for government loans, they were less apt to be approved.

Childers' work represents the first attempt by a researcher to analyze FEMA data. While the work provides useful information related to age and gender differences, the fact that FEMA does not gather demographic data on race and ethnicity limits our power to further understand women's diversity in the disaster context.

The same pattern of male power and privilege found in homes extends to the larger community where women are likely to be instrumental to the success of local volunteer and professional organizations, but rarely hold leadership positions that carry real authority. In those cases where opportunities are increasing, women are likely to face resistance. Exploratory research by Jennifer Wilson and Arthur Oyola-Yemaiel suggests some of the challenges facing women who enter the previously male bastion of emergency management:

> . . . [W]omen have been told that in order for them to be more accepted in a man's world they have to be more assertive but not aggressive because if you are aggressive you are seen as pushy . . . . If I or other women are in a room full of men who are talking and talking and making decisions but I have some important things to say also then it is sometimes very intimidating to say, "Whoa, wait, what about this" . . . in this field if you are not like that then you might as well not have been in the meeting because they don't let you talk.

At the same time Wilson discusses how changes in the field of emergency management are opening up new opportunities for women and hold promise for better integration of women's issues in disaster management.

In the community context, the result of gender-specific social and cultural differences is that, while women are likely to be strategically placed when it comes to promoting effective disaster mitigation and response, they are not likely to have adequate power and resources to do so. We end this collection with a practical contribution from Richard Krajeski and Kristina Peterson. "Our experience has taught us that women . . . play critically important roles in all aspects of disaster preparedness, response, and mitigation with all types of organizations and groups. We are particularly convinced that non-professional, historically vulnerable, and marginalized women are uniquely equipped to play important organizing and leadership roles." To this end they provide specific suggestions for effectively utilizing the knowledge, skills and leadership of community women in disaster response.

Because an established body of feminist research already exists, the disaster field can avoid classic mistakes: looking for physical differences rather than an understanding of privilege and oppression; focusing on women as a homogeneous group rather than as diverse; pitting male against female when some women possess more privileged statuses than some men; and using individual rather than social structural explanations for vulnerability. The work represented here is a positive step in a promising direction. These efforts to understand the intersection of gender with class, age, disability, race, and ethnicity move us beyond the anecdotal to documented cases with practical as well as theoretical implications.

SUMMARY

The hope of many disaster researchers is to ultimately contribute to a reduction in the effects of hazards on human populations. Beyond what it tells us about vulnerability, the study of gender in the disaster setting has tremendous potential for learning about change from the individual through the organizational levels. Interestingly, one researcher has observed that, "during crisis, the stratification system weakens . . . the permeable boundaries of roles, the shift from formal credentials to crisis-solving abilities, and the reallocation of resources, including social roles, are all crisis-engendered processes that promote the de-differentiation of gender roles within the family, the labor force, and the political system" (Lipman-Blumen 1982: 186-187). We need to further document these shifts, the conditions that promote them, the groups most likely to be affected, and how they can be extended beyond the immediate aftermath when, in fact, the situation is likely to worsen for many women.

Furthermore, group efforts to overcome crises can be better understood. After Hurricane Andrew in Florida (U.S.), groups of women came "together to share domestic tasks" and "helped elderly neighbors and friends, either directly or by connecting them with community services" (Morrow and Enarson 1994; 1996). When the area's strongest and financially richest recovery organization excluded them, women formed their own multicultural alliance, overcoming difference to create an effective collective (Enarson and Morrow 1998a). For those interested in reducing inequality, disasters represent an opportunity to improve the circumstances of marginalized persons and groups such as victims of family violence, persons with disabilities, and elderly women needing assistance.

Integrating women from across the spectrum of physical, economic, and social circumstances into the full range of disaster-related activities will result in an increased pool of ideas and talents, fuller consideration of the needs of all citizens, more effective response, and thus quicker household and community recovery. And, ultimately, our households and communities will be more resistant to future hazards.

If you wish to learn more about women and disasters, or to join in the discussion, we refer you to several sources of information and networking. A summary of the related literature appeared in Volume 14(1) of *The International Journal of Mass Emergencies and Disasters* (Fothergill 1996). The collection of international contributions on the topic of gender and disaster is now available in *The Gendered Terrain of Disasters* (Enarson and Morrow 1998b). The references at the end of this volume, along with a bibliography at the website listed below, represent an extensive set of consultative resources.

As an outgrowth of an informal meeting of interested researchers and practitioners organized at the 1997 Natural Hazards Workshop in Boulder, Colorado, a *Gender and Disaster Network* (GDN) was established. The goals of the GDN are to:

- Document and analyze women's and men's experiences before, during and after disaster, situating gender relations in broad political, economic, historical and cultural contexts;

- Work across disciplinary and organizational boundaries in support of collaborative research and applied projects;
- Foster information sharing and resource building among network members;
- Build and sustain an active international community of scholars and activists.

The 1998 meeting was attended by a diverse group of about 50 women and men of varying backgrounds and careers. Since then, several hundred researchers, practitioners, consultants and others have joined the GDN. The Network continues to meet annually at the Natural Hazards Workshop in Boulder, Colorado, U.S.A. Contact the GDN (see below) to join the list serve and to learn of other gatherings. Members met recently, for example, in Australia (2002) and Spain (2003).

The Gender and Disaster Network participated in the first "Reaching Women and Children" conference, held in Miami, Florida, U.S., in June 2000 with attendees representing hundreds of nations. Efforts are underway to launch a second *"Reaching and Women Conference."* For further information on these and other efforts, we invite you to become a member of the Gender and Disaster Network. Visit the GDN at its current Web site (*http://www.gdnonline.org*). A significant set of resources and links are available at the GDN web site including an extensive bibliography, conference papers, guidelines for action, reports, and a list of members.

In 2002, the Gender and Disaster Network established the *Mary Fran Myers Awa*rd that recognizes contributions to gendered research and to furthering women's related careers in research and practice. Mary Fran Myers of the Natural Hazards Research and Applications Information Center at the University of Colorado-Boulder received the first award, subsequently serving as its namesake. The editors hereby acknowledge her lifetime of achievements and admiringly dedicate this book to her. The Mary Fran Myers Award will be awarded annually to worthy recipients. It is an international award and those interested in nominating an individual should view information at the GDN website cited above. Three recipients of that award serve as authors in this volume: Betty Hearn Morrow, Elaine Enarson and Maureen Fordham.

In the aftermath of terrible disasters that have affected women and children worldwide, the editors and authors hope the collection will interest you and will have relevance to your work. *May you find the arguments compelling and the commitment to a better understanding of the disaster-related vulnerabilities and capacities of women contagious.*

2

INVITATION TO A NEW FEMINIST DISASTER SOCIOLOGY:

Integrating feminist theory and methods

Elaine Enarson and Brenda Phillips

INTRODUCTION

We write out of conviction that women and men are situated differently in the political ecology of disasters and that women's experiences matter. Recognizing that human experiences are never unmediated by language, society, and culture, we identify women's concrete material experiences in disaster contexts, both as explained by women survivors to researchers and in survivor narrative accounts from women, as an invaluable source of knowledge in the social analysis of disasters. Simultaneously, we realize and acknowledge that empirical experiences remain contested (Stone Mediatore 2000). The implicit grounding of disaster theory in men's lives affords a partial view which must be challenged through a woman-focused gender analysis. Studying the "gendered terrain" of disasters through women's eyes (Enarson and Morrow 1998) offers disaster scholars and practitioners new angles of vision on the complex interactions of people with hazardous environments.

We argue here that thinking about disasters from women's standpoints challenges a 'gender blind' myopia which renders invisible so much of human experience. Because how we think about disasters significantly shapes human action in hazardous environments and in crisis and reconstruction, theoretical blinders have real consequences for women and men in crisis. We offer a critique, then, that "views the apparatus of knowledge production as one site that has constructed and sustained women's oppression" (DeVault 1999: 30). Beyond critique, our goal is to suggest theoretical and methodological resources that we hope will reduce the "omission and distortion of women's experiences in mainstream social science [including disaster research], the tendency to universalize the experience of men (and relatively privileged women), and the use of science to control women" (DeVault 1999: 26). In Hewitt's terms (1998), we view feminist theory as a way of bringing the "missing voice" of women to social theory about disaster and hence to new forms of practice.

We begin by reflecting on linkages between women's studies and disaster research, identifying possible openings for various feminist perspectives. We then briefly discuss the core ideas in six interwoven strands of feminist thought, and consider how these ideas have and might in the future inform disaster research. To draw out the practical implications of new theoretical approaches, we include a summary of potential policy and planning directions (see Figure 1). In the subsequent section we turn to methodology, again asking what disaster social scientists can learn from feminist research strategies. In our summary, we identify "five good reasons" for a closer relationship, if not a trial marriage, between feminist theory and disaster social science, and outline strategies to help bring this paradigm shift to fruition.

WOMEN'S STUDIES AND DISASTER THEORY

Recognizing that feminist theory and research may be unfamiliar to disaster students, we emphasize some of the foundational connections we see with disaster studies. A primary goal of feminist scholarship is work that raises "new questions and/or formulates theory that furthers our understanding of . . . social science . . . in such a way that girls and women . . . are brought to the center of scholarship" (Glassick 1999: 5). Beyond gender, feminist scholars seek to recognize, theorize about, and analyze diversity independently and through an understanding of intersecting racial, developmental, cultural, economic and sexual social relations and institutions.

The vehicle for thinking in these ways is women's studies, the intellectual arm of the global women's movements of the late 20th century. Women's studies invites students to study women's history, literature, culture, and politics not simply to better understand the social organization of gender but to advance women's liberation. This passion for committed scholarship also defines the search for knowledge about hazards and risk and their mitigation.

Conceptual linkages also abound. Sociologists predominate in the social science of disasters, using firmly-established concepts that resonate fully within women's studies: social power, privilege, domination, institutions, culture, political economy, social change. Feminist sociologists in particular analyze the social construction of power and privilege and identify strategies of change toward more equitable social structures.

Feminist research has been described by the National Women's Studies Association (NWSA) as including the "scholarship of discovery, the scholarship of integration, the scholarship of application, and the scholarship of teaching" (Glassick 1999: 5; see also http://www.nwsa.org). Women's studies increasingly emphasizes global understanding through an interdisciplinary "scholarship of discovery," raising questions about human difference that "researchers have either ignored or not thought to ask"(Glassick 1999: 5). Discovery is also the goal of the International Research Committee on Disasters (IRCD) whose general objective is "to promote the social scientific study of disasters, especially to help increase scientific knowledge and understanding." Both work toward the "scholarship of integration" which makes "connections within and between the disciplines" and "educates nonspecialists by giving meaning to isolated facts and putting them in perspective" (Glassick 1999: 6). In the 1990s, the NWSA identified "globalizing" as a key characteristic of women's studies scholarship, consistent with the international focus of the IRCD through which "members from over thirty nations work toward a collective goal of academic research with an action focus: using knowledge effectively to mitigate disaster impact, improve planning and response, and reduce recovery needs." The NWSA report also recognizes that "feminist action-oriented research and cultural analysis is both participatory and reciprocal," as a form of scholarship that "can stimulate change and growth in communities, policies, participants and new research projects" (Glassick 1999: 5). This spirit is echoed in the IRCD which "endorses and publishes research on individual, group, organizational, community, societal and international activities to mitigate, prepare for, respond to, and recover from major crises." Global, interdisciplinary and practice-oriented work is a hallmark of both women's studies and disaster studies.

STANDPOINTS ON DISASTERS

The seen and unseen

Following critiques by Morrow and Enarson (1996), Enarson (1998), Bolin, Jackson, and Crist (1998), Fordham (1998) and others, we see gender-blinders at a foundational level in the social construction of disaster theory. A recent work edited by E. L. Quarantelli (1998) addresses a question at the heart of disaster research: What is a disaster? Contributing authors are primarily western and European, representing countries where most social science research on disasters has been written; most were also male and Anglo, again representing the dominant pattern. As we write, a more diverse group of authors are working on a broader set of definition papers at the request of the editor, who observed the neglect of non-dominant perspectives. In concluding remarks, Quarantelli urges us to clearly define the place such "new events" as AIDS and technological failures have in prevailing definitions. Famines, epidemics and droughts are a case in point. As these are typically response-oriented and "diffuse happenings both in terms of chronological time and geographic space," and because "many well-established observations findings about disaster behavior at any level of analysis, simply do not appear to apply to these diffuse kinds of happenings," it is apparent that "empirical data and theoretical ideas do not overlap very much" (Quarantelli: 260-261).

Gender patterns are a case in point. Publications on gender and disaster consistently report that women and children are over-impacted by famine, epidemics and drought (FEDs). To take one example, Kabir noted after the 1991 cyclone in Bangladesh (1995: 5) that women and girls were vulnerable to postdisaster disease "more often than men due to their poorer health and nutritional status" before the event; gender bias in some cultures also limits the caloric intake of women and girls before and during food shortages or other crises (Rivers 1982). It may be that disjuncture between mainstream disaster research and FEDs arises from inattention to gender relations and to development issues, as the dominant body of disaster behavior research focuses primarily on male populations in western, European and developed nations.

Similarly, when other contributors to the volume explicitly or implicitly suggest that disasters disrupt "the social system" in some way, we ask "whose social system?" To what extent does our existing knowledge of what constitutes a social system rest on male experience, the privilege of the western or developed world, or the perspectives of relatively high-income populations in the world? In many developing nations, ill-informed assumptions about agricultural production, food distribution, and familial roles have excluded women and their families, especially single women and women maintaining households, from effective access to relief supplies (Gell 1999; Kabir 1995). We suggest that understanding pre—and post-disaster social systems from the positions of those historically marginalized is an "excluded perspective" long overdue in disaster social science (see Hewitt 1998). In the absence of more accurate knowledge, assumptions about the relief and recovery process made without knowledge may worsen the situation.

We see promise in the effort toward consensus on definitional issues and concur when Quarantelli writes (1998: 268) that "feminist scholarship has sharply questioned traditional views of and approaches to social phenomena . . . this could surface another way of looking at disaster phenomena." As is evident below, we concur when he points to ecofeminist views and others as promising new perspectives.

THINKING ABOUT WOMEN:

New ways of knowing

Though thumbnail sketches run the risk of distortion, we offer them here to illustrate the very rich field of useful feminist thought. In the interests of space, we do not allow theorists to speak in their own voice nor cite individual works. For more, readers are directed to original sources, collected in Nicholson (1997), Meyers (1997), and Rossi (1973), among others, and to interpretive texts, e.g. Rosemary Tong (1998). Nor do we identify the many areas of overlap and debate in the lively enterprise of feminist theory-building. Following Tong (1998), we appreciate the "kaleidoscopic" richness of feminist thought, and value it not for promoting "truth" but for revealing "new visions, new structures, new relationships for personal and political life" (1998: 280) in hazardous environments of nature and of our own creation.

Liberal feminist theory

Liberal feminist thought has galvanized women's movements around the globe and remains the dominant discourse. Rooted in Enlightenment convictions about "natural rights" and human freedom, liberal feminism—first articulated by Mary Wollstonecraft (1759-1797) in response to Rousseau and others—promulgated the radical notion that women are fully human persons and are (or should be) accorded the rights and duties of citizenship. It follows that the challenge of the liberal state is to create conditions guaranteeing all women equality of opportunity in social institutions and political life. No less than men, women are governed by reason rather than nature and advance their interests and lives through education.

In this view, neither difference nor inequality are based on biological difference but understood to be socially produced and maintained through gendered structure and practice in social institutions and lifelong socialization into gendered cultures. Resulting differences in turn disadvantage women in "a man's world" which privileges male bodies, skills, ways of being and knowing, and language. The core concept of liberal feminism is discrimination and the core value a commitment to gender equality by increasing women's opportunities. "Women, their rights and nothing less; men, their rights and nothing more," read the *The Una* masthead, the voice of the 19th century US women's movement. Two centuries later, the deceptively simple proposition that women are global citizens undergirds the movement to interpret women's rights as human rights and apply international conventions guaranteeing such rights as political voice and freedom from violence both to women and to men.

Liberal feminist theory informs much of contemporary disaster social science. Barriers to women's participation—in community planning for emergencies or in political decision-making—effectively limit women's capacity to exercise full citizenship rights. Some disaster research suggests that "growing up female" and taking up feminized work roles, increases women's risk, for example when women socialized as caregivers ignore their own physical or psychological needs and put the safety of others first—or are placed second or third in cultural contexts valuing girls lives less than boys. Gendered patterns in work and use of living space help explain the common (though not consistent) finding that girls and women experience higher rates of mortality (see Ikeda 1995 for the l991 Bangladesh cyclone; Krishnaraj 1998 for the Latur, India earthquake) and of postdisaster stress (see Koranci 1995 for the 1992 Turkish earthquake), among other examples. Liberal feminism also stresses women's voluntary social action and civic "good housekeeping" role, evidenced in affluent white women's activities following the Galveston hurricane (Turner 1997) and in research on neighborhood environment action (Neal and Phillips 1990).

Disaster organizations often evoke stereotypical notions of femininity limiting women's career potential or work roles in relief efforts. Phillips' account of women in emergency management (1990), demonstrated how women's different voice reduced their credibility and effectiveness in male-dominated emergency response organizations. Gibbs (1990) documented gender bias in Red Cross/Red Crescent Societies as did Robertson (1998) and Wraith (1997) in Australian relief and emergency management agencies, and Wilson (1999) in the

United States. Enarson and Scanlon found gender bias in evacuation orders in a Canadian flood (Enarson and Scanlon 1999).

Students of disaster working in this spirit might examine how gendered divisions of labor put women and men differentially at risk in various contexts; investigate how socialization to masculinity affects the vulnerability of boys and men (e.g. in help-seeking, household preparedness, risk-taking, or coping mechanisms); evaluate organizational initiatives against gender bias in disaster practice; and incorporate women's life chances and everyday living conditions into research on postdisaster stress.

Socialist feminist theory

Socialist feminists criticize liberal thought for asking only equal access to existing power hierarchies and for focusing largely at the level of individual change. They argue that exploitation, not discrimination, is the key to women's status, and that both capitalists and men benefit from patriarchal structures built around the gendered division of labor. Women's subordination across cultures and historical periods, they suggest, rests primarily on the exploitation of their labor in the domestic realm—where women's "housework" reproduces the family symbolically, socially, and materially—and in the international political economy that segregates, stratifies, and devalues women's productive work at home and on the job. At a practical level, they are less concerned with affirmative action policy than with achieving comparable pay by challenging corporate power to reward traditionally male working conditions and job skills (e.g. outside work, operating heavy equipment) more than women's (e.g. public contact, providing personal body care). Socialist feminists have focused on women's historic struggles not simply for economic equality but for "bread and roses" earned through labor struggle and through feminist struggle against male privilege.

For students of disaster, these ideas urge attention to women's capacities and vulnerabilities in and out of the household. Women's social reproductive labor helps children and other dependents survive cyclones, recover from the health effects of toxic contamination, and evacuate from dangerous areas; their income-generating activities in the formal and informal sectors help households prepare and recover; and their community roles often include informal leadership in disaster-stricken communities. This attention to women's reproductive, productive, and community labor makes women visible as behind-the-scenes emergency responders, economic providers, community activists, and household preparers (Morrow and Enarson 1996; Enarson 1999a and 1999b; Fordham 1998; Fothergill 1999; Enarson and Fordham 2001).

Socialist feminist thought also stresses the gendered and racialized nature of poverty. Like women lacking land rights or credit, farming small plots, or employed in commercial agriculture, women employed as contingent workers (part-time, casualized, contract labor) and consigned to underpaid sex-segregated industries and jobs are economically more vulnerable to disaster—less able to replace livestock or household possessions after an earthquake in India or to buy window shutters before a hurricane in Lousiana. In some cultures, women lose dowries in floods and are left even more impoverished; lost dowries may mean lost opportunities to escape violent situations in the aftermath of disastrous environmental events. Certainly, women's high predisaster poverty rates compound the effects of economic loss, particularly for women maintaining households, as Wiest et al. (1994) discuss theoretically and Wiest (1998) demonstrates empirically in a study of women farmers heading households along the chars of Bangladesh. Women's home-based work in the informal sector (e.g. cottage industries, family day care, domestic labor) puts them at high risk of secondary unemployment when homes are destroyed or must be evacuated, and their concentration in the "helping" professions (e.g. crisis work, counseling, teaching, social work) make them significant disaster responders. In this view, both economic insecurity and patriarchal social structures increase women's risk before, during, and after disasters.

What new research questions arise? Social vulnerability mapping must include indicators of women's economic and social status in developed as well as developing nations. Social reproduction in the household should be investigated as a resource throughout the disaster cycle. Emergency managers drawing on feminist disaster sociology will not neglect to include women's home-based work in business recovery planning, and may seek to engage women as partners in emergency planning through their professional associations (e.g. teachers and nursing associations, domestic violence coalitions, women mental health workers). When disaster sociologists study household and workplace emergency preparedness, they need to examine gendered patterns of decision-making between couples and between workers and owner/managers. When studying postdisaster mobilization, they need knowledge of women's global participation in (formal and informal) labor movements and campaigns for safe working environments. Finally, theorizing disaster from this perspective maintains a sharp focus on patterns of privilege and power between women based on class differences.

Radical feminist theory

In contrast, radical feminism is less concerned with discrimination or exploitation, though it considers both, than with women's oppression. Women's subordination is rooted in a universal sex/gender system through which men seek power and control over women—and over the natural world, non-human species, and other men. Women's primary struggle is for self-determination in the face of male domination. Control over women's sexuality is seen as a base cause of subordination and physical and psychological violence a primary weapon. Men's efforts to control women's sexual and reproductive lives undergird the norm of "compulsory heterosexuality" in the intimate lives of all women and men.

Among other topics, radical feminist theory encourages the study of female resistance to male power, the symbolic devaluation of the feminine, and expressions of women's solidarity (e.g. lesbian history and culture, women's collectives and women-only institutions). Ecofeminist thought is grounded here because of men's asserted domination over nature and women's asserted connection to natural cycles and values (e.g., as birth mothers, or guardians of natural resources). In the concluding section on feminist political ecology, we return to this perspective.

In disaster contexts, these ideas again suggest both vulnerability and capabilities. Women outside patriarchal control ("protection") may be both highly vulnerable, for example experiencing restricted access to relief systems as women in seclusion, single mothers, widows, divorced women, and lesbians conspicuously lack access to male-controlled relief and recovery resources. Women on their own as new immigrants or transient migrant workers may be especially isolated, both from men and from other women, and more vulnerable to violence. This was certainly the case for the destitute women studied by Kafi (1992) and in field accounts of women in refugee camps and temporary accommodations (League of Red Cross and Red Crescent Societies 1991). In highly sex-segregated societies, women in families able to afford the practice of sequestering women (purdah) are at great risk to the degree that male honor is contingent upon constraining their public movement and contact with non-related men. Purdah is often identified as a factor limiting women's movement from private residences to public emergency shelters (e.g. in Hossain et al. 1992, and see Rosario 1997), though others point instead to male control over information, for example the use of radios broadcasting emergency warnings (Ikeda 1995).

Living alone or outside of male contexts does not cause vulnerability; it does increase it when male-dominated relief efforts or mitigation initiatives systematically exclude women. The accounts of relief workers leave little doubt that women are primarily responsible for securing essential relief resources for their households yet, in many circumstances, are unable to publicly approach non-related men distributing relief without risk of male harassment or assault (Begum 1993). From Peru (Oliver-Smith 1986) to Alaska (Palinkas et al. 1993; Larabee 2000), male "coping strategies" after disasters involve alcohol abuse and interpersonal aggression. Recent studies of antiviolence women's agencies suggest that U.S. women more actively seek protection, counseling, and legal services in the aftermath of disasters (Enarson 1999; Wilson, et al. 1998; Fothergill 1999a).

Disaster researchers working in this vein will have an interest in women alone, for example the coping strategies of rural women raising families alone on the cash remittances irregularly arriving from partners who migrated for wage work to urban centers. Other topics include the function of women's friendship and kin networks in promoting disaster resilience and women's self-organization in the aftermath of devastating environmental or technological events. Miami's feminist coalition (*Women Will Rebuild*) focused on female solidarity across class and cultural barriers to unite women against a male-dominated recovery initiative (*We Will Rebuild*), for instance (Enarson and Morrow 1998). Dismissed as 'hysterical housewives' in the US (Neal and Phillips 1990; Seager 1996), Mexico (Serrat Vinas 1998) and elsewhere, women's autonomous movements after disastrous events have helped restore community solidarity and won gains for disaster victims, for example after the Bhopal gas leak (Rajan 1999), and warrant more attention in the study of postdisaster politics.

Multiracial and global feminist theory

Just who is the 'woman' implicit in these theories? The easy conflation of "woman" with only a minority of the world's women (e.g. white, middle-class, married, able-bodied women in the North) leaves the status of racial/ethnic women across the globe undertheorized. Focusing on intersecting patterns of subordination based on race, class, gender, sexuality, and nationality, race-conscious feminist thought moves discussion of women's differences to the center of debate. Multiracial feminists observe a complex "matrix of domination" within which women's choices may be both expanded and limited. Border-crossing narratives from U.S. women of color draw attention to the ways "minority" cultures can sustain women marginalized by the dominant culture.

Racial identity and power fracture relations between and among groups of women and produce conflicting interests. Multicultural feminist thought problematizes the concept of "race" by analyzing racial privilege and power in the lives of all women, so conspicuously on display, for instance, in the social relationships of "maids and madams" in domestic service. Global feminists add a focus on the global political economy and patterns of neocolonialism privileging some women at the expense of others. The politics of tourism are a case in point. Women's labor and sexuality are exploited in low-wage tourism jobs servicing an international leisure class now including many affluent women. Though the environmental costs to tourism industries are often very high and put people in harm's way on fragile coastlines, the economic gain to low-wage workers, including large proportions of women, are very small. When threatened by a mudslide or cyclone, the immediate needs of women hotel guests may well conflict with the urgent need of racially subordinate women working in low-level tourism jobs to help themselves and their families.

Not yet influential in disaster sociology, which tends to undertheorize race and ethnicity, this body of thought challenges students of disaster to think about women's diversity and the complexity of gender, race, and class relations in the world system. Increasing numbers of women across the globe now experience disasters on their own as single mothers but, to take an example from the U.S., the poverty of the garment-industry homeworker in the Bay Area raising children on her own differs in nature and extent from the relative poverty of professional woman in San Francisco who divorce and retain custody. Latinas in the Red River Valley of the Upper Midwestern U.S. were publicly humiliated by relief workers who mistakenly identified them as migrant workers rather than long-term residents (Enarson and Fordham, 2001). Do disaster studies seek out marginalized residents like foreign domestic workers from the Philippines, maquiladoras in border enterprise zones, or indigenous women farmers when they evaluate identify or unmet needs? Is their labor considered in studies of long-term economic recovery, or racialized gender issues investigated in studies of post-disaster conflict?

Multiracial global feminist highlights the significance of racialized and gendered political-economic structures in disaster mitigation, impacts, and recovery. If not recognized and addressed, the latent assumption that "all the women [are] white, all the men [are] black" (see Hull, Scott and Smith 1982) distorts social reality and leads to disaster practices based on false assumptions. As disaster theory and practice begin to incorporate gender analysis, it is critical that these patterns of difference be part of the analysis. How, for example, are women's employment and/or livelihood options structured racially and with what effects for different women's economic security in the face of a drought or hurricane? How are Native American women and men differently impacted by hazards on rural reservations or in urban centers, and how are wealthy and poor Cuban American women, respectively, impacted by coastal storms? Women of color are often leaders in grassroots organizing around environmental justice issues (see Taylor 1997 for the U.S.). Do women from different cultural communities organize in different ways or have different priorities?

Multiracial and global feminist thought challenges disaster sociologists to specify differences as well as commonalities among and between women and men. Social organization around disasters is often raced, gendered, and classed in ways that matter and warrant empirical investigation.

Feminist development theory

Moving from a narrow focus on women in development (e.g. the special needs of women subsistence farmers in rural economies) to a more complex analysis of gender relations in global development, engendered development theory "begins from women's everyday experiences of development" (Currie and Wickramasinghe 1997). From this perspective, women struggle not only for economic survival and their full human rights but against development projects according men control over traditionally female domains or undermining traditionally female skills and resources. Situating women's subordination in global economic and cultural power structures, these theorists identify barriers to women's education, training, and productivity as barriers also to sustainable national development.

A feminist political economy of development grounds disaster vulnerability in the social relations of gender in postcolonial societies, directing researchers toward a gender-specific analysis of macroeconomic trends tending to increase global vulnerability. For instance, trade policies undermining local markets increases pressure for wage work and induces male migration from impoverished rural African households to more disaster-vulnerable urban residences and workplaces, leaving women and children increasingly dependent upon uncertain male remittances. Under different conditions, women are more likely than men to migrate (e.g. as foreign domestic workers or to cross-border maquilas).

These theorists also focus on women's skills, social networks, and local knowledge of ecologies, communities, and social histories. In communities hit by drought or by earthquake, women's active coping strategies (e.g. planting "famine crops," disposing of assets like jewelry, combining households, taking on waged work, survival prostitution, or other work in the informal economy) help people survive (among others, see Agarwal 1990). When their livelihoods depend on natural resources, they are very likely to respond proactively to environmental degradation.

International humanitarian relief practices are increasingly likely to reflect these views. Training materials, gender guidelines, and checklists for practitioners developed by Oxfam and other NGOs (see Eade and Williams 1995) are widely available if not fully utilized. The training model for social mitigation in Southern Africa developed by von Kirtz and Holloway (1996) illustrates gender-sensitive practice at the grassroots level. In another example, when the NGO Pattan addressed a massive flood in rural Pakistan, they began with gender analysis and subsequently promoted all-women village groups, the registration of homes built after the flood in the names of both wife and husband, and other initiatives toward gender equity (Bari 1998). Accepting the urgency of relief supplies, personal safety, income and women's other practical needs, the more important goal from this approach is to implement strategic responses to disaster that undermine male dominance and hence reduce women's vulnerability to future disasters.

Sociologists working in this spirit can contribute longitudinal evaluation studies of gender-fair disaster practices and, more proactively, integrate gender into action research with groups such as the Emergency Network of Los Angeles (ENLA), which engages advocacy groups for recent Central American immigrants in social mitigation projects. They can also track the long-term effects of disasters on development and gender relations, and generate gender-specific knowledge about vulnerabilities and capacities. Local emergency planners need data, for example, on the housing conditions, social networks, health, and economic status of Asian-American women in the garment industry in California, maquiladoras in El Paso and Ciudad Juarez, street vendors in Honduras, small businesswomen in Grand Forks, ND, and foreign domestic workers housed in employers' homes during a flood. Feminist development theory helps makes these highly-vulnerable groups more socially visible.

Postmodern feminist theory

Postmodern feminist theory is an engaging perspective but one we find limited by its grounding in linguistic, literary, and psychoanalytic theories and lack of applied focus. Like multiracial and global feminists, postmodern feminists reject dualistic and essentialist thinking (male/female, nature/culture), the presumption of women's collective subordination, and the presumptive power of any group of (elite) women to represent the purportedly universal interests of "women." Postmodern feminists also destabilize core concepts like "woman," seeing identity as shifting, emergent, and artfully enacted through gender "performances." It makes little sense, then, to analyze women's disaster experiences (or any other collective experiences) in general terms—a formidable limitation for most sociologists. Yet disaster sociologists would profit from this insistence on women's agency, which rejects an overdetermined notion of women as disaster "victims."

These theorists find liberatory potential in the marginalization of women as "other," as it sustains a female voice arising in opposition to dominant phallic language and imagery. Less active than other feminist theorists in public policy debates, these feminists focus on women's subversion or alternate reading of dominant texts and the production of symbolic systems privileging the otherness of femaleness. Attending to women's voices and symbols might help us see the disastrousness of daily life for many women and the routine nature of events like floods. It might foster an alternative symbolic interpretation of disasters expressed, for example, through quilting (Enarson 2000) or women's songs (Vaughan 1987).

Postmodern feminists insist on the significance of living through sexualized bodies. This perspective informed the association of men's bodies and male imagery with power and control during Hurricane Andrew (Alway et al. 1998). Male and female bodies come into play differently, for example in Larabee's cultural analysis of the Exxon Valdez oil spill (2000). Cast as a "romantic symbol of an outmoded laboring masculine body" after the Exxon Valdez spill, she suggested the ship's captain represented a working-class form of "besieged masculinity" contesting Exxon's corporate image. Conversely, the pristine wilderness despoiled by oil was cast as female and women were present as much culturally (for example, in cartoons) as physically during the clean-up and salvage period.

For disaster sociologists, more familiar with case studies of organizational practice than with postmodern cultural or feminist studies, postmodern feminism may raise as many questions as it answers. This, indeed, is the "promise" of feminist disaster sociology.

Feminist political ecology

Finally, we look with interest at the possible integration of an explicit gender perspective in the political ecology of disasters. Weaving together strands of multiracial, ecofeminist, and development theory, these writers reject a naturalized relation of woman. They seek instead to integrate gender relations into theorizing around environmental knowledge, practice, and politics and the social construction of hazard in space and time.

Feminist political ecology sees gender as a powerful and neglected force shaping environmental thinking and action, beginning with the "gender division of power to preserve, protect, change, construct, rehabilitate, and restore environments and to regulate the actions of others" (Rocheleau 1996:10). It focuses on how women have historically and in varying contexts drawn on the material circumstance of their lives, their social networks and their practical environmental knowledge to identify and respond to emerging crises, challenging both male dominance and environmental degradation in the process. As in feminist theory generally, gender is identified as a central dynamic, not an occasional or marginal factor, in "shaping resource access and control, interacting with class, caste, race, culture, and ethnicity to shape processes of ecological change, the struggle of men and women to sustain ecologically viable livelihoods, and the prospects of any community for 'sustainable development'" (Rocheleau 1996: 4).

This perspective most clearly joins gender inequalities, environmental degradation, and disaster vulnerability. As primary resource users and managers and primary household providers and caregivers, women are especially sensitive to hazardous conditions placing households and neighborhoods at increasing risk of mudslide, toxic spills, forest fires, gas explosions and other environmental and technological hazards (among others, see Steady 1998 and Cutter 1995). Joni Seager observes (1996: 280) that women are "often the first to notice when the water smells peculiar, when the laundry gets dingier with each wash, when children develop mysterious ailments—or they are the first to worry that these assaults on family safety and health are imminent. [E]nvironmental degradation *is* typically mundane: it occurs in small measures, drop by drop, well by well, tree by tree." This connection inspires women's work to mitigate hazardous conditions, secure compensation for survivors, demand corporate accountability, and challenge governmental environmental policy is evident across cultures—from indigenous women protesting uranium mining to the movement of Indian women against the Maheshwar dam in India and women's self-organization to protect livelihoods based on forestry. For further studies of women's organizing around environmental issues see, among others, edited volumes by Naples (1998), Rocheleau (1996) and Warren (1997).

Feminist political ecology encourages the long view and holistic analysis "connecting all the dots." For example, in Thailand new dams flooded valleys, destroyed towns, devastated wood supplies used for housing construction and food production, depleted local resources, undermined familial capacity to survive, and caused families to send children off to urban factories—or brothels misrepresented, at the height of the AIDS crisis, as factories. As Buddhist monks say "first the forest died" and now a generation of Thailand's young are threatened (Usher 1994).

From this perspective, feminist political ecologists analyze gendered environmental knowledge and survival strategies in drought-prone regions (Wangari et al. 1996), for instance, and female leadership in grassroots movements against the destruction of forest resources (Agarwal 1997) or toxic waste disposal (Krauss 1996). Fordham's perspective on gender vulnerability in European contexts is grounded here (1998, 1999). Without accepting an essentialist identification of women and nature (see Agarwal's proposal a materialist environmentalism, 1992), disaster sociologists can examine the gender politics of community organizing around environmental degradation.

We conclude by noting the resonance of the political ecology framework adopted by some disaster social scientists (e.g., Oliver-Smith 1998; Peacock et al. 1998) with feminist theory; both emphasize intersecting relations of power as people interact with their political, economic, and physical environment. Political ecologists insist on an "ecologically grounded, social scientific perspective within a political economy framework" (Oliver-Smith 1998: 189) and close analysis of social relations and sociocultural systems mediating relations between people and their environments: "Human-environmental relations are always structured and expressed through social relations that reflect the arrangements by and through which a population extracts a living from its surroundings" (Oliver-Smith 1998: 189). It remains to understand how differently humans may relate to uncertain environments when the division of labor and cultural systems are so profoundly gendered. With risk reduction and disaster mitigation as our focus, theorizing about disasters must incorporate women's knowledge and resources as well as their vulnerabilities, and on female as well as male ways of knowing and acting.

NEW WAYS OF ASKING QUESTIONS

Disaster research results from social interactions, sets of established procedures, and work within institutionalized systems. Because knowledge is socially produced, we must focus not only on the process of conducting research, but on the sets of relations and institutions within which research is undertaken (DeVault 1999). Debates linger over whether or not feminists offer new data-gathering or analytical techniques; certainly they offer a critique of the politics of knowledge—how it is produced, by whom, for whom, and with what effects (DeVault 1999)—rather than a cookbook feminist methodology. Most agree that the processes through which knowledge is produced and research conducted must not reproduce privilege. In this spirit, we call upon disaster research to engage in a self-reflective, critical critique of the degree to which traditional research processes—like mainstream theories—may deny difference and reproduce dominance.

The feminist critique of positivism

Feminist research critiques the tendency of positivism, seen as an objectifying framework "reducing humans to social facts" (Gorelick 1996: 37), to deny women voice. As Gorelick writes (1996: 37) "the old top down methods of politics and science will no longer do." Socialist feminists have also articulated a critique of positivism serving the "interests of the ruling class" or who challenge authority (Smith 1996) through the university system. Ample evidence exists of exclusionary practice, for example pressure to publish (or perish) in dominant journals only and the institutional practice of "taming" faculty with radical or nonconforming views (Smith 1996). Reward systems like annual evaluations, promotion, and tenure clearly support positivistic research, a method of inquiry assumed to produce "objective" knowledge. Working outside this positivist tradition often leads to marginalization as knowledge claims are decried as "political" and findings only "exploratory." Though generalizability is not the intent of qualitative or participatory action research, it is charged with lack of generalizability. This caste-like marginalization comes as no surprise to disaster researchers whose work is not as generously rewarded as other fields.

Substantively, positivistic inquiry can also lead to a univariate, highly atomized analysis, as in "sex as a variable" studies dominant in most disaster research. In a classic study, Fritz and Marks (1954) reported on National Opinion Research Center studies of seventy disasters. Their work focused on interviews in eight of those field trips, the first known study of sex as a variable in disaster research. Sam Prince included women in his pioneering studies of disasters, identifying but disregarding gender differences in response to the Halifax explosion (Scanlon 1999). Interestingly, Fritz and Marks identified social conditions rather than sex as explaining those slight variations between men and women that were apparent and decades passed before researchers looked seriously at sex or gender in disasters. Thirty years later, Benin (1981) found disparate death rates based on sex in two Soviet earthquakes and Rivers (1982) documented gender differences in death and disease rates in famine, which he attributed to sex discrimination.

More recently, Schroeder (1987) examined the vulnerability of Hausa women in northern Nigeria and southern Niger in a pioneering societal level study of gender and disasters. He found that social conditions limit women's abilities to prepare for and recover from drought including low pay, commercial vulnerability to inflation, less control over the means of production, educational restrictions, seclusion, dependency on males, child labor, loss of parental custody through divorce, inheritance discrimination and inattention in governmental programs. Schroeder's study marked a significant departure in analyzing women's disaster experiences, moving from the sex as a variable approach to a structural analysis.

Qualities of feminist inquiry

What alternative research strategies and qualities characterize feminist research and how might these be applied to disaster research? Qualitative methods are somewhat more likely in feminist investigations though both quantitative and qualitative methods are found useful for different research questions. Not the method, per se, is at issue but the "commitment to finding women and their concerns . . . to provide a fuller and more accurate account of society" (Devault 1999: 30, also citing Nielson 1990). Debate centers on the degree to which qualitative methods can make women more visible, offer women anonymity (safety?) in discussing sensitive topics and a fuller, *contextualized* "voice"—and perhaps be less reflective of institutionalized privilege.

Regardless of method, feminist research strives to be *revelatory*, *explanatory* and *liberatory* about the research process and outcome, and the environment in which it occurs. Feminist research is also *reflective* as researchers rethink research strategies and methodological paradigms. *Reciprocity* with research subjects is assumed—at the very least, to share results or engage in give and take within a set of social relationships during research. As Carty writes (1996: 132): "[W]e had to earn their trust. We promised to share our findings with them (and did). For some of them who were taking high school or college courses at night, we often helped them with assignments."

Feminist research often starts with what Carty terms "seeing through the eye of *difference*." Her work in the Caribbean culture of her birth used qualitative methods, but failed. Traditionally, our qualitative interview training compels us to remain quiet and let the "subject" talk. But research must be also understood as something that occurs within an "interlocking system of oppression." In Carty's experience, such an approach was interpreted by subjects as colonialist. Feminist research calls on us to consider *context*. Research across differences (such as global inequality between First-World researchers and Third-World research subjects) must reflect social, economic, and political realities. Carty's "subjects" also expected her to "hang out, interact, join groups, listen, share" (1996: 123), and otherwise challenge barriers between the privileged "researcher" and the objectified "subject."

Thus a more holistic way of understanding undermines power inequalities between researchers and subjects making so much research exploitative. An alternative to positivism, the "naturalistic" paradigm assumes the existence of multiple realities (e.g. based on social differences and global inequalities), holistic investigation (context), mutual participation of researchers and participants (seen as active and powerful, not passive objects of inquiry), and the use of thick, rich description to allow readers to make their own judgements regarding generalizability (re-read as applicability and transferability; see Erlandson et al. 1993 and Lincoln and Guba 1985). This contextual, holistic, and multiple realities approach may provide a leveling of "hierarchies of power and control in research relations" (DeVault 1999: 31). This leveling process supports strong feminist commitments to ethical treatment of subjects that cast inequality between researcher and objectified subject as not only inappropriate, but likely to distort reality.

The liberatory function of feminist research resonates with the commitment of many disaster researchers toward improving policy and practice. "Feminists seek a methodology that will support research of value to women, leading to social change or action beneficial to women" (DeVault 1999: 31). If the ultimate goal is an improved society or set of social relations or the elimination of inequality based on social differences, then particular research strategies may be appropriate. Some feminists—among them increasing numbers of disaster researchers—have turned toward participatory research that involves the transformation of subjects into research team partners. Because historically divisive relations exist between practitioners and researchers in disasters, more participatory studies may hold promise as a linking strategy that integrates voice and agency, transforms respondents from objects of inquiry to active subjects and affirms the goal of liberatory research. Participatory action research in particular fits as a linking strategy in that it seeks "democratization of the knowledge process—people normally shut out from research and information become involved in the research itself, learning how to obtain information and how to use it," affirming that "the goals of research are to engage in action that reverses inequalities, empowers the have nots, and ultimately transforms society so power is based in grass roots organizations and individuals" (see Community Development Society, http://comm-dev.org/par-is.htm).

Similarly, feminist scholarship calls for collaboration with local groups toward social change, recognizing "activism by and on behalf of women outside academic institutions as producing a great deal of knowledge and contributing a significant perspective within women's studies scholarship" (nwsa.org). Participatory research includes facilitating and supporting indigenous research. For example, anthropologist Paula Palmer worked collaboratively in a participatory action research project with indigenous women Juanita Sánchez and Gloria Mayorga (Palmer et al. 1993) to interview Bribri women and men on environmental sustainability projects. More recently, the National Emergency Commission of Costa Rica has worked with the Talamanca Bribri to map landslide hazards.

We do not assert that only women can use feminist ways of knowing to help build a new feminist disaster sociology, nor do we propose a definitive all-purpose "feminist method." But we do promote ways of knowing which:

- facilitate global research;
- further feminist, interdisciplinary inquiry;
- transform researcher relations;
- challenge established university systems for treatment of feminist and disaster research;
- foster equitable, participatory teams that support indigenous research;
- strengthen researcher/practitioner relations, and involve practitioners in research;
- apply basic feminist principles to the research process: leveling, ethics, reflexivity, holistic, contextual, difference, privilege, reciprocity, research relations;
- systematically address the characteristics of feminist scholarship: discovery, integration, application, compensatory, liberatory/ social change.

USING FEMINIST THEORIES AND METHODS IN DISASTER SOCIOLOGY

Five good reasons why

Drawing on the theoretical insights and methodological principles of feminist scholarship can only make disaster sociology better—more relevant to world conditions and more insightful about the social organization of communities in crisis. When we examine gender relations in the social construction of disasters and take women's lives as seriously as men's, we will simply know more and what we know will help people more.

Figure 1 (below) indicates a number of practical implications following from the theories discussed above. Recognizing that not all disaster practitioners are eager to embrace feminist theory, we hope these action guidelines will make these ideas user-friendly. We further suggest five substantive reasons why feminist theory should be read and integrated into disaster sociology:

First, *contextualizing gender* is essential. Feminist theory helps avoid the dead ends of analyzing gender as a demographic variable or as an aspect of personal identity. Gender becomes meaningful in historically—and culturally-specific contexts and can no longer be examined in isolation from social class, race/ethnicity, age, ability, sexuality, culture, nationality, or other social relationships of power and privilege. As there is no single or simple meaning to gender and no universal set of gender relations, it follows that disaster research cannot account for gender by integrating "sex" into a set of demographic variables. Gender is certainly implicated in the precarious situation of a char-dwelling Bangladeshi widow facing another flood or the efforts of emergency managers to communicate with undocumented migrant women or the sheltering of single women and their children. But so are race relations, international labor policy, kinship patterns, and cultural constraints. Integrating gender holistically is part of the hard work ahead.

Second, *analyzing gender in men's lives* as well as women's challenges us to think harder about gender. We need a richer understanding of gender in men's lives to examine social relationships between women and men. The social invisibility of race in the lives of dominant white populations is paralleled by the invisibilty of gender in men's lives—or, more accurately, in our theorizing about men's lives. As we begin to look more closely at women's realities in disasters, we need a close-up and personal look at men's lives as men, examining how men's feelings and action before, during, and after disasters are informed by the social psychology of gender and gender identity, gendered patterns of communication and affect, the gendered division of labor, gendered popular culture, gendered development patterns, and gender power in political life, complex organizations, households, and interpersonal interaction.

We anticipate resistance to theorizing about men and gender in disasters but note that gender is implicated in male injury and mortality rates during disasters, in rates of postdisaster stress, in the capacity of households to prepare for and mitigate the effects of disaster, and in the coping strategies of individuals and groups. Thinking about hegemonic masculinity (Connell 1995) helps us think more clearly about how non-dominant men in various cultural contexts can and cannot act to prepare their communities and homes against disaster, can and cannot challenge vested interests locally and nationally, and can and cannot work collaboratively across class, racial/ethnic, and gender lines. The contemporary construct of the (U.S.) "emergency manager" as male and also middle-class, middle-aged, able-bodied, credentialed, and Anglo can and must be challenged by disaster researchers investigating forms of community leadership and the actual management of crisis in homes and neighborhoods and workplaces.

Third, feminist theory in disaster sociology closes the analytic gap between *gender equity, disaster vulnerability, and global development patterns*, both in advanced capitalist and emerging nations. In the first instance, this supports the contemporary shift in theory and, to a lesser extent in practice, toward decentering ad hoc emergency response and relief and bringing sustainable development values into postdisaster reconstruction. A broadened, more sharply political approach to risk reduction through mitigation and vulnerability reduction must also insist upon social mitigation and address the root causes of social vulnerability. Crisis response and reconstruction strategies which reaffirm women's subordinate position and fail to address the driving forces of gendered vulnerability arise from a series of political choices, and effectively shutter the proverbial "window of opportunity" for more equitable reconstruction. Engaging the ideas, politics, and practices of gender and development theorists and the new feminist political ecology supports the trend toward vulnerability reduction and development-oriented crisis response and reconstruction.

Fourth, *identifying gender bias* in the organization contexts in which disaster plans are made and interventions imagined and realized will expand opportunities for women and for men. Program managers more knowledgeable about barriers to women relief workers, the needs of single fathers and mothers during crisis, factors reinforcing stereotypical job assignments for women and men, and deeply embedded cultural systems disempowering women in the workplace are better equipped to advance gender equity in disaster work. Sustained initiatives to expand paths of recruitment into disaster organizations will bring a wider range of women and men into disaster work and enrich the resource base of planning and response organizations. Disaster sociology using feminist theories and methods to understand the gendering of organizational culture and practice in disaster work can make a significant contribution to this process.

Fifth, *engaging communities* in designing, conducting, evaluating, and utilizing the findings from research is a hallmark of feminist scholarship when fully realized. Integrating feminist theory into disaster social science supports a revisioning of relationships between researcher and community in disaster investigations. Again, this echoes and affirms the international call from developing nations and impacted communities to redirect research dollars toward community-based action research and to "translate" findings for broad audiences of interest and practice. As we argued above, feminist methodology also calls for subjects rather than objects in research, for seeking knowledge with liberatory potential, and for space to hear the survivor's voice.

MAKING PARADIGM SHIFTS HAPPEN

We have identified resonating linkages between women's studies and disaster research, including common ground in methodological process and outcome, a global and cross-cultural perspective, interdisciplinarity, and the twin vision of seeking social transformation. We also note the increasing presence of gender-focused researchers in the field, especially regarding gender and development theorists writing from developing nations. An international collections of readings (Enarson and Morrow 1998; and see Fernando and Fernando 1998) and several special journal issues have been published (Morrow and Phillips 1997; Reardon 1993; and Walker 1994); a plenary discussion at a recent national conference included gender equity; a bibliographic review was published (Fothergill 1996), and social scientists have worked with practitioners in a several recent conferences on gender and disaster. But the connection is tenuous. It is also worth noting that feminist theorists are conspicuously disinterested in disaster studies as currently written.

We do anticipate and advocate more gender-sensitive theorizing about disasters—and, with less certainty, anticipate that future disaster practice will increasingly reflect feminist ideas and ideals. We also anticipate and advocate a more fruitful alliance disrupting the current alienation and separation between (mainly) women writing feminist theory and (mainly) men writing disaster theory. To help build this new community of scholars, we conclude with a number of practical steps geared to change in academia and disaster organizations. Among other initiatives, we support:

- Exploiting the potential of the existing Gender and Disaster Network website by offering updated bibliographies, case studies, and working papers; fostering information exchange through the listserve network; linking with relevant disaster agencies and university-based researchers in research proposals, course development, and other strategies appropriate to an electronic network.
- Increasing the presence, visibility and influence of diverse women (non-academics as well) on editorial boards; cross-organizational invitations such as inviting NWSA members to the annual Natural Hazards Workshop; presenting on gender and disaster at environmental justice and sustainable development conferences and at feminist theory conferences;
- Fostering international collaboration, for example through international and regional workshops on gender and disaster; and collaborative projects involving researchers and practitioners in developed and emerging societies;
- Instituting an international, university-based five-year curriculum transformation project to integrate gender scholarship across the curriculum. In the US this would include

adult education, distance education, FEMA higher education courses and training, and certification programs. Workshops to help faculty identify existing gaps or biases, access new resources, revise syllabi, and develop new courses would be needed, and expanded library resources with translated publications in this area. Strategies for institutionalizing cross-departmental dialogue include engaging disaster and gender researchers in jointly sponsored independent studies, internships, field research projects, colloquia series, etc.

- Actively expanding efforts to recruit more women and men from nondominant social groups into disaster scholarship. This involves resourcing institutions of higher education to recruit, support, and retain nontraditional students. Recruitment of students to disaster studies should be expanded in women's colleges and universities and in departments and programs attracting large numbers of women (e.g. education, health, social work). Summer internships, colloquia series, mentoring programs and other strategies should be developed which attract female students in women's studies, urban planning, environmental studies, international relations, geography and other fields. Campus-based networks of disaster researchers should be developed or strengthened to foster informal social relations with new and established scholars in areas not currently involved in disaster work (e.g. gender studies, ethnic studies, area studies, gender and development).

- Fostering feminist scholarship in disaster studies formally and informally. Special journal issues on gender provide new scholars increased opportunities for publication, but gender must also be mainstreamed, for example through regular conference sessions, a gender-and-disaster caucus, and student paper competitions recognizing excellence in writing in this area. This might also entail developing and publicizing an international roster of consultants, teachers, and researchers, book reviewers and others with expertise in gender and disaster.

CONCLUSION

Writing disaster sociology "as if women mattered," to borrow Marjorie Waring's felicitous phrase, invites researchers to feminist theory and method. Disregarding women's specific experiences impoverishes our analysis of disaster-impacted communities; ignoring gender in men's lives shortchanges boys and men in crisis; and neglecting to account for gender in relation to class, race/ethnicity and other power relations in social life before, during, and after disasters is just bad sociology. With this in mind, we hope to have demonstrated how feminist theories, so rich with insight into women's and men's experiences in hazardous environments, can strengthen disaster sociology. Certainly, "correcting the inequitable distribution of resources and power between men and women is the only way to achieve sustainable development, and reduce the effects of a natural disaster" (Kabir 1995: 6). But gender-focused disaster studies can be a resource in what is ultimately a political transformation. We hope our readers agree there are ample grounds for collaboration between feminist scholars and disaster researchers. It remains to bridge the gaps and start the work.

Figure 1: Policy and Planning Direction from Feminist Theories

Liberal feminism

- Identify the specific practical needs of women and girls throughout the disaster event;
- Analyze gender stratification and segregation patterns in all disaster organizations (e.g. emergency management offices, humanitarian relief organizations, community-based and faith-based NGOs) and work affirmatively toward equal opportunities for women;
- Recruit and retain women staff in decision-making roles in disaster planning and response organizations, targeting women in disaster-vulnerable populations;

- Integrate gender analysis across the curriculum in postsecondary coursework and in training programs for emergency planners, responders, and relief workers;
- Diversify emergency management workplaces by fostering the development of gender-focused coursework on traditionally female campuses, mentoring female students, and recruiting female students in fields like graduate social work;
- Target women-owned businesses and female-dominated nonprofits in business recovery programs;
- Monitor relief and recovery programs for gender bias in access to services and decision-making roles.

Socialist feminism

- Collect data on the root causes of women's economic insecurity and social status for use in local-level vulnerability and capacity assessments;
- Incorporate data on women's unpaid domestic work and community work in vulnerability assessments;
- Target low-income women and women maintaining households for economic recovery assistance, including migrant workers, homeworkers, domestic workers, the self-employed, and undocumented workers;
- Engage working women's associations and unions in community-based disaster mitigation;
- Affirmatively recruit and retain low-income women in emergency management professions and training programs, and in community partnerships with practitioners.

Radical feminism

- Engage woman-dominant households particularly in mitigation, preparedness, and relief projects, including single women, widows, single mothers, lesbians, and foreign domestic workers;

- Anticipate and address the risk of increased physical and emotional violence against women and partner with anti-violence women's groups to mitigate these effects;
- Anticipate the need in some circumstances for outreach to sequestered or especially isolated women, including increased hiring of female relief workers;
- Capitalize on women's community-based organizations knowledgeable about locally vulnerable women (older women, women with disabilities, immigrant women) and utilize their networks and resources in disaster planning and interventions.

Multiracial and global feminism

- Work through women's organizations to identify patterns putting women of color at greater risk; build informal networks between disaster organizations and these CBOs;
- Foster formal and interpersonal social networks between women active in antiracist, social justice, and environmental organizing and women in disaster agencies;
- Identify and utilize the institutional and interpersonal resources of women's groups involving women of color, e.g. in preparedness exercises, project evaluation, research initiatives, vulnerability assessment;
- Facilitate the active participation and leadership of women from subordinated racial/ethnic or cultural groups in disaster planning and response at the local, regional, national, and international levels;
- Affirmatively recruit and retain women from under-represented racial/ethnic groups into community-based mitigation coalitions, emergency management professions, humanitarian relief management roles, and international leadership roles.

Feminist development theory

- Expand vulnerability analysis to include women's economic status, kinship relations, cultural proscriptions, age and racial/ethnic stratification, family structure, housing conditions, health and other vulnerability factors;
- Develop and monitor indicators of women's disaster vulnerability before and after disasters through environmental conditions, working conditions, social and political rights, literacy, health and nutritional status, etc.;
- Assume women are primary economic actors and distribute relief sources accordingly;
- Design operational guidelines reflecting gender power differentials in disaster decision-making and in access to and control over key survival and recovery resources;
- Mainstream gender issues into international, multisectoral disaster planning and response, e.g. through training and accountability structures;
- Develop and reward the capacities of disaster organization staff to utilize gender analysis in all aspects of program development, implementation, and evaluation.

Postmodern feminism

- Foster grassroots cultural productions which express alternative interpretations of local hazards or disasters;
- Analyze symbols such as flags, quilts, handmade signs, humor and videos that represent women's symbolic interpretations of disaster events;
- Work proactively with women representing local and national media to bring gender-specific perspectives into media accounts of disasters;
- Monitor disaster relief appeals for exploitative images of women as victims.

Feminist political ecology

- Draw on women as natural resource users and managers in environmental mitigation initiatives;
- Increase outreach and networking between disaster agencies and women in environmental justice and sustainable development organizations;
- Include women in planning and environmental science professions and caucuses on local mitigation and preparedness initiatives;
- Target women as informal neighborhood leaders around community health and safety issues for partnership with emergency practitioners;
- Integrate gender analysis into mitigative environmental strategies and assess sex-specific impacts, for example regarding access to land, workload and time, and social power.

3

THE INTERSECTION OF GENDER AND SOCIAL CLASS IN DISASTER:

Balancing resilience and vulnerability

Maureen Fordham

INTRODUCTION

Those who experience disaster are widely regarded as an undifferentiated group, labeled "victims." In the immediate crisis period, it is difficult for professionals to differentiate, except crudely, between varying levels of need and still carry out urgent duties and responsibilities. However, it soon becomes apparent that some are hit harder than others and that disasters are not the great levelers they are sometimes considered to be. Close examination reveals complex variations within, and not just between, social groups broadly understood as middle- and working-class. This paper examines the intersection of gender and social class in two major flood events and argues for a more nuanced appreciation of these factors, at both the conceptual and the practical level, to be incorporated throughout the disaster process.

Too often, those who are subject to the impact of disasters are conceptualized as belonging to a homogeneous group called "victims," but this apparent similarity conceals considerable difference: difference in terms of gender, class, race/ethnicity, age, sexual orientation, physical and mental ability, culture, etc. Dealing with difference represents a significant challenge for disaster managers, one that remains largely unrecognized or suppressed in favor of a sometimes spurious egalitarianism which attempts to treat everyone the same. In this sense difference has been problematized. However, this paper argues that recognizing difference in disaster is part of the solution, not the problem. Equality, inasmuch as it is consistent with social justice, cannot be achieved by ignoring differences; this simply reinforces the dominance of already dominant groups (Phillips 1997: 143). Rather it will be achieved (partly) through recognizing other voices and moving to reduce marginalization. Nevertheless, there remains a danger that an *emphasis* on difference, rather than a recognition and incorporation of it, will divide not unite (Harvey 1993) and may lead to a reinforcing of competition over resources.

Seeking a more nuanced approach to disaster management should not be interpreted as an adherence to a "faddish" political correctness nor an acceptance of post-modern critiques of grand narratives and universalizing theory. Rather, it is presented here in the context of a recognition that resilience to disaster comes often from dependence upon, and reciprocity within, small and changing networks of individuals (see Peacock et al. 1997 for similar conclusions), within and between varying social groups. The recognition of these differences can lead to a redistribution, not just of resources but also of risk and exposure to harm, and to the enabling and reinforcing of coping strategies within a broader context of social justice (accepting that a universally agreed definition of that concept is problematic). However, it must also be recognized that the notion of community itself is contested and can represent exclusion as well as inclusion (Young 1990; Massey 1994).

GENDER AND DISASTER

Disaster research focusing specifically on gender is a small but growing field (see Enarson 1998; Ferguson and Byrne 1994; and Fothergill 1996 for recent reviews of the literature and research issues).

Most of the work in this area is located within so-called "development" or "Third World" studies (see, for example, Agarwhal 1990; Ali 1987; Begum 1993; Blaikie et al. 1994; Dreze and Sen 1989; Jiggins 1986; Kerner and Cook 1991; Rivers 1982; Sen 1988, 1990; Vaughan 1988; Walker 1994;), but increasingly it is recognized that a gender-sensitive analysis is necessary for understanding the industrial (or post-industrial) nations of the North (Bolin 1982; Enarson and Morrow 1998; Fordham 1998; Fordham and Ketteridge 1995, 1998; Morrow and Enarson 1994, 1996; Neal and Phillips 1990; Scanlon 1996). In much of this work, the focus is specifically on making *women* visible in disasters and on the ways that women are vulnerable to, and made more vulnerable in, extreme events, whether floods in Bangladesh (Ahmad 1994) or Britain (Fordham 1998), hurricanes in the U.S. (Enarson and Morrow 1997), or earthquakes in India (Maybin 1994; Tokle 1994). A male-dominated official disaster response milieu (Myers 1994; Fordham 1998) has been slow in recognizing women's particular needs and experiences in disaster. However, these experiences are embedded in socially constructed modes of living which make women (and others) chronically vulnerable in their everyday existence (Blaikie et al. 1994; Hewitt 1997), necessitating more fundamental social change. Thus, the research trajectory must now bring traditional, redistributive, and social justice issues together with a recognition of difference.

EQUALITY/DIFFERENCE

The paired categories of equality and redistribution on the one hand, and difference and recognition on the other, are seen as mutually exclusive aims of conflicting projects which broadly can be stated as socialist (or, even more broadly, "Left") and identity politics, respectively. A socialist, redistributive politics, which has been characterized as "universalist" and "for *all* human beings" (Hobsbawm 1996: 43), has been challenged, nevertheless, for privileging class above or even to the exclusion of other axes of social division—particularly gender—and thus rejecting "difference." Furthermore:

> [T]he differences that are suppressed are differences from those who occupy positions of power and who have the authority to define knowledge . . . . Thus, to qualify for equality means becoming indistinguishable from the authors of this viewpoint: white, Western, bourgeois men. And the spurious claim to universality effectively creates excluded, minoritized groups. (Bondi 1993: 86)

A cultural politics of identity resists and challenges dominant, universalist notions of the human subject and is part of "an emancipatory politics of opposition" (Bondi 1993: 86). However, it too has been criticized as, inter alia, a divisive, fragmenting process which reduces the potential of reaching a critical mass capable of political action: "[I]dentity groups are about themselves, for themselves, and nobody else" (Hobsbawm 1996: 44).

Attempts have been made to deal with "the redistribution-recognition dilemma" (Fraser 1995: 70) in theoretical terms through a suggested coalition drawing on the transformative potential of a socialist politics of redistribution linked with a deconstructive cultural politics of recognition (Fraser 1997: 28). Separatism is seen to be a political "dead end" while strength lies in coalition (cited in Adams 1994: 346). However, the difficulties of forming such a coalition of "multiple, intersecting struggles against multiple, intersecting injustices" (Fraser 1997: 32) are acknowledged. It is through this difficult coalition, a collective project but one not without conflict (Phillips 1997:.153), that the route to social justice lies.

Recognition of difference is closely associated with the feminist challenge to the masculine, universalizing theory of the Enlightenment project (Di Stefano 1990) which emphasizes rationality and objective truth. However, it has itself fallen prey to its own form of biological and cultural essentialism in which the female subject has been fixed rather than continually re-created through processes of change and construction. But, notwithstanding the importance of biological factors in partly explaining women's subordination (through reproductive labor), women's oppression also has a material basis (McDowell 1986, p. 31) and is not reducible to biological difference. The concept of a universal female experience has been seen as "a clever confidence trick" (cited in McDowell 1986, p. 313), but much feminist theory presents gender as a variable of human identity independent of other variables such as race and class (Spelman 1988 in Gould 1997, p. 149).

However, concepts of difference, often located within a postmodernist discourse, have been challenged by black, lesbian and working-class feminists, claiming feminist theory has been dominated by white, middle-class, heterosexual women (see, for example, hooks 1982; Davis 1982; Evans 1997; Lorde 1981, 1984; Rowbotham 1973; Threlfall 1996; Walby 1990; Walker 1984). While difference between women is now more widely accepted, nevertheless there has been some reaction that this differentiation has resulted, depending on your position, in either a dangerous fragmenting of the women's movement or in a maturing process of greater inclusiveness and radical possibility. "Postmodern culture with its decentered subject can be the space where ties are severed or it can provide the occasion for new and varied forms of bonding" (hooks 1994: 427).

GENDER AND CLASS

This paper looks particularly at gender and class because of their observed significance in the two case studies to be discussed and because of their relative invisibility, in different ways, in disaster and feminist studies. Skeggs argues that "class as a concept and working-class women as a group have almost disappeared from the agendas of feminism and cultural theory" (Skeggs 1997: 2). In disaster research, both categories of gender and class are accepted individually as important explanatory variables in different sub-disciplinary areas and at different times but less frequently are recognized *together* as having some salience in understanding the creation of inequality and vulnerability. The aim here is not to claim overriding primacy for these two social categories over others but merely to attempt to make manageable the complexity of particular empirical findings in which, for example, race/ethnicity are not salient but gender and class are. The paper does not offer a neat, summative theoretical proposition (the small number of interviews and the lack of representativeness do not allow this) but rather offers initial observations that challenge simple constructions of class and gender and point toward the need for more finely-structured observations in the field and by disaster managers. It is acknowledged that traditional descriptors of class have been contested from both general sociological (Clark and Lipset 1998; Hout et al. 1998; Prandy 1990; Saunders 1990) and specific feminist perspectives (Skeggs 1997; Mahony and Zmroczek 1997; Walby 1990). However, here is not the place for an extended discussion of social stratification theory and its problems and so this paper adopts a broad definition and understanding of class which locates interviewees into one of two classes, middle or working. This simple class position is based on inter alia: the individual's, i.e., women in their own right and not subsumed under that of an assumed male head of household, relationship to the means of production (Miliband 1987; Westergaard and Resler 1976;) to which of the British Registrar General's categories they belong, i.e., related to unskilled, skilled, and professional occupations (OPCS 1992); and also including a cultural model of class based on "capital" (economic, cultural, social, and symbolic) movements through social space (cf., Bourdieu 1986: 114, 291). This position is in some opposition to Walby's position that the concept of class should not be used to cover non-economic forms of inequality "since to do so would be to wrench the concept too far from its heritage" (Walby 1990: 13).

Interviewees were not asked to which social class they felt they belonged but rather were assigned to a class (either working or middle class) on the basis of a combination of several of the following factors: their job/profession and/or that of their partner where relevant; whether they owned or rented their home; where they lived; and level of education, lifestyle, and manner (Abbott and Sapsford 1987). Thus, typical middle-class characteristics were: home-ownership; living in areas with medium to high land/property values; having post-compulsory education; and having, now or previously, a professional occupation (social worker, business owner, etc.). Typical working-class characteristics were: having a tenancy, living in social housing; having little if any post-compulsory education; and having, now or previously, a manual or semi-skilled occupation (cleaner, hairdresser, etc.). However, in neither case were categories fixed and immutable.

VULNERABILITY AND RESILIENCE

The study of hazards and disasters has been guided for many years by the so-called "dominant paradigm" (Hewitt 1983) which places a major focus on the hazard agent and the individual response to it. However, an alternative "vulnerability paradigm" has been developing which places its focus on differential vulnerability to hazard and disaster and the contextualizing of disaster within everyday vulnerabilities (Blaikie et al. 1994; Varley 1994; Hewitt 1997). This paradigm recognizes interlocking systems of vulnerability in both physical and social space—"geographies of vulnerability" (Hewitt 1997, p. 164).

The development of the vulnerability paradigm has similarities to that of feminist theory where the early stage of the project was to recognize and document the ways in which women, as a group, were subordinated and oppressed. However, the imposition of this static condition of "victim" was seen to be both partial and disempowering, and so the feminist project shifted its emphasis towards difference and resistance. The vulnerability paradigm is also moving from an identification of social causation and the recognition of vulnerable groups ("victim") to a more nuanced understanding of how social groups (defined by gender, age, race/ethnicity, etc.) differ between and within themselves and how they are never simply victims, but also survivors and active agents.

It is as a contribution to this latter point in the paradigm's development that this paper is addressed. The questions it asks are not just what makes women vulnerable to, and in, disasters, but also, more positively, what creates resilience?

CASE STUDIES

Two case studies are used primarily, arising from major floods in Scotland: Perth in 1993 and Strathclyde in 1994. The early stages of this research were undertaken as part of the European Union-funded "EUROflood Project" co-ordinated by Middlesex University (Ketteridge, Fordham, and Clarke 1996; Ketteridge and Fordham

1996; Penning-Rowsell 1996; Penning-Rowsell and Fordham 1994) in which gender analysis was merely a part. A more specific gender and vulnerability focus has developed subsequently (Fordham 1998; Fordham and Ketteridge 1998).

A series of in-depth, qualitative interviews were carried out at various periods (from three months to four years) after the events and supported by a number of informal meetings and interviews with professionals connected with the events. The initial interviewees were mostly working-class women from large social housing estates who had been impacted throughout the disaster process in ways invisible to disaster managers. However, their relatively homogeneous social position raised the methodological question of whether these women's experiences were identifiably and primarily gendered or dependent upon their class position. More interviews were undertaken subsequently with middle-class homeowners and professionals from various locations in the same flooded regions to explore this specific social class dimension, and it is this which forms the basis for this paper.

In an additional study area, twelve interviews were carried out in August 1997, one month after major flooding occurred in the Moray region of Scotland (Fordham 1998). These were with men and women, working- and middle-class, professionals and victims/survivors. Occasional reference will be made to these where relevant.

The most recent research began from an initial assumption that working-class disaster victims would be impacted harder and for longer than middle-class victims. On a continuum from vulnerability to resilience, the working-class community would be located at the vulnerable end and the middle-class community at the resilient end, purely on the basis of access to resources (with resources recognized to be not simply economic but also cultural). While this was generally the case, the reality, as with most research, revealed a much more complex matrix rather than a simple binary opposition. However, in identifying strengths in working-class communities and weaknesses in middle-class ones, this paper should not be read as a denial of fundamental inequalities or special pleading on behalf of middle-class disaster victims. The argument is not that social class has no analytical power but rather that it must be interrogated closely to reveal an often hidden diversity.

Beyond social class, vulnerability-creation and resilience-building are also dependent upon sometimes inter-linking—sometimes divergent—networks of individuals and groups within the wider community. A parallel (but much larger) research project in the U.S. on Hurricane Andrew (Peacock, Morrow, and Gladwin 1997) arrives at a similar conclusion, that "a community is an ecological network of groups and organizations linked through divisions of labor based on contingent relationships" in which competition and conflict are inherent (Peacock and Ragsdale 1997: 24). While evidence was found, in both Hurricane Andrew and the two case studies presented here, of the "therapeutic community," so also was its opposite: "While co-operation certainly exists, recovery typically entails sets of negotiations that can best be characterized as competitive, potentially conflict-ridden, and stressful. Many of the network's social units occupy similar niches, placing them in competition for scarce resources and services" (Peacock and Ragsdale 1997: 25). It is important not to see these networks as static but rather dynamic and contingent. Disaster management itself is an agent of change in this landscape and must be alert to its effects. This is discussed further below.

The next section attempts to set out, in simplified form, some of the socio-spatial variation within a given disaster-hit community. The class factor is the main focus here (see Fordham 1998 and Fordham and Ketteridge 1998 for the specifically gendered perspective on these case studies).

"Rivertown"

Figure 1 shows a simplified community called "Rivertown" in a landscape of flood risk. It is intended to illustrate some of the complexity hidden in commonly used categories and concepts such as "community," "working-class," "middle-class," etc. Rivertown is clearly a fictitious community but one based on specific case study areas in Scotland, and the examples and verbatim extracts given below are real examples. Nevertheless, it remains a simplified representation of ideal types and it is accepted that for all the examples given, there will be many exceptions.

Figure 2: "Rivertown"

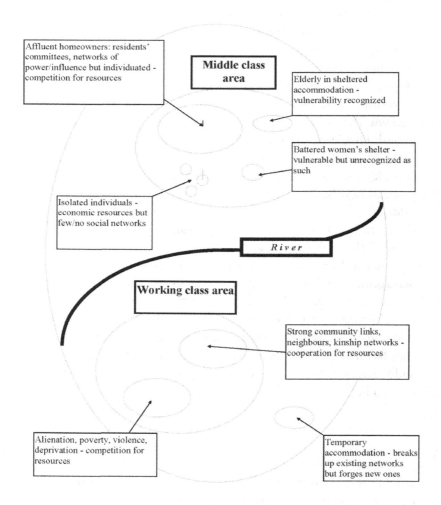

Affluent homeowners: residents' committees, networks of power/influence but individuated - competition for resources

Middle class area

Elderly in sheltered accommodation - vulnerability recognized

Battered women's shelter - vulnerable but unrecognized as such

Isolated individuals - economic resources but few/no social networks

River

Working class area

Strong community links, neighbours, kinship networks - cooperation for resources

Alienation, poverty, violence, deprivation - competition for resources

Temporary accommodation - breaks up existing networks but forges new ones

Rivertown can be regarded from the outside as a community (the problematic status of that term is accepted), but it contains within it a complex array of sub-communities, neighborhoods, and networks which are often socially and spatially distinct. In disasters, the geographic "labels" used to name them are often deceptive, tending to conceal more than they reveal. Particular locations are used to name disaster events because such areas may be well known, representative of the dominant social group, where the major damage was caused, or just where the media first located themselves. This can impose an erroneous homogeneity on the total disaster-hit area and can make invisible the smaller, often socially and politically subordinate groups and locations. Similarly, if "Rivertown" is the label given by the media to, in this case, a particular flood event, it may only be representative of one particular group, to the detriment of others. Even Rivertown is heterogeneous and must be subject to deconstruction.

In most localities, there are obvious physical differences between the easily recognizable working—and middle-class areas. In Rivertown, the former is distinguished by (frequently large) estates of tenanted social housing, often of architectural uniformity; the latter, by owner-occupied properties, generally small in number, often of some architectural variety. While physical distances may be small between these two locations, the inhabitants remain strangers to each other, with, sometimes surprisingly, little understanding of each other's experiences and needs.

The working-class community

In the working-class community there may be differences, spatially delineated and historically determined, which work for or against vulnerability limitation. The working-class community in Rivertown is divided into three different sub-areas for illustrative purposes.

The first working-class sub-community comprises alienated individuals or small groups living in poverty, violence, and deprivation. Here, women are survivors from everyday crises and have to be resilient, but disaster events can finally overwhelm their coping strategies. Here there is competition for resources, and information concerning the availability of disaster relief supplies sometimes does not pass further than the household or close family. Disaster management does not operate as expected because the emergency services (police especially) are not seen as sympathetic, and community members' first call for help goes instead to social workers and counselors who are outside the emergency response loop. Thus help is delayed, and individuals find later that they have inadvertently bypassed the main support services and missed out on support that others received.

Local authorities often have lists of cheap hotel and Bed and Breakfast (in Britain, unlike in the U.S., refers to less expensive rooms) accommodation for use in times of emergency such as floods or, more frequently, to house homeless people. When extreme events occur, they have to telephone around to find more. Because resources are limited (and, arguably, sometimes because of value judgements about those in need), these places are at the lower end of the quality scale and may not have been officially "vetted" for suitability and standards. While it appears to those outside the situation that social housing tenants have been well and efficiently provided for, an insider's view is often at variance:

> They sent us to the X Guest House. We went there and thought "great, this is lovely, clean." Because upstairs was immaculate, spotless. They took us down to show us the rooms . . . it was filthy. The bedding, there was cigarette burns all over it, there was urine stains all over it . . . . There were cooking facilities but only at a certain time . . . . They wouldn't put the heating on. When we left the [flooded] house, we left with nothing, just what we had on . . . . I asked the landlady if she could give us a wee towel, and she said no, they didn't supply the towels because the tenants who'd been in were stealing them, and I said, but we're flood victims, I'm just asking for a towel to wash ourselves and we'll bring it straight back up. I said the kids are filthy, they're needing [to be] washed. So for four days and four nights, we couldn't get back into our own houses to get the kids' clothes, we didn't know there

were places we could go to, to get clothing . . . . Nobody
had told us these things, that you could go to certain places
to get clothing, and things that you needed . . . . It felt
as though they weren't doing enough for us . . . [a flood
had] never happened to us before, so they didn't know
what they were doing . . . . Social Work department, the
Housing, you know, these people didn't know what they
were doing, they were just as confused as we were.

This gives an insight, not just into the plight of flood victims, but of
homeless persons who have to face this prospect daily. Clearly, when
extreme events occur, there is a major demand on accommodation
that has to be met with whatever is available. However, before (or soon
after) placing highly traumatized individuals and families in temporary
accommodation, it is vital that certain minimal checks are carried out.
Public money is being used to pay for this particular form of private
enterprise, and minimum standards must be instigated.

The flood-hit Rivertown may be further internally divided
through disaster management decisions for the allocation of relief
funds. The management of collections of many thousands of pounds
for disaster victims is always highly political and very sensitive. In
Rivertown a decision was made to allocate funds according to need, to
those without insurance, for example, rather than simply according to
flood experience. The "Flood Fund" became re-named the "Hardship
Fund," and, while this may appear a just and efficient use of always
limited funds, the result here was to stigmatize those without insurance
and anger those in possession of it. It became a significant cause of
conflict within the community to the extent that neighbors no longer
spoke to each other afterwards.

> The community has been cut right down the middle,
> because people got a lot of money.
>
>   *   *   *
>
> It was just from one side of the road to the other side of
> the road . . . . The [river] did a lot of damage but money
> done more.

*   *   *

> Once they came home [from the temporary accommodation] and you saw . . . I mean there was a lady, and I've seen her house, and I mean I would kill for her house, kill for it! [said laughing]. And this is what everybody is saying. People who weren't insured got better houses, better than they ever had. Everything was new. I would kill for that!

Those without insurance are seen by the insured as irresponsible in not choosing to protect themselves against future flood risk and therefore not deserving of relief funds. However, in some high-crime areas, flood insurance (with premiums set on crime statistics, not flood risk) is unavailable to the poorest members because it is too expensive; it is not necessarily the case that they *choose* not to buy insurance.

An example from the 1997 Moray floods is indicative of the problems that can arise in the use of temporary accommodation that normally has a specific function. One family (a lone mother with two children at home) was placed in a homeless persons' hostel. While this property was newly built, structurally sound, clean, and well decorated, its usual tenants were subject to strict rules which were also imposed on the flood victims. There was no personal telephone (one was available in the Warden's office where there was no privacy); tenants had to check in and out, including all visitors (this was very difficult for the children and their friends who also had to check in and out each time). No visitors were allowed after 11:00 p.m.; tenants had to report if likely to be out late; the key to the dwelling could not be taken off the premises. No alcohol was allowed on the premises, and staff came in daily to check for damage.

As a council tenant she had no choice but to accept this accommodation. She could not choose to go anywhere else. And choice, or the lack of it, is the key differentiating factor between the middle-class and working-class areas and people. While some of the difficulties faced by middle-class flood victims are set out below, nevertheless, at a general level, they are less vulnerable through their ability to exercise choice and a degree of control over their lives.

The second working-class area has strong community links, neighbor and kinship networks:

> I went down, got my pensioner [senior citizen] and put most of her stuff up[stairs], and I said "Right, lock up and come and stay with us."
>
> *   *   *
>
> [In] the flooding everybody coped together, "Can I help you?", "I've got clothes there," "I've got this here." Because everybody was in the same boat. And everybody helped everybody out. You know, "I've got stuff over here," "I've got a kettle you could have." . . . Yeh it was great . . . there was a great community spirit.

In such communities, neighbors/relatives check that all have received the call to evacuate before themselves evacuating, and there is co-operation over resources (when one hears of free clothing being given to flood survivors, they tell the others so all can benefit). Because many working-class communities are situated in large estates, vulnerability is reduced through strength of numbers and the support systems (both official and unofficial) which accompany them. Because of the large numbers in one place, emergency services prioritize the area for evacuation; after the flood, insurance companies may set up mobile offices to give help and advice to claimants, and the local authorities often set up a "Flood Team" to give advice on claiming from flood or hardship funds. However, a more negative aspect may be a process of "massification," where people feel that they are never treated as individuals with specific needs but always as an undifferentiated group—"flood victim." They are made to feel grateful for what they are given even when it is inadequate or misplaced.

Existing community networks are sometimes disrupted by disaster management itself when people are split up and moved away to temporary accommodation while their disaster-damaged homes are repaired. Women who care for sick, disabled, or elderly relatives and neighbors or provide unpaid child care for their grandchildren perform a vital—though insufficiently acknowledged—community function:

> I was kind of worried about my Ma as well because the days [the home help] wasn't in I would go down . . . to make her supper, then I'd be down to put her to bed, because she's disabled. But with all that happening I couldn't go near my Ma.
>
> I'm [wanting] somewhere where me and my daughter can be next to each other. Just for the sake of me watching the bairn [child] for her, she would need to pay a childminder and she's not got the money, and I wouldn't like anybody else to watch my grand-bairn, it's my only one, my first, I wouldn't like anybody else to watch her.

But even simple friendships provide a lifeline for unemployed women alone or with young children at home on a daily basis:

> I feel kind of lost just not being next to Jean. We were next door to each other. Just being away from her I've felt lost. Just so alone . . . . It's only wee silly things. They mean that much to you, but obviously people don't see it that way because they've not been through it . . . but all the wee things, they mean that much to you and suddenly not to have them any more, it can upset you . . . . If it happens to me again, I'm not coming out of my house . . . . It's not on.

Where some choice can be exercised over the location of people in temporary accommodation it is important that women are not separated from their support networks. However, there is the potential for new networks to be forged in these more distant locations. Women in temporary accommodation in a caravan park formed new networks in the laundry area where 50 families had to share one, later two, washing machines (Fordham 1998; Fordham and Ketteridge 1998):

The camaraderie amongst the women was second to none. All folk were in the laundry. But none of these women could identify any of the others' partner! They'd be sitting in the caravans at night and a man would pass. They wouldn't be able to say who it was. Because the men lived in solitude. They went out to work, came back and sat in the caravan. There wasn't the same mix, the men didn't mix on the site.

And similar disruptions and bondings occur when people return to their repaired homes: "It was strange coming back here because the neighbor we did know [before the flood], we did'na know again, if you know what I mean. You forgot about them, you just had to make friends with them again . . . it was like starting again." Thus, working-class communities show an internal diversity of experience which may manifest itself as either vulnerability or resilience.

The middle-class community

The middle-class community can also be seen to be divided into several sub-communities. The first is the more (stereo)typical, containing relatively affluent homeowners with access to economic resources, insurance, networks of power and influence in the wider community, and social and cultural capital. These resources tend to make them resilient. For example, they are better able to replace lost belongings, to influence future mitigation proposals in their interest, and, through their class position, to command respect (see Skeggs 1997 on the importance of respectability to working-class women). Action groups, set up to campaign for flood defense works, are often gendered and dominated by the men in the local area who assume responsibility in this, the more public, domain. However, a key defining value of individualism, usually seen by the middle-class as a major strength, can be a weakness in disaster and can increase vulnerability. The middle-class victims of disaster must act as individuals to protect their interests with insurance companies, builders, letting agencies for temporary accommodation, etc., and in competition with each other. Some have compared their own experiences unfavorably to working-class communities (see also Morrow 1997: 167, for similar findings) who had agents working for them as a group and who appeared to have had better conditions and services secured for them:

> Where it's council property that's affected they will get work done quicker than what they would if it's private property. I think you're left very much on your own. "Well, too bad," you know, "you get on with it." This is the attitude I think.

> *   *   *

> And what we found here was all the help was focused on X [working-class housing estate]. I mean we got no help whatsoever . . . . Everything was focused on X . . . nothing got filtered out here . . . and that got on our nerves.

> *   *   *

> They [the Flood Team] did a lot, I know, they organized a lot for the kids and all that kind of thing but I felt that it was for people that were with the council. I didn't think it was really for us . . . "Us"! That sounds really snobby but you think that they're actually less fortunate than you whereas they're not . . . if you'd bought your house then you weren't quite as welcome to go to get benefits and things like that. That when you went they were all looking at you and saying "Tut! Greedy person" sort of thing, you know "you can manage yourself" whereas you don't always manage yourself.

Some middle-class residents had difficulty finding temporary accommodation while their homes were being repaired. They were in competition with the other flood victims, and good property nearby was hard to find. They found themselves forced to take low quality, rented houses which were dirty and in poor repair—well below what they normally considered to be an acceptable standard. This they contrasted with the powers of local authorities to get access more easily to large numbers of better quality properties for their tenants. (The working-class interviewees, however, often had other views on the properties made available to them; see above.)

The second, middle-class community sub-division is elderly sheltered or wardened accommodation where age and infirmity make the residents potentially vulnerable. Ironically, however, such places are usually well known in terms of their exposure to risk; they appear on relevant lists and generally are among the first to be contacted ("rescued") in times of disaster. Thus, this particular sub-community becomes less susceptible through its visibility and identification as vulnerable. However, this is not always the case, and emergency responders cannot be complacent about this and assume that someone has contacted the residents, as this example from the working-class community illustrates:

> By this time [the water] was coming in, all the drains were coming up, so I thought, "Right, I'll get out the back." It was worse out the back, I couldn't get out there either. So I've one of those alarm phones and I pressed the button and, they're very, very good, so she said, "How can we help you Mrs A?" I said, "This place is being flooded." "Yes," she said, "We're watching it on the television!" "Well," I said, "would you please get somebody to get us out!"

This experience was told with some humor, but it could have had serious consequences. Sheltered housing, as in this case, is normally single story with no upper floors to which to escape, and in Rivertown the floodwaters rose with considerable speed and to a depth sufficient to drown.

Thirdly, an elderly middle-class woman on her own in an outlying fragmented community or isolated location, even if she has financial resources and insurance, is potentially as vulnerable and in need of help as a woman in a large working-class community which may not have the same financial resources or insurance but may have access to social networks such as neighbors, family, and welfare support workers. Post-disaster resources are often located—for very good reasons—in those locations deemed to be, numerically, hardest hit, but there is a danger that pressing needs on the small or individual scale will be neglected as this example illustrates:

> There was an emergency number we had seen in the paper and we phoned this number and . . . very cheeky he was too and he said, "Oh we're very busy in X [large social housing estate], it's flooded there too." And I said, "Yes, but I'm flooded here and I'm an old lady," I says, "and I live on my own," and I mean by this time I was literally on my own because nobody could get down . . . . "Oh, leave your name and we'll get back to you." Never heard from them yet! At the time all I wanted was somebody to come in and give a little bit of an ear or just a little bit of comfort or tell me what to do or tell me how to do things.

Such women alone can be very vulnerable during a disaster (having few or no neighbors to call on for help to move property to safety or to help them evacuate) and afterwards in terms of access to information and psychological support.

Fourthly, there may be women victims of domestic violence who may be invisible in their own households or, potentially, more visible in shelters for battered women. This is a group not as yet widely recognized in disaster management (Morrow and Enarson 1994; Enarson 1998) and therefore potentially vulnerable:

> Severe weather events . . . isolate women at home in unsafe environments without working telephones or accessible roads; contact with crisis counselors may be cut off and court-ordered protection unavailable when major disasters disrupt or destroy lifeline services, including law enforcement agencies. (Enarson 1997: 2)

Domestic violence is not confined to a particular social class, and such cases could be found anywhere. Where a refuge is known to exist, then its particular vulnerability in time of disaster should be recognized and acted upon (Enarson 1997). But effective progress in this initiative depends on prior networking between relevant groups to reduce women's vulnerability (Neal and Phillips 1990).

Thus the middle-class women, perceived to be at the resilient end of the vulnerability-resilience continuum through their access to resources, may not always be so. They may be isolated and cut off from social networks which might aid them—perhaps through physical distance, perhaps because of the social stigma attached to seeking help from welfare agencies, perhaps as the result of individual life events and emotional/psychological difficulties. Their material position may aid resilience, but they may still be in need of counseling or advice or other kinds of support.

POLICY IMPLICATIONS AND RECOMMENDATIONS

This paper examines gender and, more specifically, social class in two major flood events and argues for a more nuanced appreciation of these factors, at both the conceptual and the practical level, to be incorporated throughout the disaster process. Disaster management decisions are often influenced by an over-simple conception of their social setting and fail to recognize the internal diversity of communities that may demand greater, fewer, or different resources. A recognition of difference, as suggested above, can lead to more efficient, effective, and sympathetic resource allocation. This need not result in an absolute increase in funding or staffing but rather a rethinking of some resourcing decisions. These points are expanded under separate headings below.

Empowering the victims/survivors

Those who experience floods and other disasters can (and often do, if allowed) make their own contributions towards management. Too often, professionals enter the disaster area with the intention of taking complete control and overriding existing networks and abilities (this is particularly the case in working-class areas). Placing people in emergency rest centers and administering to them in a top-down fashion can be disempowering and often demeaning. A better way of thinking about such emergency provision is in terms of an enabling function that gives victims/survivors greater control and the space to make a positive contribution. This is beginning to be recognized by some disaster workers, generally those in the social work field:

> For God's sake! You've got resources! You've got 300 people sitting here! Traumatized they may be but they're not incapables. Yesterday they were running households, they were managing . . . that hasn't been destroyed overnight. They still have those qualities and maybe we should be the ones that's giving them those back. [Social worker, part of the Flood Team]

*   *   *

> It seems like a very "social work" kind of thing to say but I think its important that people don't get overrun in terms of the decision making process. That people have various capacities to make decisions, we all have those capacities and we should make sure that folks will be allowed to make those decisions and we should not make those decisions for them. But . . . I'm not saying we shouldn't give them support, advice and help. It's remarkable how some people . . . they realize there's a crisis, they call out, "What're we going to do?" With a bit of advice and a bit of help they reach their own decisions about what they want to do and that seems to me perfectly correct that they did that. Other people, with less resources, couldn't make decisions and in a sense we sought to make more decisions on their behalf. I suppose. With the less resourceful folk. [Social worker]

Retaining self-esteem

Official provision, however well-intentioned, can be unpalatable and, because of that, may be subverted. One elderly flood victim/

survivor revealed that she continued to attend a weekly "drop-in" center, set up by a social services department to provide community support for flood victims/survivors, not because she still had need of it but to support the social workers who were running it! It is important for people's self-respect that they are not always on the receiving end but feel that they are in a position to give. This woman retained self-esteem through the belief that she was the one that was providing.

The right person for the job

Furthermore, while this paper has focused on some of the diversity and the conflicts within the victim/survivor community, there is equal diversity and conflict within the disaster management community. Disasters are high profile events, and they can make or break people's professional careers. They are perceived by some to be "plum jobs": "Disasters are sexy! Professionals often get involved, not out of altruism but out of a recognition that they can see an opening, they are empire building, then they get in there and close the doors to other people who genuinely want to lend a hand." [Social Worker].

Some professionals are not the right persons for the job. They are there for a variety of reasons and skill and experience may not be included; neither is a willingness to relinquish control. Placing more control with the communities themselves is necessary to ensure the correct identification of problems and needs from a community perspective (see Maskrey 1989). These needs, and the accompanying provision, are also likely to be diverse; what is suitable for one group may not be suitable for another. If provision is made that is unsuitable, then it means resources are being wasted.

The need to understand social theory

This adds to the skills necessary for emergency/disaster managers and calls more for an understanding of social theory in disaster management than an extension or improvement of technical abilities. This is normally the province of social workers, often at the later stages of the disaster process, but the research presented above suggests a need at all stages and for all disaster workers. Clearly resources are not infinite, and choices must be made about where to allocate them. The bulk of resources must still go to the areas containing the largest numbers or the hardest hit (in terms of physical damage or danger), but other groups and individuals outside this area must also be evaluated for need. We cannot assume that a woman in a middle-class area, with some capital and insurance, will necessarily be resilient in an extreme event. A minimum level of support must be available, should it be necessary. But neither can we assume that a working-class woman is without all resources or the ability to articulate her needs. A sensitivity to difference is required.

CONCLUSION

Disasters are not the great levelers that they are sometimes claimed to be, but neither are they understood in terms of a simple code of social stratification. This is not to deny that social class remains a key determinant of vulnerability and that working-class communities generally will be materially more affected, but rather to claim a greater variability than disaster managers sometimes recognize. Gender-sensitive analyses also show a differential experience and response, but much more work remains to be done in this area, particularly with men's experiences. This paper argues for a more nuanced appreciation of these factors, at both the conceptual and the practical level, to be incorporated throughout the disaster process.

4

GENDER AND DISASTER:

A synthesis of flood research in Bangladesh

William E. Lovekamp

INTRODUCTION

Despite the wide body of literature on disasters and their impacts, there has been a persistent "gender silence" in disaster work (Bhatt 1995:3; Enarson and Fordham 2001; Fothergill 1998). Bolin, Jackson, and Crist (1998: 29) argue, "the voice of women is indeed the most noticeable absence in the literature." This gender silence is systemic as it is very evident within the larger political arena and social structure. As Siddiqui (2001: 1A) states "still they [women] are subjects of discrimination in every day life and cannot achieve minimum humane respect from the male-dominated social systems." Gender is a critical variable that researchers have too often ignored. A gender-neutral stance is frequently taken in disaster research which causes the differential impacts and experiences of disasters to be overlooked and men's experience is considered to be representative (Fordham 1998). Furthermore, the research community has only recently admitted that "exposure to risk of disaster is shaped by overarching social structures of caste and class, race and ethnicity, age and physical ability, and sex and gender" (Enarson and Morrow 1998:2). We must acknowledge that vulnerability to disasters varies for men and women, people of different racial and ethnic backgrounds, and across social classes. "Equality . . . cannot be achieved by ignoring differences; this simply reinforces the dominance of already dominant groups" (Phillips 1997:143).

This paper explores how gender intersects with the disaster process and the larger socio-political arena by examining the current literature and illustrates the importance of examining gender in disaster research with specific regard to Bangladesh. Khondker (1996) highlights key issues recurrent of disasters in developing countries that serve as general thesis statements for this research. The first is an awareness of the vulnerability of women's economic activities, particularly in rural, agricultural sectors. Second, women's response, recovery and indigenous coping strategies are often unique and need to be considered. Third, social and cultural norms and unequal access to assistance may perpetuate and deepen gender inequality.

I make use of a nine-stage disaster typology in this paper to ensure adequate coverage of the entire disaster cycle and to systematically highlight the aforementioned set of issues. The typology or theoretical construct of the disaster cycle is as follows: (1) exposure to risk; (2) risk perception; (3) preparedness behavior; (4) warning communication and response; (5) physical impacts; (6) psychological impacts; (7) emergency response; (8) recovery; and (9) reconstruction (Fothergill 1996:34). This typology is based on the cyclical model of the human ecological perspective that uses the following categories: preparedness, response, recovery, and mitigation. These refined categories allow for a more detailed analysis of research, illuminate gaps in our knowledge base, and highlight issues of gender and stratification (Fothergill 1996). This typology has been used to synthesize research on race and ethnicity and gender in the United States (Fothergill 1996; Fothergill, Maestas, and Darlington 1999). This research attempts to integrate a cross-cultural dimension into the theoretical construct by providing an overview of disaster research addressing the intersection of gender and disasters in Bangladesh.

We can learn a great deal about the intersection of gender and disasters through systematic examination of Bangladesh, as it is one of the most disaster prone countries in the world. "Both natural and manmade disasters erode development opportunities of this country tapping an estimated 60 percent of her 120 million people in poverty and leaving them vulnerable to future risks" (Khondker 1996: 281). Demographically, Bangladesh is a country that is slightly larger than England and approximately the same size as Wisconsin, but with a population of 120 million, it has one of the highest population densities in the world (Alexander 2000: 202). Research emphasizes an identifiable link between disasters and population density when examining the economic costs. Furthermore, "since the 1960's, economic losses from natural disasters on a global scale have tripled, while insured losses have quintupled"(Barton and Nishenko 1997: 1).

The country of Bangladesh and her people fall victim to floods, tropical cyclones and storm surges, droughts, and tornadoes almost yearly. Floods are indisputably the most frequent and devastating natural disaster in Bangladesh (Alexander 2000; Paul 1997). Bangladesh consists of a deltaic floodplain of approximately 250 rivers and on average, flood waters inundate anywhere from twenty to forty percent of the total land area (Alexander 2000: 202). In addition, the country is located at the north end of the Bay of Bengal and is situated at the delta of the Ganges, Brahmaputra (sometimes referred to as the Jamuna), and Meghna rivers. These rivers are the major contributors to flooding in the country.

The people of Bangladesh must deal with several different types of floods such as flash floods, local floods, normal floods, major floods, and storm surge floods on a regular, almost annual, basis. These floods have a variety of effects. They can damage crops and properties because of high water flow velocities that exceed the carrying capacity of the river systems, or generate water volumes that overwhelm drainage capacity and cause localized flooding. The rivers can also rise owing to ice and snow melt from the Himalayan mountain ranges to the north, heavy amounts of continuous rainfall, and the opening of dams (barrages) in the neighboring country of India (Khan 1998: 221). Furthermore, cyclones bring heavy rains and cause water levels to rise in the oceans which causes water to back up into the deltaic areas during the post-monsoon period (October-November) and the pre-monsoon period (April-June) (Khan 1998: 221; Shahjahan 1998: 41).

My hope is that the integration of women's voices into the various stages of the disaster process will create an opportunity for social change and lead to women's increased empowerment in Bangladesh. In what follows, I provide a synthesis of relevant literature within each stage of the disaster cycle.

RESEARCH FINDINGS

Exposure to risk

This section examines literature on women's exposure to risk in Bangladesh and supports the notion that vulnerability to disasters is unequally distributed across classes, racial and ethnic groups, and genders. Survey findings of flood damages from Bangladesh suggest that the poor, who are primarily women and children, are the socioeconomic group most at risk and affected by flooding (Ikeda 1995; Paul 1997; Shahjahan 1998). Most of these poor women live in rural areas and rely heavily on agriculture as their main source of income. "Fifty-five percent of the labor force is dependent upon some form of agricultural employment and approximately 90 percent of women still work in agriculture" (Hanchett 1997: 43). The poor and women often live in high-risk areas, rural and agricultural, because they cannot afford to live in the cities or areas that are at lower risk. They also have a more difficult time recovering from disasters owing to their lack of financial resources. Sometimes, they cannot even afford to restore or rebuild their homes to the pre-disaster state, purchase food, or obtain adequate health care. Other times, they must pursue new and different economic ventures in other areas for survival. Some people must resort to living on charlands which are basically sandbars that emerge as islands as a result of silt deposits and are very vulnerable to flooding, erosion, storms and sandcarpeting (Chowdhury 2001:4). The estimated population of the chars in 1993 was approximately 630,000, which constitutes a 47% increase in population from 1984 (Chowdhury 2001:5). Simply put, the poorest of the poor seek survival in charlands placing them in an extremely vulnerable situation.

In his study of three communities in Bangladesh, Raymond Wiest (1998: 71) found that "char and embankment zones have nearly three times as many women-headed households as noneroded zones" where men are most often absent. Men often leave in the home in search of relief materials, work, or simply abandon women and children further increasing their vulnerability. He appropriately calls this abandonment "the flight of men and the plight of women-headed households" (Wiest 1998:68).

Furthermore, rural women in Bangladesh are often economically vulnerable in floods, partially due to the allocation of micro-credit loans. Theoretically, these loans empower women by increasing their autonomy and decision-making within the household, promoting more social interaction, and enhancing their economic status by generating extra income. However, while micro-credit loans are theoretically viewed as helpful in the development of Bangladesh's economy, these loans reinforce the cycle of poverty and debt and potentially increase women's vulnerability to future disasters. These loans "are largely targeted at women from the poorest sections of the population; they lend small sums of money to individuals as members of groups and rely on group liability to ensure loan repayment" (Kabeer 2001: 63). In 1995, more than 3 million poor women received small loans (Steele, Ami, and Naved 2001). Some of the largest NGO's (nongovernmental organizations) responsible for issuing micro-credit loans are BRAC (Bangladesh Rural Advancement Committee), Grameen Bank and ASA.

Floods also often disrupt the normal flow of income, which increases women's vulnerability. Bangladeshi women rely heavily on agriculture, and flooding often destroys cropland, kills farm animals and causes land erosion. Following the 1998 floods, some women were unable to continue their income-earning activities such as selling vegetables, sugar cane or selling clothes (Rashid 2000: 248). This income disparity also makes it very difficult for women with micro-credit loans to keep up with their payments. Micro-credit lenders usually expect women to repay their loans over a two-year period on a weekly basis (Steele et al. 2001). In most instances, women are still expected to repay their loans even when normal activities are disrupted.

During the floods of 1998, micro-credit NGOs channeled disaster relief loans to flood-affected people and micro-credit workers maintained weekly contact with members and offered interest free consumption loans to members in flooded areas (Hashemi and Ahmed 1999). Furthermore, repayments were deferred in some flooded areas and BRAC, Grameen Bank and other NGOs provided fresh loans and rescheduled repayments to help decrease the burdens on flood-affected people (Hashemi and Ahmed 1999). Despite their efforts, many women still "complained that they were having difficulties repaying loans and had resorted to borrowing from different people (loan sharks and relatives) to repay these loans" (Rashid 2000: 248).

Finally, the importance of women's roles in everyday family life is often ignored and unrecognized, and women are expected to carry the primary burden of caring for the household. Women's role as principal caregivers places them at higher risk to disasters. Paul (1997: 104) notes that the fulfillment of women's traditional gender-based roles in the overwhelmingly patriarchal culture of the country becomes even more difficult during disasters. They are still expected to take care of their families' emotional needs, take care of the children, cook, maintain family health, and procure safe drinking water, along with many other vital tasks. Women have the primary responsibility of protecting the family and home and are responsible for most of the activities that are required to restart a normal life after a flood (Nasreen 1999: 36-37). Furthermore, women's gender assigned tasks usually become more difficult, while men's responsibilities are suspended during floods (Nasreen 1999: 36). Although some research suggests that the gendered division of labor and traditional gender roles break down during disasters, more recent research shows that women's roles expand during disasters (Fothergill 1999).

Future research should continue to explore vulnerability of micro-credit and repayment problems after disasters as Grameen loan delinquency rates are rising (Pearl and Phillips 2001). We also need to expand research of cultural factors that continue to place women at risk. Finally, despite the fact that most of Dhaka was flooded in 1998, very little attention has been directed at urban flooding in Bangladesh.

Risk perception

This section examines how men and women differentially perceive risk. Fothergill (1996: 37) states that women tend to perceive disasters as more serious and risky than do men and speculates, "it is possible that women are more concerned because of their relative lack of power and control in society." Cutter et al. (1992: 10) have found that women and men perceive the world differently and conclude that men are risk-takers, while women are risk-avoiders. One contributing factor to the gender differences in risk-taking behavior may be linked to women's role as family caretakers. Women look after children and the household while men may leave the home and relocate to cities or nonflooded areas to find employment often never sending money back to their wives or returning home. This might lead women to internalize the risk of disasters more seriously as they are left at home to take care of the family (Paul 1997). Furthermore, during the 1991 cyclone and tidal surge in Bangladesh, many respondents stated, "We hear the cyclone warning No. 10 (great danger level) several times a year. But, usually nothing serious happens. So, we thought that the water would not come" (Ikeda 1995: 182). In other words, they do not believe they are at great risk for a catastrophic disaster. This area however, has received very little research attention. We need to begin by investigating whether men and women perceive risk differently, examining factors that contribute to these perceptions, and whether their risk-taking behaviors are related to gender and poverty.

Preparedness behavior

Preparedness behavior involves preparatory efforts and mitigation against disasters. It includes activities such as "formulating, testing, and exercising disaster plans; providing training for disaster responders and the general public; and communicating with the public and others about disaster vulnerability and what to do to reduce it" (Mileti 1999: 215). Preparation for disasters also varies according to gender. Women seem to be more active in preparing their families for disasters and work at the grassroots, community level more than men. This is often perceived as an extension of their traditional gender roles and responsibilities (Fothergill 1996: 38). Many contributors to the online conference of the United Nations Division for the Advancement of Women noted, "women's domestic responsibilities situate them to act proactively to reduce risks and protect the most vulnerable" (Enarson 2001: 5). Just before the Bangladesh cyclone of 1991 made landfall, women were responsible for "packing clothes and valuables, getting household possessions to the roof and feeding the children while men took care of securing livestock, protecting paddy stock and securing the home" (Ikeda 1995: 183). Despite their efforts at the community level, women are not as well represented in more formalized sectors of disaster mitigation. Men are visible in formal emergency management positions (Wilson 1999). Women's efforts to mitigate against and cope with disasters generally take place behind the scenes (Enarson 2001: 6).

In a study of Bangladeshi women's participation in agriculture and their participation in governmental flood adjustment strategies, Susan Hanchett (1997: 54) found that "many female household heads in [the] sample owned land, but had no men to represent them despite their presumably strong interest in agriculture." Furthermore, Hanchett attempted to convince the men on the Flood Action Plan (FAP) Board to include Bangladesh women but they objected to her proposal. They perceived women's work as extraneous to the serious business of increasing agricultural production and changing water management and also "assumed that if women had any interests in the flood/agriculture situation, there would be men to represent them in discussions" (Hanchett 1997: 54). This example illustrates that women's concerns are often overlooked and women are poorly represented in the formal sector when preparing for disasters.

Structural flood adjustment strategies generally take one of two forms. One structural approach to flood mitigation is to control flooding by building large reservoirs in the mountainous regions of the rivers so the amounts of water flowing through the farming regions of the country can actively be monitored and regulated. Another is to construct embankments to prevent, divert, and/or regulate flooding.

Many people argue that these structural adjustment measures would not produce significant beneficial results compared to the financial costs of the projects. "A massive investment of as much as U.S. $60 billion in dam construction would produce a reduction of as little as 0.4 metres in flood peaks in Bangladesh" (Haque and Zaman 1994: 72). Alexander (2000: 207) argues, "human use of the land must inevitably adapt to (floods) and any attempt to thwart it is likely to fail." Another problem is that approximately 90% of the water in Bangladesh originates from outside of the country's geographical boundaries. Hence, Bangladesh has been trying to establish a link with India so that they may share canal-waterway rights. This link would hopefully allow Bangladesh to have more control over the flows of water and dams (barrages) within their boundaries currently controlled by outside forces. Also, construction of embankments along the major rivers would require a principal expenditure of as much as US $10 billion (Bingham 1989: 42). These embankments also may provide the people living in the flood-prone areas with a false sense of security and they may fail to take the necessary preventative measures. Furthermore, damage is often more severe in areas within embankments than in areas outside it (Thompson and Sultana 1996; Paul 1997). Embankments built to control water flow also increase silt deposits and reduce the carrying capacity of rivers. Finally, embankments have the possibility of depriving farmers of the benefits of the natural flood season.

Despite the knowledge we have on disaster preparedness, we need to investigate the role of organizations and cultural forces in mitigating against floods. A few studies, for example, have found that powerful elites often control the placement of shelters and many of the poorest and most vulnerable populations find them to be inaccessible (Khan 1991; Kafi 1992). Extensive research is needed to examine women's involvement in grassroots mitigation efforts. We also need to explore whether structural attempts at flood control lead to increased dependency upon large multinational corporations that fund projects rather than empowerment. Finally, we must examine how to integrate disaster projects and development projects together so that they serve those in need most effectively (See Guarnizo 1993).

Warning communication and response

Warning communication and response includes the dissemination and reception of disaster bulletins, watches, and warnings as well as actions taken in response to warnings. Most disaster researchers concur that women and men perceive disaster warnings differently and also respond to them differently. Fothergill (1996: 39) states, "women are more likely to receive risk communication, due to their social networks, and to respond with protective actions, such as evacuation."

Bangladesh has also sought to increase the effectiveness of warning systems. As part of the Flood Action Plan, the United Nations and the government of Bangladesh established a national flood forecasting office located in Dhaka, the Flood Forecast and Warning Center (FF & WC). The purpose of this center is to forecast floods and report on daily water levels and rainfall summaries during the flood season (Kachic 1998: 71). However, researchers at the center conclude that despite providing accurate and timely forecasts and warnings, still no comprehensive national effort exists to disseminate this information once they have issued forecasts and warnings.

Furthermore, not everyone takes the warnings seriously and simply do not respond to them for various reasons. Studies of the 1991 cyclone reveal that although most people were informed of the approaching cyclone four to twelve hours prior to landfall, almost no one evacuated before the storm surge (Ikeda 1995). While men were more aware of cyclone warnings, had more information regarding the locations of shelters, women often had to obtain warning information from men, and "the decision whether, when and where to take refuge was made mainly by men" (Ikeda 1995:183). Men and women alike did not seek shelter because they tended not to believe the severity of the storm warnings, were fearful of property theft if they did seek shelter, and often did not have access to nearby shelters (Ikeda 1995). Khondker's (1996: 286) study of women's flood experiences in villages of Bangladesh found that out of forty female respondents interviewed, twenty-four placed household possessions in a safer place, twenty elevated homes to keep them from the floods, eight people moved their livestock and children to higher ground, and only four respondents left their homes and went to shelters after hearing warnings. Also, in countries such as Bangladesh, it is not uncommon for women who are confined to the house or family plot to have no access to disaster warnings through radio, TV, or other medium (Rodriquez as cited in Enarson 2001:5).

During the cyclone of 1997, 28% of the people did not leave their homes for fear of looting in their homes, 42% waited inside their homes "in faith of God's mercy," and 52% of the people did not take shelter because of inadequacies of relief shelters like "security for women and sanitation" (Staff Reporter 2001). We need to examine more extensively the constraints faced by women in gaining access to warning systems, the effectiveness of flood forecasting centers dissemination of information, and the use of this information once it is received.

Physical impacts

The physical impacts stage refers to populations' hardest hit and examines who suffers most from disasters. Women often suffer from physical impacts of disasters more than men. Floods pose a great number of health risks to women, as they tend to be the most vulnerable group (Blaikie, Cannon, Davis, and Wisner 1994: 133). Women face the problem of providing their family with clean drinking water during floods because wells are often consumed by contaminated floodwater and often have to travel great distances to find fresh water for their families (Ahmed 1999b: 28). If they cannot find fresh water, they are often forced to drink contaminated water, cook with floodwater, bathe and walk through floodwaters to get to work. Also, exposure to flood waters increases the risk of diseases such as diarrhea, viral fever, jaundice, and skin diseases. Of the 918 people that lost their lives as a result of the 1998 floods, more than half died as a result of health problems such as diarrhea (Ahmed 1999a: 151). Another problem that leads to higher risk of health problems is the lack of adequate plumbing or the disruption of normal sewage systems during floods (Ahmed 1999b: 28). Families that do not have the financial resources to readjust their sewage lines, if they even have proper sewage facilities, are forced to use other, more unsanitary means. Commonly, families pack waste into plastic bags and throw them out into the water (Ahmed 1999b:28). Nahar's story illustrates the complexities associated with women such as lack of access to sewage facilities.

> The most common method (when going to the restroom) is to sit on the edge of the raft, but modesty (and the patriarchal structure) prevents women from relieving themselves in view of others. Nahar tried to control her need for toilet facilities by eating as little food as possible; and she only went to the toilet at night. (Hanchett 1997: 54)

Moreover, Rashid and Michaud (2000) also found that during the floods of 1998, many women felt shame and embarrassment regarding publicly relieving themselves and would wait until late at night. Adolescent girls were concerned and ashamed about being exposed to the 'public eyes of men' while bathing, going to the toilet and sleeping (Rashid and Michaud 2000: 59). During menstruation, women are considered to be dangerous and dirty. During the floods of 1998, many women did not have adequate or proper facilities, which led to increased feelings of shame and increases in health problems (Rashid and Michaud 2000: 68).

Scarcities of food and nutrition that commonly exist for women and children as a result of gender inequality in Bangladeshi society are often more extreme during floods. In Bangladesh for instance, a female child receives twenty percent fewer calories than a male child due to the unequal distribution of food within the family (Hena 1992: 71). During floods, this scarcity can lead to increased health problems associated with a lack of nutrition (Paul 1997: 104; Paul 1999). Furthermore, governmental healthcare facilities and other organizations often cease to exist in the wake of a flood and women take on the role of health care providers. For instance, during the floods of 1998, women had knowledge about "certain medicinal plants and they used herbs, roots, and bark to cure family members from different types of diseases" (Nasreen 1999: 38). The situation is much the same on charlands as "institutional health care and sanitation facilities are very poor and health care of families is heavily dependent upon the traditional knowledge and practices (home remedies) of women" (Chowdhury 2001: 9).

Furthermore, mortality rates were consistently higher for women in virtually every age group after the 1991 cyclone as the death rate for women ages 20-44 was 71 per 1000 compared to 15 per 1000 for men (Chowdhury et al. 1992: 104; Chowdhury, Bhuyia, Choudhury, and Sen 1993). An interview of a father told the story of holding on to his son and daughter as tightly as he could so as not to drop them in floodwaters. When he could no longer hold both of them he "helplessly released one—[his] daughter" (Haider, Rahman, and Huq 1991: 64). In yet another example, a father of five daughters and one son trapped by floods released his daughters one at a time so that his son could survive (Akhter 1992: 64). This differential mortality rate is due in part to gender inequality that is built into the culture of Bangladesh, with women dependent on men for information dissemination, and unequal access to warning communication.

Rates of sexual violence and domestic abuse against women tend to increase in times of disasters and adolescent girls are often subjected to sexual harassment as they venture outside of the home to search for shelter or work (Anam 1999; Honeycombe 1994; Kafi 1992; Rashid and Michaud 2000; Wilson, Phillips, and Neal 1998). Anam (1999) states, "due to the floods domestic violence has increased as unemployed, jobless men vent their frustration on their wives" (p.30). These issues are mere realities for many women after disasters.

Despite having a fair amount of research on the physical impacts of floods, governmental response to higher crime rates and violence during disasters has not been thoroughly examined. We also need to continue exploring how women's health related problems, mortality rates, domestic violence and sexual abuse during disasters are related to larger patterns of gender inequality in Bangladesh.

Psychological impacts

Disasters can also cause both short and long-term emotional stress and trauma for victims. In general, the literature shows that men and women do not experience the same types and levels of psychological stresses. Women and children tend to experience more emotional trauma and anxiety, while men may be more likely to "suffer from alcohol abuse in times of disaster" (Fothergill 1996: 1999). Women also tend to exhibit higher levels of posttraumatic stress disorder than men following disasters (Ollenburger and Tobin 1998). Studies imply that higher levels of stress and anxiety are most often associated with women more than men because of women's roles as primary caregivers. One interesting finding after Hurricane Floyd demonstrated that women in counties that were moderately to severely affected reported lower levels of social support and sense of purpose than men (Van Willigen 2001: 75).

Given such general U.S. findings, very few studies have examined psychological aspects of floods in Bangladesh (Paul 1997). One study examined the effects of floods on children's behaviors and found that stressful events play a causal role of the development of behavior disorders in children (Durkin, Khan, and Davidson 1993). Yet in another study, a woman expressed that she was emotionally scarred more than her male counterpart because of the loss of her children in strong flood currents during the 1991 cyclone. She stated ". . . and my children slipped away from me" and felt "a man is a man, but what am I without my children?" (Bari 1992: 57). Another account tells of a mother and father who lost their only child during the floods. The mother went into a deep depression from the shock of losing her daughter (Rahman 1992:18). As women are often responsible for supporting the psychological needs of the family (Paul 1999), there is a definite need for more research on the psychological effects that floods have on women and children in Bangladesh and possible intervention strategies.

Emergency response

The emergency response phase is the immediate aftermath period of a disaster, from hours to approximately a week after the disaster event (Fothergill 1996). Within emergency response, "there is evidence of a gendered division of labor, with women helping more in the home, and men assisting more often outside the home" (Fothergill 1996:

44). Women use creative and indigenous means to survive, keep their families safe, and protect their homes and other economic assets as many daily functions become much more complicated because of floods. Preparing food for the family becomes a great challenge for women and calls for more creative ways to get the job done as cooking areas are submerged under water. The narrative of a woman who struggled through the 1998 floods exemplifies such creativity.

> Nahar had a lot of trouble with cooking. She first tried putting her mud stove (chula) on the banana tree raft, but when she started cooking the heat from the stove burned the raft.
>
> Then she moved the stove onto a broken wooden chair, but the chair also got burned from its heat. Finally, she got a broken 'tin' pot, set the stove on top of it, put the whole thing on the raft, where she was then able to cook without worrying. (Hanchett 1997: 54)

She was also successful in wading through the floodwaters to find bricks so that she could elevate her bed above flood levels and provide her family with a place to sleep (Hanchett 1997).

Research regarding relief efforts provides mixed conclusions. Some research stated that after the floods of 1988 and the devastating cyclone and tidal surge of 1991, people from every walk of life participated in relief efforts including the government, non-governmental organizations, the business community and many community groups, volunteer organizations and individuals. "Every organization collected relief goods: dry food, clothing and medicine; even water in plastic containers" (Rahman 1992: 19). However, other research suggests that women rarely ventured to relief centers to collect relief goods and only men were involved in relief work (Hena 1992: 72; Khondker 1996: 288). The cultural norms of Purdah, which prevents women from engaging in activities outside the household and emphasizes their responsibility of taking care of their children and home, discouraged many women from going to relief centers. Furthermore, relief simply did not reach women in remote areas (Hena 1992: 72).

Hence, we need to examine the effectiveness, location, and utilization of relief centers. Also, we must comparatively examine different areas of Bangladesh as this may account for mixed results regarding relief. We also need to continue researching both grassroots and organizational emergency response patterns and effectiveness. For instance, it seems that there is virtually no research examining the effectiveness of emergency response teams providing aid to disaster victims.

Recovery and reconstruction

Although recovery and reconstruction are two different stages of the disaster cycle, they are treated dependent of one another here. Typically, disasters are thought to be relatively isolated events that have a rather distinctive recovery phase and longer-term reconstruction phase. The recovery phase is typified by the one year period after the disaster when some sense of normalcy returns and the reconstruction phase can last several years and is characterized by rebuilding infrastructure and communities. In Bangladesh, however, the processes of recovery and reconstruction often overlap because of the annual nature of floods. Therefore, it can be argued that Bangladesh rarely advances beyond the recovery phase.

Research on recovery and reconstruction shows that, in general, women are more likely to seek the support of their family in recovering from disasters, while men often feel stigmatized when asking for assistance from family (Fothergill 1996). Research also shows that because women rely on social networks, they are able to cope with and survive during flood times. Largely because of cultural practices, it is the "role of women to borrow small things such as food or fuel or small amounts of money . . . which helped them survive" (Nasreen 1999:33). Despite this, Morrow and Enarson (1994) found that poor and minority women are most often the last to recover.

Many Bangladeshi people, particularly women, participate in non-structural measures of flood control such as community based flood control, evacuation, sheltering, and other grassroots strategies to safeguard themselves and recover from floods. Over time women have learned to adapt to and recover from floods in the most effective ways that they know and their accomplishments should not go unrecognized. For example, they build their homes on sandbars, levees, and platforms, build miniature levees and embankments, and pile sandbags and bricks around their homes(Hossain, Dodge, and Abed 1992). They have also adapted by planting different varieties of rice depending on the type and severity of floods. During the floods of 1998, "many shopkeepers rearranged their shops on platforms high above the water level" and others traveled in boats to sell products (Ahmed 1999b: 26).

Furthermore, Alexander (2000: 203) emphasizes, "Bangladesh is an overwhelmingly agricultural country with 68,000 villages and nearly three quarters of employment in farming and fishing." People in these communities have grown very accustomed to coping with floods. Flood control efforts have been wide ranging, and Bangladeshi people have adopted many different survival techniques. However, women's participation in these activities has often been overlooked. We need to continue to explore how the building of dams and embankments would affect people that have adapted to living with floods in creative, indigenous ways. Why has women's participation in flood control at the grassroots level not been incorporated into future disaster mitigation policies? How do NGO programs targeted at controlling floods compare to governmental flood control programs? Finally, we need to examine the effectiveness and importance of community-based organizations such as the Disaster Mitigation Institute, SEWA, and Duryog Nivaran in creating a link between communities and national level disaster organizations.

DISCUSSION

This paper has examined many aspects of women's unique experiences with floods in Bangladesh and supports the notion that gender is a significant variable that cannot be left out of current and future disaster research. Some might feel that the use of an extended typology of the disaster process is inadequate because various elements of disasters cannot be neatly packaged into stages. I agree that every stage of the disaster process is interconnected in a multitude of ways and cannot easily be separated. I would argue however, that the typology used in this paper serves as a foundational framework for synthesizing what we know about gendered flood experiences in Bangladesh and for illuminating areas in need of more extensive research. Finally, we cannot be satisfied with an overview of existing literature, as we still do not know enough about gender roles in disasters worldwide. Future research and additional empirical work must fill knowledge gaps in the literature and continue to theoretically examine gender dynamics in disasters. We, as researchers, must strive to bring about an acceptance and integration of women's experiences and knowledge into all phases of the disaster process and acknowledge the importance of gender in our work.

5

WOMEN, AGING

AND POST-DISASTER STRESS:

Risk factors

Jane C. Ollenburger and Graham A. Tobin

INTRODUCTION

There is a substantial literature looking at relationships between age and hazards (Bolin and Klenow 1982-1983; Cutrona et al. 1986; Huerta and Horton 1978; Krause 1987; Phifer and Norris 1989; Russell and Cutrona 1991). Many of these studies suggest that older individuals may experience more stress and relatively greater personal loss than younger persons during disasters. However, our research has produced some conflicting results to these earlier findings. The issue of age is mitigated by physical and mental health conditions that significantly influence stress responses (Ollenburger and Tobin 1995; Tobin and Ollenburger 1994). For instance, individuals in poor health, and who have difficulty getting around, are restricted in the actions they can take to mitigate hazard losses, which can lead to higher stress levels.

In addition, gender interacts with age since older individuals, especially those living alone, are proportionately more likely to be women. Furthermore, the economics of aging place many women in extremely vulnerable positions, which influences their ability to cope with the unexpected consequences of natural disasters. This economic vulnerability of women, who may be the sole support for themselves and/or for their children, has been described as the feminization of poverty (Ollenburger and Moore 1993). It reflects the economic position of women throughout the life cycle from teenage unemployment to the loss of economic support when divorced or widowed. The cumulative effects of unpaid care-taking roles, part time employment histories, lack of consistent benefits, and the economic losses due to divorce or widowhood are exacerbated throughout the life course and leave many older women with little or no economic security for their later years. Consequently, natural disasters can perpetuate the poverty trap for women as demonstrated by some of the recent research looking at women and other marginalized groups in hazardous areas (see, for example, Cutter 1995; Enarson and Morrow 1998; Khondker 1996; Melick and Logue 1985-1986; Rivers 1982; Wiest et al. 1992).

The goal of this research is to develop a model of community and individual characteristics that will provide a framework through which long-term impacts of hazardous events can be more fully understood. The current focus on personal stress responses to flooding, especially those associated with older women, is part of a larger longitudinal survey of how stress and anxiety fluctuate over time and under different hazardous conditions.

RESEARCH METHODOLOGY

A detailed investigation was undertaken of flood victims in Des Moines, Iowa, in 1993; this cohort was subsequently described as the high exposure group. First, a stratified random sample of flood victims was drawn based on census records, large-scale maps, and telephone directories, and an introductory letter mailed to prospective respondents. An in-depth telephone questionnaire was then administered by trained interviewers from the Center for Family Research in Rural Mental Health at Iowa State University approximately four months after the flood. One hundred and six questionnaires were successfully completed with each interview lasting up to 40 minutes. There was a refusal rate of 15 percent.

Three months later, a large-scale control survey was undertaken in Des Moines and surrounding communities. This survey, again conducted by the Center for Family Research in Rural Mental Health, incorporated many of the same items of the original survey as well as further questions concerning psychological morbidity and level of flood exposure. A total of 1,735 surveys were completed; these served as the control group.

The survey instruments included questions on personal and family characteristics, socio-economic traits, details on flood experiences, individual life style, physical and mental health status, and several standard measures of stress. Health effects were ascertained using several standard techniques, including a portion of the Rand 36-Item Health Survey from the Rand Health Sciences Program (Hays and Hays 1992; Stewart and Ware 1992; Ware and Sherbourne 1992). Screening questions were used to determine anxiety, depression, and post-traumatic stress disorder (McFarlane 1988; Steinglass and Gerrity 1990), and a nine item scale from the Center for Epidemiological Studies Depression Scale (CES-D) (Radloff 1977; Burnam et al. 1988) was used to rate depression. Finally, an "impact of events" scale was utilized to assess more carefully the psychological response to traumatic life events (Zilberg et al. 1982).

The study area

The Des Moines metropolitan area has experienced many small floods in the past, especially in the neighborhoods of Valley Junction and Frisbee Park, when Walnut Creek, the Raccoon River, and the Des Moines River have moved out of their banks. In 1993, the flooding was particularly severe with many buildings under ten feet of water and a number of homes and businesses completely destroyed. By the end of summer, 2,100 residences and 350 businesses had been inundated (Bryson 1994), and total losses in Des Moines were estimated to be $716 million (Tobin and Montz 1994; Wegner et al. 1993).

RESULTS

Background information

The questionnaire surveys provided valuable baseline data on the immediate impacts of the flooding on residents (Table 1). Not surprisingly, there were several differences between the two groups. Residents in the high exposure area were most directly affected by the flooding, although many in both groups experienced access problems because of flood water. Many residences were extensively damaged, and repair estimates ranged from a few dollars to $80,000; 66 percent in the high exposure area stated that it would cost more than $10,000 to repair the damage. The median cost estimate for repairs for this group was $17,000 (Tobin and Ollenburger 1996).

Table 1. Characteristics of Respondents

Variable	Control Group	High Exposure Area
AGE		
Range	19 to 91	23 to 85
Mean Age	52.13	52.5
MARITAL STATUS		
Married or Living Together	67%	62%
Divorced or Separated	11%	14%
Widowed	14%	14%
Single	8%	10%
GENDER		
Male	34%	43%
Female	66%	57%
NUMBER OF PEOPLE IN		
HOUSEHOLD	22%	20%
Lives Alone	37%	32%
Two people in house	15%	23%
Three people in house	26%	25%
Four or more		

Variable	Control Group	High Exposure Area
EMPLOYMENT		
Full Time	51%	48%
Part Time	13%	6%
Retired	25%	27%
Homemakers	6%	6%
Unemployed	3%	8%
Disabled, Student, Other	2%	5%
EDUCATIONAL ACHIEVEMENT		
Less Than High School	10%	25%
High School Degree/GED	37%	54%
2 yr Degree/ Voc. Tech Degree	31%	16%
Bachelor's Degree	16%	5%
Advanced Degree	6%	—
FLOOD IMPACT		
House Flooded	13%	100%
Property Flooded	20%	100%
Previous Flood Experience	18%	37%
SAMPLE SIZE (n)	1735	106

Relief was forthcoming from a variety of sources, including financial compensation through the U.S. Federal Emergency Management Agency (FEMA), from state emergency agencies, and from volunteer organizations. However, only 43 percent of the high exposure respondents were insured against flood losses. The presence or absence of insurance or relief aid to cover losses may play an important role in alleviating or aggravating post-hazard stress.

Risk Factors

Gender and Age

Women experience heightened risk exposures during natural disasters as a result of various societal and cultural norms including gender inequity and overall social roles (Fothergill 1996). The two primary influences on this risk exposure are women's care-taking roles in the family and women's overall socio-economic status. Women are more likely to be living in poverty and have fewer economic alternatives to cope with the effects of a hazardous event. In addition, elderly individuals may also have heightened risk factors due to health difficulties and limitations in mobility. Since the life expectancy for women is longer than for men, aging and gender issues are interconnected.

Family living environments

Data on family living environments showed several significant differences between the situations for men and women that might affect stress levels. For instance, in the high exposure group, 75 percent of men compared to 59 percent of women were married. Women were much more likely than men to be widowed (19.2 percent compared to 1.8 percent) or divorced (12 percent compared to 8 percent) [$\chi^2 = 28.42$, df=6, p<.001]. There was also a significant difference between marital status and number of people in the household [F=20.70, df=2, p<.001]. Individuals who were married or living together averaged 3.08 persons per household; individuals who were separated, divorced, or widowed averaged 1.90; and those who were never married averaged 1.71 household members. The average age of individuals living alone was 59 years, and, not surprisingly, more women (23 percent) than men (15 percent) were in this situation. There was also a correlation between age and number of members in the household with the oldest age groups having one or just a few members [F= 7.4967, df=8, p<.0001].

These data reinforce the notion regarding the vulnerability of women, particularly of those who reside in disaster prone areas. First, women living alone are more likely to be divorced, separated, or widowed, whereas men living alone are more likely to be single. Also, men who live alone are more likely to be younger, and women living alone are more likely to be older. In addition, divorced women are more likely to be heading households with two or more individuals. This reflects the trend of men being more likely to remarry and women, as they age, being less likely to remarry. Also, women are primarily responsible for childcare responsibilities, especially after a divorce.

Health status

Three groups of variables pertaining to health (physical health characteristics, physical mobility, and mental health characteristics) were collected from both cohorts. Physical health data were derived from a series of questions that focused on general health criteria such as number of visits to the doctor, number of days stayed in the hospital, medicines taken, types of illnesses, and so on. These data were used to provide a composite picture of respondents' overall health characteristics.

Responses to these questions revealed a significant relationship between gender and health. Men were more likely to indicate their health was excellent or good, whereas a larger percentage of women indicated their health was only fair or poor [χ^2=7.73, df=3, p<.05]. Similarly, there was a inverse relationship between age and health status. The average age of individuals who indicated their health was excellent or good was significantly younger than for individuals who indicated their health was fair or poor [F=13.48, df=3, p<.001]. Thus, the inter-relationships between age, gender, and physical health results in potentially more stress attributes for women. Women were significantly more likely to have poor health, and they were significantly more likely to have experienced health limitations which in turn affects their mobility [χ^2=18.98, df=2, p<.001].

Since women were more likely to have health limitations which affect their mobility, it is logical that they were also significantly more likely to have moderate or extreme limitations to their mobility compared with men [χ^2=13.04, df =4, p<.01]. Again, age plays an important role in explaining the relationship between the extent of the limitations and gender [F=2.49, df=4, p<.05]. Those respondents who indicated that their limitations were moderately severe generally were older.

Economic status

There was a significant difference in the economic status of men and women. In the control group, 70 percent of men and only 45 percent of women were employed full-time, while 10 percent of the women were employed part-time compared to 5.4 percent of the men prior to the Midwest floods. Also, women were significantly more likely than men to be retired or disabled [χ^2 =15.28, df=3, p<.002]. The data showed clearly that women consistently had lower incomes than men. Of the high exposure group, 19 percent reported that they were temporarily out of work, and an additional 1.3 percent were permanently out of work as a consequence of the flood. Of these, 92 percent of men and 56.5 percent of women lost income [χ^2=8.55, df=1, p<.005]. In addition, 26.4 percent of the women and 12.2 percent of the men had other household members who lost income due to the floods [χ^2 =4.85, df=1, p<.05].

POST-DISASTER STRESS

Natural disasters do not lead to a major breakdown in mental health despite widespread media reports to the contrary, and most academic studies report that severe incapacitating emotional breakdown from disasters is rare (Baisden 1979). Nevertheless, while sweeping mental illness may not be the norm, hazard victims do experience considerable stress, increased anxiety levels, and depression that may be prolonged and quite disabling under certain circumstances.

There are a number of factors which have proven significant in predicting stress following a natural disaster. These include age (Cutrona et al. 1986; Ollenburger and Tobin 1995), previous experiences with natural disasters (Norris and Murrell 1988; Solomon et al. 1989), physical and mental health (Perry and Mushkatel 1984; Canino et al. 1990), and socio-economic status (Baisden 1979). Although gender has also been shown to be a significant factor in predicting stress levels with women exhibiting higher stress responses then men (Solomon et al. 1987; Tobin and Ollenburger 1994), it is the cumulative effect of family environment, care-taking roles, health, mobility, and age that more clearly defines the issues for women.

Stress and anxiety responses to flooding

As would be anticipated, individuals responded to the flooding in their respective communities with various levels of stress manifested in forms of depression and anxiety. To assess the degree of stress, respondents were asked to indicate if they had experienced any of the following since the flood: trouble sleeping, hands trembling enough to bother them, loss of appetite, feeling weak all over, shortness of breath, and wondering if anything is worthwhile anymore. The responses were combined into a stress-anxiety variable. The data showed that, when individuals had simply been inconvenienced for only a short time by the flood, their stress responses were minimal compared to individuals who had experienced extensive damage to their home and property.

Another measure of stress can be determined from the extent of medication taken for anxiety and depression. Only 1.8 percent of the men and 5 percent of the women took medication to help them sleep before the flood; yet, following the flood, 4.4 percent of the men and 12.4 percent of the women took such medication. Indeed, women were significantly more likely than men to require sleep medication after the flood [$\chi^2=4.97$, df=1, p<.03]. Similarly, before the flood, 4.4 percent of the men and 5.8 percent of the women took medication to calm their nerves; after the flood, these percentages increased to 6.2 and 12.4 respectively.

Symptoms of Post-Traumatic Stress Disorder

Post-Traumatic Stress Disorder (PTSD) refers to psychological stress associated with major trauma. Its application to post disaster difficulties is fairly well documented (Madakasiru and O'Brien 1987; Wood and Cowan 1991). PTSD can be triggered by any event outside of normal human experiences which causes extreme psychological distress. Responses generally include intense fear, helplessness, unresponsiveness, and re-experiencing the event through dreams or nightmares. Individuals suffering from PTSD generally avoid stimuli that remind them of the event (American Psychiatric Association 1987).

Following the flooding, it was found that 71 percent of the high exposure cohort exhibited signs of post-traumatic stress disorder (Tobin and Ollenburger 1996). It should be stressed that women, particularly those who had families and those with less formal education, were more likely to show signs of PTSD than any other group. To extend this analysis, a logistic regression model was used to determine risk factors that might lead to PTSD following the flooding (Table 2). The model estimations were determined in four iterations and correctly explained 73.79 percent of the presence of PTSD among individuals in the high flood exposure area [$x^2 = 17.78$, df=5, p=.0032].

While individuals living in the high exposure area of Des Moines exhibited a high incidence of PTSD, minority females in poor or fair health were the group most likely to show PTSD symptoms. Females were 2.66 times as likely to experience PTSD compared with males. Minority respondents were 1.41 times as likely as non-minority members to indicate PTSD symptoms. In addition, individuals in good health were 5.34 times as likely as individuals in excellent health, and individuals with fair or poor health were 7.22 times as likely as individuals with excellent health to exhibit symptoms of PTSD.

Table 2. Risk Factors for PTSD in High Exposure Area

VARIABLE[1]	B	S.E.	Wald	df	Sig.	Exp(B)
Age	-1.31	.5762	5.1748	1	.0229	.2696
Sex	.98	.5066	3.7265	1	.0536	2.6590
Minority	.34	.6527	.2778	1	.5982	1.4106
Health			11.5291	2	.0031	
Health(1)	1.68	.6212	7.2800	1	.0070	5.3442
Health(2)	1.98	.6346	9.7014	1	.0018	7.2185
Constant	-.70	.7538	.8625	1	.3531	

[1]   Codes for independent variables include: Age: 0=Younger than 65, 1=65 and Older; Sex: 0=Male, 1=Female; Minority: 0=Non-Minority, 1=Minority; Health: 0-0 Excellent, 0-1 Health(1)=Good; 1-1 Health(2) Fair Or Poor.

Interestingly, younger individuals were more likely to exhibit PTSD than individuals 65 years of age or older. This pattern is consistent with some earlier disaster research which identified older individuals as more "seasoned" with the flood experience. Also younger individuals often had more family concerns such as the care of young children which increased their anxiety related to the flood consequences (Tobin and Ollenburger 1994).

In order to test whether or not the flooding was the key factor in creating the incidence of PTSD among this population, a similar analysis was conducted on the control group. This group included individuals who had varying degrees of exposure to the floods. The level of exposure was coded into three categories: no exposure; minimal exposure including loss of services but no damage to home, property, or person; and high exposure including damage or loss to property, home, job, and/or personal injury.

Table 3 describes the logistic regression model with the inclusion of the exposure variable predicting PTSD among the control group. All of the independent predictors are defined the same as in the first model. This time the model was able to predict 80.40 percent correctly [x^2 =571.08, df=7, p=.0000], clearly demonstrating that level of exposure is the most significant predictor for PTSD. Individuals with a high level of exposure were 562 times as likely to exhibit PTSD as compared with those with no exposure. Even individuals with minimal exposure were 357 times as likely to exhibit symptoms of PTSD when compared with those individuals who lived in the community but were not directly affected by the floods.

Table 3. Risk Factors for PTSD in Different Flood Level Exposure Areas

VARIABLE[1]	B	S.E.	Wald	df	Sig.	Exp(B)
Age	-.02	.1724	.0139	1	.9061	.9799
Sex	.21	.1518	1.8842	1	.1699	1.2317
Minority	1.08	.2549	17.9317	1	.0000	2.9433
Health			7.2885	2	.0261	

VARIABLE[1]	B	S.E.	Wald	df	Sig.	Exp(B)
Health(1)	.58	.2277	6.4877	1	.0109	1.7858
Health(2)	.25	.1573	2.5591	1	.1097	1.2861
Exposure			44.8171	2	.0000	
Expose(1)	6.33	.9864	41.2051	1	.0000	562.1779
Expose(2)	5.88	1.0031	34.3207	1	.0000	356.4786
Constant	-7.09	.9920	51.1090	1	.0000	

Factors mitigating symptoms of extreme PTSD

In this study, there were two significant predictors that decreased the severity of PTSD—maintenance of employment and the perception of positive outcomes from the flood experience. The presence of insurance to help cover losses and health problems and the presence of family and friends near enough to help the recovery process were also important variables.

A large percentage of the respondents felt that there were significant positive outcomes as a result of the flooding. Four potential positive outcomes were identified in the surveys undertaken following the Midwest Floods. These included: more involvement in the community, made new friends, brought the family closer together, and increased cooperation and helpfulness in the neighborhood. Indeed, 80 percent of the respondents indicated they felt there was more cooperation and helping in the neighborhood following the flood, 68 percent had made new friends, 59 percent felt the floods brought their family closer together, and 42 percent indicated they became more involved in their community (Table 4). More men than women indicated that they became more involved in the community, made new friends, and found more cooperation and helpfulness in the neighborhood. However, women were more likely to indicate that the flooding brought the family closer together. The long-term consequences of this, however, need to be studied in detail.

Table 4. Positive Outcomes from the Midwest Floods

Positive Outcome		Yes	No
More Cooperation and Helping in the Neighborhood			
	Total	80%	20%
	Males	85%	15%
	Females	76%	24%
Made New Friends			
	Total	68%	32%
	Males	78%	22%
	Females	60%	40%
	$[\chi^2=6.42, df=1, p<.02]$		
Brought Family Closer Together			
	Total	59%	41%
	Males	57%	43%
	Females	61%	39%
More Involved in the Community			
	Total	42%	58%
	Males	52%	48%
	Females	33%	67%
	$[\chi^2=5.9, df=1, p<.02]$		

CONCLUSION

Both gender and age play significant roles in interpreting the stress responses to natural hazards. Research on post-flood disaster stress has consistently found that women exhibit higher levels of stress when compared to men. This relationship, as demonstrated here, appears to be the result of a complex web of factors including the presence of children, marital status, the structure of the family unit, age, socio-economic status, health, and the level of social involvement. In addition, the use of a large-scale control group sets this study apart from many others and supports the notion that different degrees of flooding generate different levels of stress with particular emphasis on older women.

Family structure is of paramount concern since large families, especially with young children and single-headed households, experience multiple concerns during a disaster, leading to higher stress levels for all members of the household. Also, single-headed households are more likely to be female-headed households, and they are more likely to be individuals with limited economic options following a hazardous event. Their ability to cope with high levels of post-traumatic stress is more limited.

The interaction of gender and age exacerbates the dilemmas faced by vulnerable individuals during disasters. As we indicated earlier, individuals living alone are more likely to be older, female, and divorced, separated, or widowed. Older women are also more likely to suffer from health and mobility limitations, increasing their vulnerability during and after a disaster. In addition, divorced women are more likely to be heading households with two or more individuals, and women are primarily responsible for child-care following a divorce.

In addition, more attention should be given to the interaction of gender with other factors including income, health, and race. For instance, this research confirmed that minority women in poor or only fair health were more susceptible to stress than most other groups. It would seem pertinent, therefore, to address those structural constraints that might exacerbate problems for such individuals. In this regard, for example, the availability and distribution of relief aid following disasters may play significant roles.

Therefore, the concerns of women during disasters are multifaceted, potentially encompassing concern for children and family, employment, financial constraints, and possibly care-taking for elder relatives. Given this complex framework, it is not surprising that women generally experience higher levels of stress following natural disasters.

6

DOMESTIC VIOLENCE AFTER DISASTER:

Voices from the 1997 Grand Forks flood

Alice Fothergill

INTRODUCTION

Two facts are generally uncontested regarding the abuse women receive from their intimate male partners. First, the home is not always a safe place (e.g., Dobash and Dobash 1979; Walker 1979; Gelles 1997). Second, because woman battering frequently occurs in the context of the home and is stigmatized, it is a largely invisible offense (e.g., Belknap 1996). However, the phenomenon of woman battering is so widespread that it is considered by some scholars as the most frequent form of family violence (Levinson 1981). Indeed, it has long been recognized that calls for woman battering are among the most common police calls (Goldstein 1977). Research on woman battering was almost non-existent until the second wave of the feminist movement in the 1970s.

To date, however, the research on woman battering in post-disaster communities is still almost non-existent. In the disaster research community, many question whether rates of woman battering increase in a disaster. Thus, although this question has been frequently asked, it remains largely unanswered. There is no simple or straightforward way to determine the rates, and there have been no systematic studies or controlled population surveys that support a direct causal relationship of the disaster events on woman battering rates. However, there are some studies and reports on domestic violence in disasters that deserve attention. In this paper, I summarize the sparse existing research on woman battering in the context of disasters, and then I present findings on woman battering in my research on disasters using the Grand Forks (Grand Forks, North Dakota and East Grand Forks, Minnesota) flood of 1997.

LITERATURE REVIEW

To date, only two studies focus on the issue of woman battering in the context of disasters. First, Wilson, Phillips, and Neal (1998) studied community organizations' perceptions and responses to domestic violence in Santa Cruz after the Loma Prieta earthquake, Lancaster, Texas after a tornado, and Dade County, Florida following Hurricane Andrew. Second, Enarson (1998) surveyed 77 domestic violence organizations in the United States and Canada, 41 of which had some disaster experience, to learn about their disaster planning and experience. Other disaster studies have mentioned the issue of woman battering in tangential, less focused ways. Finally, other woman battering research, not addressing disasters, also poses relevant issues to the phenomenon of woman battering in disaster sites. In this section I summarize these studies: those focusing directly on woman battering in disasters, those disaster studies where woman battering is not a central theme, and those woman battering studies which are not about disasters, but pose important points relevant to woman battering in disaster sites.

Attempts to measure the impact of disasters on battering rates

Some research has examined the issue of whether woman battering increases in a disaster. Wilson and her colleagues (1998) found that Santa Cruz reported large increases in domestic violence, the city of Lancaster, Texas reported no noticeable increase, and in Dade County the data were mixed, although they suggested an increase. Enarson (1988) found that those domestic violence programs that experienced a disaster indicated declining service demand during the impact period, as women could not get to the services, but an increased demand after that, which was complicated by a decrease in organizational resources. For many domestic violence programs the demand for services was mostly from existing clients, not from women seeking help for the first time. Morrow and Enarson (1996), in their research on women in Hurricane Andrew, did not focus specifically on the topic of domestic violence, but reported that social service providers felt strongly that family violence had increased. Morrow (1997) reported that there was initially a drop in domestic violence injunctions after Hurricane Andrew, perhaps due to the inaccessibility of government services, but then the number of injunctions increased substantially. Based on their experiences in disasters in Australia, several social service providers reported that increases in domestic violence rates are "repeatedly found" during disasters and their aftermaths (Honeycombe 1993: 29; Dobson 1993). Contrarily, there is evidence that crime rates in general drop after a disaster, and that prosocial rather than antisocial behavior characterizes disaster periods (Quarantelli 1994), therefore some may feel that woman battering rates would decrease.

While evidence is limited, the common perception is that battering rates increase since the demand for services increase. It is difficult to know if the battered women seeking assistance are mostly existing clients, meaning they sought help for their battering situations prior to the disaster, or new clients, implying that the disaster brought on physical violence in relationships that were not abusive before the event. If indeed all the clients are existing ones, then technically the number of battered women does not increase, and the increased demand is indicative of the clients all needing help at the same time. Another scenario may be that many women were in domestic violence relationships prior to the disaster, but had never gone for assistance, so they count as new clients, but are actually not new victims.

Community responses and preparedness to woman battering in post-disaster sites

A few previous studies have addressed community responses and the preparedness of organizations to woman battering. In non-disaster times, battered women are often overlooked as victims by the public at large, the criminal processing system (e.g., the police and court professionals), and service and health agencies and professionals (e.g., physicians, social workers) (e.g., Dobash and Dobash 1979; Belknap 1995; Gelles 1997), so it is possible that they are overlooked after disasters as well. Wilson et al. (1998) report that the community, domestic violence, and disaster organizations in their study that were aware of the existence and extent of domestic violence prior to the disaster were more sensitive to the presence of postdisaster violence. Therefore, if a community defines domestic violence as a problem pre-disaster, it will be more able to identify and respond to it following the event. Wilson et al. (1998) argue, then, that a community's ignorance of a domestic violence problem could increase women's vulnerability, and possibly contribute to more injuries and deaths after a disaster. Enarson (1988) found that most grassroots women's organizations are not prepared for a disaster and few domestic violence programs participate in local or regional planning groups. These women's organizations, however, are interested in increasing their disaster readiness. Honeycombe (1993) advocates that disaster workers are trained and become informed on issues of woman battering in order to be prepared for increases in this violence. Thus, there are both domestic violence organizations ill prepared for a disaster, and disaster organizations and communities poorly prepared for domestic violence situations in disasters.

The antecedents of disasters purported to be related to subsequent woman battering

A significant amount of public opinion, professional responses, and research agendas have attempted to understand the *causes* of battering. While there is a strong history of blaming the victims for the battering perpetrated against them (see, for example, Dobash and Dobash 1979; Tong 1984), more recent research has attempted to understand what places men (and women) at risk of becoming batterers or escalating their existing battering practices. Some disaster research has found that men use more alcohol after a disaster (Green 1993), which some believe would increase domestic violence rates (Pleck 1987). Yet Kantor and Straus (1987) examined the role of alcohol as a cause of woman battering, and concluded that excessive drinking is associated with higher woman battering rates, but alcohol use is not an immediate antecedent of battering. Dutton (1988) identified the *excuses* and *justifications* batterers frequently use to deny wrongness and responsibility for their battering behavior. Dutton found that batterers use situational characteristics, such as being drunk or fired from a job, to *excuse* their behavior, and characteristics about the victims, such as not having dinner ready or allegedly having an affair, to *justify* their abuse. Thus, a disaster crisis could be used in this manner, to excuse their behavior, and to blame the flood for losing control. For example, Morrow and Enarson (1996) interviewed one woman whose husband, who beat her so badly that she had to be hospitalized, lost control because he could not handle the effects of the flood, which included losing household belongings, not having enough food to eat, and losing his job, because his business was destroyed in the flood (from Enarson 1998). Experts in the field maintain that perpetrators are very much in control, stating that crisis conditions do not cause the abuse, nor do they cause men to lose control. Gelles (1997) notes that stressful social factors such as poverty and illness may be related to violence and abuse, but the abuse would not occur if there was not widespread social and cultural approval of violence in the home.

Differential vulnerability and battering experiences

Some women may be more at risk to woman battering than others. In addition, of those women who are battered, their social status and resources affect their subsequent vulnerability. For example, women with disabilities may be more vulnerable to battering. Women with disabilities are much more likely than women generally to be victims of physical and sexual assault, and almost all the perpetrators are men who are known to the women (Sobsey 1994). These women face a high incidence of violence and abuse in their lives in general as they have seen as being of little worth, invisible, and less than human (Chenoweth 1996). Compounding this, the violence disabled women experience is largely unknown and invisible since they often experience societal marginalization, powerlessness, and exclusion (Chenoweth 1996). In disasters, therefore, disabled women may be at increased risk to woman battering.

Poor women are also more at risk. In disasters in general, research has found that poor women's concerns are not taken seriously, and they lack the resources and support necessary for recovery and reconstruction (Morrow and Enarson 1996). Poor women may also be more vulnerable to woman battering. Schwartz (1988) argues that the "universal risk" theories are so popular, primarily in an effort to see women as a unified group under patriarchy and to repudiate past class biases in research, that researchers have overlooked how working class and middle class women have distinct experiences with battering. In fact, empirical studies have shown that there is more woman battering in low-income, low socio-economic status families (Okun 1986). Schwartz (1988) argues that if you examine the effects of both patriarchy and capitalism, it is clear that there is not a universal risk to all women, but that socio-economic status is related to chances of victimization and consequent treatment and resources. Thus, some women *are* more vulnerable than others.

How the quality of intimate relationships are impacted by disasters

Disaster studies have found that disaster events can affect gender roles and relationships between men and women. Ketteridge and Fordham (1998) found that women, many of whom had gained a new self-confidence during a flood disaster, separated from unsupportive partners. This is relevant in that many women in battering relationships lack the confidence to leave their abusers (Gelles 1997). Alway et al. (1998) found that men's role as protector and provider is threatened in a disaster, a pertinent finding in that domestic violence concerns issues of male dominance and control. Davis (1998) found married couples with strong relationships prior to a disaster reported their relationships were stronger after the disaster. In contrast, couples who reported weak relationships prior to the disaster generally reported that their relationships were even weaker after the disaster. Her results are in alignment with many in the disaster research community who believe that disasters speed up or exaggerate, but do not drastically alter, social processes, structures, and relationships. Interestingly, however, Davis found the stronger couples experienced more tension and strain during the disaster, while the weaker couples reported feeling closer during the acute period of the disaster. While her results do not address domestic violence specifically, they do touch on some relevant issues concerning conflict between intimate partners.

The five issues covered in this literature review—measuring battering rates, community and organizational responses to woman battering, the antecedents to battering, differential vulnerability, and changes in intimate relationships in disasters—are all areas in need of research in disasters and will all be addressed in this study.

SETTING AND METHODS

This exploratory study is part of a larger feminist ethnography of women's experiences in a disaster. As a feminist ethnography, this research included multimethods, including interviewing, observation, participation, and archival analysis, all employed in an effort to make women's lives visible and their voices audible (Reinharz 1992). As a feminist ethnographer, I used fieldwork to get closer to women's realities, and in alignment with feminist research in general, I work towards three goals in this research: "(1) to document the lives and activities of women, (2) to understand the experience of women from their own point of view, and (3) to conceptualize women's behavior as an expression of social contexts" (Reinharz 1992: 51).

My setting was Grand Forks, North Dakota, and East Grand Forks, Minnesota, two adjoining towns on the Red River that experienced a flood of historical proportions in the spring of 1997, after a winter of severe blizzards. The disaster, which resulted in the mandatory evacuation of all residents of both cities, approximately 60,000 people, cost hundreds of residents their homes and the entirety of their belongings. In addition to their homelessness and loss of material possessions, the flood victims experienced unemployment, a lack of childcare services, the dismantling of routine and stability, the separation of family members, the loss of schools and neighborhoods, and uncertainty about the future. Clearly, this disaster was physically and emotionally exhausting for the residents and was a highly stressful crisis.

For this study, I conducted sixty in-depth interviews with forty women of various ages, social classes, professions, and marital statuses, to learn about their experiences in the flood. Twenty of the forty women were formally interviewed twice, and several were informally interviewed three or four times. The first interviews took place relatively soon after the event, in the summer months of 1997, and the second follow-up interviews generally took place a year later. In addition to the interviews, I conducted extensive observations. I spent as much time as possible with women, both women I had interviewed as well as other women in Grand Forks, observing, and participating in, their lives. With these women, I attended community events, family potlucks, religious services, neighborhood barbecues, and other informal outings and settings. Finally, I analyzed newspaper articles and interviewed representatives of the Grand Forks domestic violence prevention center and gathered relevant materials and statistics from their organization.

For this paper, I present an analysis of interviews with two women from the sample who reported domestic violence. These two cases do not necessarily represent all women who experience domestic violence in disasters, although case studies in general are often able to provide insights into general understandings of a social problem (Stake 1994). In addition, case studies are considered useful and valid for investigating a phenomenon in its real-life context (Yin 1984). I believe a case study is appropriate for shedding light on this almost unknown phenomenon: battered women's experiences in the context of a disaster. The findings I report revolve around the context of woman battering in the lives of women in disasters; exploring the realities of two women's lives to highlight the kinds of problems some women will face in a disaster. Thus, I intend for these two in-depth accounts to provide insight into what these experiences can mean, how they unfold, and how battered women can be assisted in disasters.

The current study focuses on two women, Karen and Liz (all names have been changed to protect identities). While these two women were the only women who spoke to me about their experiences with woman battering, there may have been other women in my study who also experienced this violence. Due to the stigma and invisibility, along with what is known on woman battering rates, it is likely that other women in my study were also battered but did not report it to me or anybody else. Indeed, Karen did not reveal her situation to me until our third face-to-face interview, after we had known each other for over a year and exchanged phone calls and letters, which illustrates the need for us to establish trust before she could confide in me. One limitation with these case studies is that both women are white so there are no racial implications, but the women do represent the racial demographics of Grand Forks, and the two women varied substantially in their class status. It is necessary in future research to keep in mind that the experiences of battered women of color are likely confounded by race (e.g., Miller 1989; Abraham 1996; Belknap 1996).

In this paper, I will begin by presenting the information I gathered from the Grand Forks woman battering organization in order to give a larger context to the woman battering situation in Grand Forks, and then I will allow you to hear Liz's and Karen's words directly, thereby letting their voices contribute to the conversation on domestic violence in disasters. As social scientists know, police records, official statistics, and even survey research results do not often match the stories told by women who have been victims of physical violence, and thus it is critical that we let women speak for themselves (Erez and Belknap 1998). It was through such traditional grassroots efforts, from listening to women, that wife abuse was first discovered in the early 1970s (Gelles 1997). It makes sense, therefore, that listening to women now will help us to discover how intimate violence plays out in a disaster.

FINDINGS

Increase in demand, decrease in services

The Community Violence Intervention Center, the organization for battered women in Grand Forks, provided me with information that helps illustrate how the demand for services increases at the same time that their resources are lower than normal. The Center provides many battered women's services, such as crisis counseling, legal referrals, and assistance with obtaining protection orders. It does not run a shelter, so battered women must use the homeless shelter in town if they cannot find other housing. The number of protection orders, which are issued to protect women from their perpetrators, are a good illustration of the demand for services. The Center found that prior to the flood, during the period of January to March 1997, there were twenty protection orders issued. However, after the flood, during the same period of 1998, January to March, there were thirty-three protection orders that needed to be filed to protect women in domestic violence situations, which indicates a substantial increase.

In terms of the amount of available resources during this same time period, we can analyze the number of volunteer hours, which is the total amount of time given to the Center by local residents who volunteer their time. In the first time period, January to March 1997, volunteers gave 3,475 hours to the Center, while in the second time period, January to March 1998, they were only able to give 1,903 hours of their time. These statistics allow us to see a period before the flood in 1997, and the same period after the flood, in 1998. An increase in the number of protection orders may be explained several ways. The increase may indicate a rise in violence, or a greater propensity to report the violence, or a woman's greater inability to handle the violence on her own. No matter which, the increase in protection orders clearly represents an increase in workload for the Center employees. In addition, we see that volunteer hours are down, even six months after the event, as volunteers are still working on repairing their own homes and lives. By having fewer volunteers to help in the office, the staff finds itself with even more work.

The staff had additional work for several other reasons. The homeless shelter, which serves battered women, was lost in the flood, so staff had to find housing for battered women at local motels. This was a difficult task, considering that most residents of the city were also in need of housing at that time. The staff reported that overall there was a huge demand for services from a combination of existing and new clients. They also told me that some women, not having any resources, called their batterers for assistance during the disaster—and as a result found themselves back in an abusive relationship after the flood. The staff also reported that the local jail let some batterers go during the evacuation period, which frightened and angered the battered women and the Center staff. This occurrence is important as it illustrates the community's role in enabling the violence. For all of these aforementioned reasons, it is clear that while the demand for services increased, the personnel and financial resources had decreased substantially.

Entering into domestic violence

Karen is a 42-year-old slender white woman who has lived in Grand Forks her entire life. She is a college-educated social worker who has been married for 20 years and has two children, aged 6 and 13. She and her family lived in a modest, well-kept two story wood house on a quiet tree-lined street of single-family homes. The family members, who evacuated in the flood, were not hurt physically. When they returned to their home several weeks later, however, they found that their basement level, which had been their family room and the hub of family activity, was lost in the flood waters. In addition, Karen's elderly in-laws lost their home, which was several blocks from Karen's, and all of their belongings.

Things were very tense around the house, Karen explained to me. Greg, Karen's husband, became more and more angry—at the flood, at the city, at the Corps of Engineers, at his family, and most of all, at his wife. Karen assumed that his anger would subside as time passed and the town and their home were rebuilt. Instead, Greg's anger grew with each month following the flood. Indeed, a year after the flood his anger erupted into violence and he began beating Karen. She explains how the situation began:

> Over the last year, almost every day, it's been sort of a slow onset of sort of a paranoia about, first of all, other men, of which there are none. And then he started getting more aggressive about it, going through my work papers, it got so bad that I couldn't go anywhere. He's never had a very good temper, but it's gotten really bad. Pretty much isolates me from my family. The first year after we were married there was an incident, but nothing until now.

While he had always had a bad temper and was always highly critical of her, Greg had not been physically abusive to Karen in twenty years, and she had not contemplated leaving until the physical violence began after the flood. She explains how she decided to leave:

> The crystallizing incident took place on Mother's Day, May 9th. That's when Greg was pushing me and Jonathan walked in and lunged to defend me. He had a clenched fist, ready to hit his dad. He looked like he *wanted* to hit him . . . My son had had enough of his yelling. He yelled at him daily. I think Jonathan felt like that's my mom and I'm going to protect her. I realized I had to go.

Karen's 13 year old son Jonathan wanted to protect his mother, and he also expressed to Karen that he wanted them to get away from his father. Many children in domestic violence situations become very protective of their mothers, and their willingness to leave a violent father helps the woman decide to leave (Dobash and Dobash 1979; Ferraro and Johnson 1983).

In Karen's description of what was happening in her home, we learn that the flood may have been the main, or at least a large, contributing factor, for the onset of the violence. She describes how the flood affected her husband:

He likes things ordered and when things are out of order
he doesn't like it. So the flood was a nightmare for him.
It's not like his temperament completely changed with
the flood, but I definitely do consider us to be a flood
casualty. The flood did bring on his anger.

But Karen continues her story:

He was kind of already on that path. He's always had
a short fuse. He was getting worse with age instead of
better, I can't explain that. His anger was always thinly
veiled, and he was always highly critical, picking on me
all the time.

After the violent attacks after the flood, Karen decided to leave and
she moved out and got a restraining order. She explains how it feels
to have left the situation:

I got a protection order that he violated three times. Now
he's being charged by the state with stalking. He can't do
too many more things before he ends up in jail. I haven't
regretted my decision to leave for a minute. It's so much
better now. Nobody wants to do this, but in the long
run it's better for everybody. I feel like a huge weight has
been lifted.

Karen perceives that Greg was already heading towards committing
more violence, and that if it was not due to the flood, it may have easily
been triggered by something else. However, it is important to note that
he was physically violent once in their marriage nineteen years earlier,
and then again right after the flood, but not at all in between. Several
months after she left Greg, she thinks back on her experience:

You know, when I used to think about women who were
victims of abuse, that if you were privileged to some extent,
then your experience would be vastly different. And now

> I think not. I think not. Because no amount of privilege
> can stop that person. You know? I am no better off than
> an uneducated, poor, Native American, ethnic woman.
> I am no better off really in that respect. Apparently,
> when a man in our society gets in that mindset, there
> is so much latitude for them to act out, to do damage,
> that a reasonable person can't imagine would be allowed
> to continue. You can be smart, articulate, educated,
> competent, but it doesn't matter, it doesn't help.

Karen came to the difficult realization that being somewhat affluent
and educated did not protect her from her husband's violence, no
matter her race or economic background. She was acknowledging her
own vulnerability, the vulnerability of all women in our society, and
the power differences between men and women. Karen noted that she
was also vulnerable financially:

> Somewhere in the last year he started putting money
> somewhere. I think he was hiding it. I've never been
> somebody that worries that much about money. The truth is
> that my name is not on any of our assets. I don't know how
> that happened. It's just not something that I attended to.

Yet despite her financial concerns, Karen did have resources available
to her, such as middle class family members who were willing and
able to take her in and support her. In addition, with her educational
background and occupational status, she knew that her job was
secure. These factors may have helped Karen to leave immediately
after the beatings, something many battered women are not able to
do. Thus, while Karen's status did not protect her from becoming a
battered woman, it did help her successfully deal with the situation
once she was in it.

Karen felt that the flood brought on the violence, but that in a
way that was good, in that she could deal with it sooner rather than
later. Although this is similar to Lenore Walker's (1979) contention
that some battered women actually behave in ways to precipitate what

they view as an inevitable beating by their batterers, Karen's case is different in that she did *not* do anything to precipitate the violence. However, she reported feeling relieved that the disaster event had done so. In a recent conversation with Karen she expressed regret that she did not leave Greg earlier, in that he had been mean to her and the children for years. She believed that if the flood had not brought on the violent incident, there would have been a more violent, and more dangerous incident down the road. She explained:

> I think when you're living in it you make all kinds of excuses, you try to find a way to frame it that is not quite as damaging. You have to rationalize it or you can't stay. There you are one day, with your kid thinking they have to beat their dad to protect you. I really think someone in my family would've gotten hurt. Maybe me, maybe one of my kids. I would rather have it be me. And considering that, it's better sooner than later . . . I think I stayed too long. I should have known better. But, now, I'm really excited about what I'm doing now, and my kids are safe.

Today Karen is living in a small apartment with her two children, working and going to school at night for an advanced degree. She lives in fear as Greg continues to stalk her, drive by her apartment late at night, follow her in his car, and on one occasion broke her door and entered her apartment. It is difficult, if not impossible, to know if his violence would have occurred if the flood had not happened. Karen believes it probably would have happened, but maybe further down the road. The important thing to consider is that Karen needed assistance—a protection order, counseling, housing—in the midst of the disaster crisis. Without this assistance she may not have been able to leave or keep herself and her children safe.

Leaving domestic violence

Liz, like Karen, is also a Grand Forks native, white, and in her early forties, but she is less privileged than Karen in many ways. Liz has lived in poverty all her life and is disabled from a car accident, leaving her unable to walk without assistance and unable to work. She grew up in an abusive household and has been in abusive relationships since she was a teenager. Her partner of the last nine years, and husband of the last two, Fred, has beaten her many times, landing her in the hospital with serious injuries on several occasions. Liz described a particularly bad beating two weeks before their wedding that left her hospitalized:

> I came home from shopping and he was intoxicated. I didn't start screaming, I didn't start yelling. I asked him to leave. The police had told me not to confront him. He began throwing things, screaming at me, threatening to kill me. Then he lunged at me and he grabbed me by the collar of my shirt and started shaking me. I remember screaming at him "You're killing me!" Then I lost consciousness. When I came to I was on the recliner, and he was hitting me on the head with his fist and screaming at me. At this point I was going in and out of consciousness . . . The police took me to the hospital and people were staring at me. My neck was so swollen, my face was so swollen, I think I was in shock. He nearly severed my spinal cord. The doctors said had he shaken me one more time, he would have severed my spinal cord and I would have been dead. They called the counseling center, and the advocate came, the poor girl, and I was her first call ever. I felt so bad for her.

Liz explained why, after this serious assault, she decided to marry Fred:

> The invitations were out, and he said it would never happen again. This is someone you love, you want to believe it is the last time. But, I mean, I just can't tell you why I went ahead with the wedding. I mean I really can't answer that question, because I don't know why I did. But I did.

After going through with the wedding, Liz suffered extensive physical abuse:

> The police have been to our house so many times, it isn't even funny. I mean he is a man that has nearly killed me I don't know how many times . . . But I have always been minimizing the physical abuse. I repressed a lot of the memories of the beatings. Until the flood, then all the memories came back.

Despite the beatings, Liz was emotionally attached to Fred, and did not have the confidence or independence to leave him. She explained that she felt "afraid" when she was not in a relationship.

Just prior to the flood Fred entered a resident drug and alcohol treatment program. Liz, therefore, was on her own during the flood, and had to deal with a difficult evacuation period and the loss of her home by herself. Her basement apartment was flooded with ten feet of water and raw sewage. In photos she showed me of the damage, the walls, furniture, and carpet appeared to be painted black, but were actually covered with sludge from the flood waters. The apartment, which tested positive for several types of bacteria, had to be gutted, and all the contents had to be thrown away. She described her feelings about the loss:

> The night I got into town, the third of May, was when I found out that I had lost everything. I mean, I was about as vulnerable as I could be. It's been terrifying, especially when I've been hungry and there is no money. And I didn't have the money to replace anything.

Liz had to face the destruction of the flood in addition to the continuing crisis of poverty. She believed surviving the flood without Fred was the reason she discovered she was strong and competent enough to survive without him. She discussed her new-found strength:

> But I've been really lucky with the flood. I've learned so many good things through this. I have really worked on

> myself and reevaluated things. I've taken the flood as an
> opportunity to grow personally. I have found an inner
> strength that will carry me through anything. How else
> could I have made it through this? I now know that I can
> count on myself. I can trust myself. It's been painful and
> I've been lonely . . . I still love him with all my heart, and
> there are many things about him that are very wonderful,
> but there's his dark side and that dark side will cost me my
> life. I'm just not willing to pay that price anymore.

The experience empowered Liz and gave her a sense that she can make
it on her own, something she never believed before. Liz was not only
dealing with domestic violence and poverty, but also a physical disability.
In my conversations with Liz, she discussed how her disability affected
her flood experience, describing here her evacuation with her 21-year-
old daughter, her son-in-law, and her two young grandchildren:

> When my daughter and I evacuated we went to the air
> base. But they wouldn't take me because they said all of
> their accommodations for people with disabilities were
> full. So they turned us away. They told me to get in my
> car and keep going . . . So we drove on to Devil's Lake, and
> the shelter there said the same thing. No accommodations
> for me. We couldn't believe it. And I have no proof if they
> were actually full or not or if they didn't want to deal with
> extra needs. We go on to Rugby, same thing, we got turned
> away. It was about one thirty in the morning and we pulled
> into Minot . . . They told us that they weren't giving any
> assistance to Grand Forks flood victims and we should
> get back in our cars . . . I said "Where am I supposed to
> go?" . . . And I'm standing there in my *pajamas*.

Liz eventually found a place to stay until her apartment was rebuilt,
but her disability still posed additional considerations. She explained
how her disability affected her ability to leave the town where her
abuser lives:

> I've had to get over my stubborn will, and realize that I
> have a chronic illness that is progressive. I live with intense
> physical pain, and intense physical symptoms, that I can't
> control. I don't have a choice there, but I have to learn to
> listen to my body. And when it says stop, I have to stop.
> That's one of the reasons I can't leave here, even though
> he's [Fred] here. My doctor's here, and I can't start all
> over finding doctors. And I need to be near my daughter
> because she knows how to take care of me.

As Chenoweth (1996) found in her work, women with disabilities
need to combat their isolation and exclusion to prevent being victims
of male violence. Liz continued her story, and acknowledged that the
Grand Forks Violence Intervention Center, and Amelia, a staff member
there, helped her tremendously:

> When he got back to town, I'd call Amelia all the time.
> Boy, did I need them then. If I couldn't make it in, we'd
> do the counseling over the phone. I used this time for
> personal growth. It wasn't easy. Had the Center not
> been there, or my daughter, you know, I wouldn't have
> made it. There were times in the middle of the night
> when I've needed the Center and called. I can't give
> up my counseling when I'm in the same town as my
> husband.

In addition to noting the importance of the Center, Liz was also
admitting that the flood, and the struggles involved in recovering
from it, may have had positive consequences. In my research, many
of my participants expressed positive consequences of the disaster,
such as new skills acquired, and personal strength and confidence
discovered. Liz revealed how her personal growth and inner strength
carried her through the disaster and how, with the help of the battered
women's organization, she was able to leave a life of violence. She
described how she felt to be free from battering, over a year after
the disaster:

> For the first time in my life I feel free. I can go where I
> want. I can do what I want. I don't have to look over my
> shoulder anymore. I don't come home, turn the key in
> the lock, and get beaten. Now I can do whatever I want.
> No one is going to tell me you can't do that. And No one
> is telling me I'm ugly and No one is telling me that the
> world is falling apart 'cause of something I did.

The flood disaster may actually have been the catalyst Liz needed to leave the abusive relationship and gain a better awareness of herself. Ferraro and Johnson (1983) found that catalyst events have been found to be important for helping women leave batterers. Yet while Liz was free of the violence, she was still faced with extreme poverty after the flood. Liz described her situation:

> I'm applying for disability and boy I hope I get it. I have
> no income. I can't eat three times a day. I just go hungry.
> Luckily I do get a housing voucher because of the domestic
> violence. I lost all my clothes, my furniture, everything.
> I mean, I have no money, no money. I have three dollars
> and 96 cents in my checking account.

A year after the flood Liz was back in her basement apartment, living on her own, and had just started to receive disability payments. She was still seeking counseling to help her hold on to her new strength and keep Fred from reentering her life. Looking at her experience with the domestic violence and the disaster, Liz had an image of what had happened:

> I'm starting a new life. So I'm going to take that flood,
> and all that abuse, and when the flood waters left Grand
> Forks, well, *that was my old life leaving*. All the abuse left
> with the water. That's how I look at it.

Research has found that battered women often have low self-esteem and a very poor self-image, which contributes to their feelings of dependence and powerlessness (Gelles 1997). Therefore, if a disaster provides an opportunity for a shift in one's view of oneself, and an increase in self-confidence, then this could help women leave domestic violence. As Liz explained to me, the disaster put things in perspective, it forced her to determine what is important in life. Enarson and Morrow (1997) found in their work on Hurricane Andrew that a woman planned to use disaster assistance money to buy a bus ticket out of town and out of an abusive relationship. Thus, disasters can provide, both financially and psychologically, an opportunity to leave an abusive relationship.

DISCUSSION AND CONCLUSION

Woman battering situations are diverse and complex. Knowing and examining the full social and individual context of a battered woman's life is considered essential to understanding her domestic violence circumstances and choices (Dutton 1996). In this exploratory study, I emphasize the context of woman battering in disasters, using two case studies to shed light on the realities of two women's lives, thereby showing not the frequency, but the range and variation, of some of the *kinds* of problems women will face in a disaster. Based on the existing data on woman battering in disasters, and from my own study and the work of other disaster researchers, I have several recommendations concerning future directions for theory, methodology, and policy.

Disaster contexts are an important theoretical site for studying women's lives and for understanding their experiences from their point of view or standpoint, and for conceptualizing their behavior and experiences within a full social context. This research contributes, for example, to feminist theories that address the intersections of race, class, and gender in women's lives (e.g. Collins 1993) and how these statuses contribute to their vulnerability or marginalization. In this study, I am able to address social class and disability issues, and some of the data challenges the "universal risk" theories of woman battering by showing that some women's status does affect their vulnerability. For example, one of the case studies helps to shed light on the battering experiences of disabled women. This is an important addition to the literature since the experiences of violence for women with disabilities are not often heard (Chenoweth 1996) and the intersection of gender and disability in general is not well explored in research (Thomson 1994). Also a challenge to universal risk theories, the case studies presented here help illustrate how lower-class and middle-class women may have different experiences as victims of domestic violence. For future research on woman battering in disasters, I would recommend that in addition to disability and class, the role of race and ethnicity be examined in order to contribute to the feminist theoretical knowledge on what exactly the intersections in women's lives mean for them and how they contribute to their marginalization.

In addition, as social scientists we can contribute to general domestic violence theories by studying the disaster context. Domestic violence is acknowledged as a social problem, but the experience of being battered is not well understood (Ferraro and Johnson 1983). Examining intimate violence within the context of a natural disaster could provide insight into domestic violence behaviors in general. For example, we can begin to understand how batterers use the disaster as an excuse and justification for the violence. Past research has found that some battered women also blame an external force, such as drug addiction or pressures at work, for the situation (Ferraro and Johnson 1983). In that way, the violence is seen as a temporary situation that could be overcome, and the women can deny that the abusers want to hurt them. Thus, battered women may frame disasters as an "external force" rationalization, as Karen did to some extent in her interview. As disasters are important research sites, I believe domestic violence theories could be advanced by further research in the disaster context.

I have several thoughts on methodological directions for future research. I advocate the broadening of research questions to go beyond asking if woman battering rates increase. I also suggest that we utilize more ethnographic, longitudinal methods to more fully understand woman battering in disasters. For example, an in-depth, longitudinal study would help us to determine when in the disaster battering is most severe. This study and the limited existing research on woman battering in the context of disasters indicate the increased demand for services may occur even months after the disaster. For example, in Enarson's (1998) survey of domestic violence organizations, many reported increases six months to a year later. Yet I learned that the Community Violence Intervention Center in Grand Forks, which had their hotline number forwarded to a cell phone so that evacuated staff scattered across Minnesota and North Dakota could continue to receive calls, received many calls for help in the acute period of the crisis. Future research may try to understand at what point in the disaster process there is a need for services, so communities can prepare to help women at that time and so that researchers can get a better understanding of the disaster process.

Lastly, I recommend that we use the data presented here to help direct future policy regarding woman battering in disasters. Karen and Liz provide important illustrations of why we need to focus on the fact that there is an increase in the demand for domestic violence services after a disaster. If we were to assume that their stories were typical of many other women, we might say that Karen and Liz cancel each other out—one woman left a domestic violence situation, one woman is in a new domestic violence situation—and thus, we could see how domestic violence rates remain stable. If we only look at statistics, however, we might miss the larger issue: *both* women desperately needed domestic violence services.

In light of the demand for services, social service providers need to be prepared and be given assistance from the larger community. Enarson's (1998) study found that while the demand for services increased, the financial help, from private funds and government, was very short-lived. In addition, fundraising is very difficult after a disaster. She also reports that the domestic violence organizations have staff overload, as the women on staff have also experienced a disaster, and many of them have to work on their own homes and help their own families recover. Grand Forks is experiencing both staff overload and a shortage of funds. Several years after the flood, the Center was able to raise enough money to open a shelter for battered women and their children, a new office, and a new visitation center set up for abusers to visit with their children and to provide a safe place for parents to turn over their children for home visits. As a result, the Center staff now feels that they are a highly effective organization and are able to serve approximately 2000 clients a year.

In addition, I suggest that women's service providers be better included in community disaster planning. The woman battering organizations need to be better prepared for disasters and the emergency management organizations need to be more aware and sensitive to woman battering issues. As Wilson et al. (1998) state, communities need to be aware of the domestic violence issue prior to the disaster event in order to be effective after a disaster. This points to the need for domestic organizations to be represented in disaster planning and to be included as an important component of the disaster recovery community. Finally, I propose that we view disasters as a window of opportunity for the community to address woman battering. Disasters are often a time of change and possibility, thus allowing the community the opportune time to acknowledge and assist women in woman battering situations. I argue that communities should take disasters as an opportunity to make long-lasting changes to their policies and structures so that woman battering organizations and shelters receive sufficient support and that women receive the help they need in both disaster and non-disaster times.

7

WOMEN AND HOUSING ISSUES
IN TWO U.S. DISASTERS:

Hurricane Andrew and the Red River Valley flood

Elaine Enarson

INTRODUCTION

Writing about the chronically homeless from a disaster perspective, Kai Erikson links place, housing, and identity (1994: 159):

> One can find asylum in a barracks or a dormitory, a prison cell or hospital ward, a crisis shelter or a flophouse. One can double up in the margins of someone else's household. But a true home—a place of one's own—is an extension of the individuals who live in it, a part of themselves. It is the outer envelope of personhood. People need location almost as much as they need shelter, for a sense of place is one of the ways they connect to the larger human community. You cannot be a member unless you are grounded somewhere in communal space. That is the geography of self.

Research across the disciplines has demonstrated that this "geography of self" is constructed in gendered space: geographers explore how differently women and men use space as well as time (e.g., Rose 1993); sociologists and anthropologists how women work and earn inside the home (e.g., Tinker 1990; Boris and Prügl 1996); and historians how women have organized to secure safe housing in toxic-threatened environments (e.g., Rodda 1994), create "safe space" from male violence (Schechter 1981), and enhance personal autonomy through equitable land and property rights (e.g., United Nations Centre for Human Settlements/Habitat 1990). In short, housing matters to women.

Located self-evidently at the heart of what is lost in disaster and what is understood as recovery, housing also matters to emergency planners. Political, economic, and cultural issues in evacuation, emergency shelter, temporary housing, relocation, and reconstruction have long interested disaster researchers (e.g., Aysan and Oliver 1987; Bates 1982; Davis 1978; Oliver-Smith 1990; Peacock et al. 1987; Quarantelli 1982;). Recent studies from the United States have identified lack of affordable housing as a factor in the slow recovery of low-income neighborhoods hit by earthquake (Bolin 1993); documented ethnic and class conflict over culturally appropriate temporary shelter and reconstruction (Bolin and Stanford 1991, 1998; Phillips 1993;); and addressed the post-disaster housing needs of the homeless and elderly (Eldar 1992; Phillips 1991). A gendered perspective on disaster and housing is conspicuous by its absence.

This paper examines housing as part of a larger project to illuminate "shadow risks and hidden damages" (Hewitt 1995) and to specify root causes reproducing women's disaster vulnerability in developed nations (Blaikie et al. 1994), among them the gendered division of labor, economic dependency, male violence, and housing insecurity. I begin with a theoretical grounding of disaster housing in gender relations and global development patterns and then focus on the United States, drawing on Census data and qualitative field studies to address two key questions. First, what structural trends and patterns suggest women's housing insecurity in this context? Second, what emergency management issues emerge from empirical investigations of women's disaster housing experiences? I draw examples from two U.S. case studies to illustrate how housing in the disaster context is a highly gendered issue. The final section outlines women's housing needs and strategic interests and offers guidelines to practitioners.

WOMEN'S HOUSING INSECURITY AND DISASTER VULNERABILITY IN DEVELOPING COUNTRIES

Gender and development studies in the world's poorest nations provide a useful perspective for analyzing women and housing crisis in the United States. The gendered division of labor accords women responsibility for maintaining safe and clean households and for using and managing life-giving environmental resources; this role is pivotal when communities face severe housing damage or loss (Steady 1993). Secure shelter is also an essential foundation for women's autonomy in every society and its absence an indicator of crisis (Tinker 1990). Impacted both by gender inequality (economic dependence, male violence, unequal access to land, tools, credit, and training) and by global development patterns (increasing poverty, hyperurbanization, changing family structures, environmental degradation, migrant labor, and population displacement), increasing numbers of women around the world are insecurely housed on marginal lands (Chant 1996; Momsen 1991; Moser and Peake 1987; Sweetman 1996).

Global studies of disaster-impacted communities demonstrate the salience of housing issues for women throughout the disaster cycle. Women's more homebound lives make them more vulnerable to injury or death under some conditions. For example, the practice of sex segregation placed women and children, but not men, indoors when dwellings collapsed in the 1993 Latur earthquake (Krishnaraz 1997). Women's losses may also be economic as women's home-based work increases internationally. In the 1985 Mexico City earthquake, the majority of houses destroyed were headed by low-income single women who supported their families through informal sector work based in and around their houses (Dufka 1988). During the emergency shelter phase, cultural barriers may place women more than men at risk; where the norms of female seclusion are strictly enforced, for example, emergency evacuation warnings are less likely to reach women, and community shelters are less accessible to them (Ikeda 1995). Later, women more than men may find it difficult to leave accommodations meant to be "temporary," as Geipel (1991) noted in the case of senior women following an earthquake in rural Italy.

International studies also document women's active participation during the rebuilding stage, both materially and as political actors. Following the Latur earthquake, Indian women organized in neighborhood groups to monitor construction work for corruption, collectively purchase construction materials, and build model homes adapted to their needs (Krishnaraj 1997). Women also shape the politics of reconstruction in impacted communities. Following a recent earthquake in Colima, Mexico, Serrat Viñas (1998) found women highly active in organizing community resistance to enforced relocation, echoing the activism of women around housing issues in the wake of the 1985 Mexico City earthquake (Momsen 1991: 101).

Gender and development theory draws a useful distinction between women's "practical needs" to meet the demands of daily life and their "strategic interests" in challenging gender inequalities (Molyneux 1985; Moser 1987). The gender-aware disaster practices of Pattan, an NGO working with flooded Southeast Asian communities, led it not only to meet women's practical needs by rebuilding houses but to record ownership of these new homes in both partners' names (Bari 1998), arguably rebuilding a more egalitarian and hence less disaster-vulnerable community. I return below to this paradigm of women's practical needs and strategic interests in disaster housing.

Comparable investigations of women's housing issues have not yet been conducted in the wealthy nations of the industrial world, though such work would contribute substantially to a more cross-cultural and gender-inclusive disaster social science (Enarson 1998). In the next section, I review social trends and population patterns suggesting that everyday life in the United States puts rising numbers of American women at risk during environmental or technological disasters.

Root causes of women's housing vulnerability

An aging population is a feminizing one. In the United States, over half of all women over 75 (and 20 percent of men) now live alone (Ollenburger and Tobin 1998: 101). The number of *senior women living alone* is expected to increase by 39 percent among women aged 55 to 64 and by 11 percent among women 75 or older (Schmittroth 1995: 221). Though aging is not a uniform process, the physical disabilities of age increase the likely disaster vulnerabilities of the elderly (Eldar 1992), and disaster planning with their needs in mind is essential. At all income levels, private residences, extended care facilities, and retirement facilities house large numbers of widows and other senior women likely to require assistance. While self-protection is a major theme in U.S. disaster preparation campaigns, senior women on their own may well lack the assistance or resources needed for home preparation, evacuation, or reconstruction.

The traditional nuclear household residing in an owner-occupied home is the focus of most disaster planning and preparation. Yet approximately one-quarter of all U.S. households are now either *sole-female* or *female-headed households* (Ahlburg and DeVita 1992). In the decade ahead (2000-2010), the fastest rate of increase for women heading households is expected among those under 25, a group of young women already subject to higher poverty rates and therefore likely to be insecurely housed (Schmittroth 1995: 224). At the other end of the life cycle, half of all elderly women live on less than $9,500 (Ollenburger and Tobin 1998: 100). Many live alone and draw on very meager resources to prepare or repair their homes.

Low-income female-headed households are increasing. Just over half of all poor households are headed by women (54 percent), an increase of 46 percent between 1970 and 1991 (Nunez 1996: 12). In 1993, over a third of all female-headed households lived below the poverty line, five times the poverty rate of married couples (Schmittroth 1995: 511). The racial dynamics of poverty in the United States put racial-ethnic minority families at greater risk of substandard housing before disasters; poverty rates for single mothers in 1997 ranged from 37 percent for Anglo women to 46 percent and 54 percent for

African-American and Hispanic women respectively (U.S. Bureau of the Census 1997).

Women in public housing are especially at risk. While projects vary in the degree to which they are safely located, retrofitted, or maintained, on balance the rising maintenance costs in aging structures have resulted in a deterioration of the nation's public housing stock (DeParle 1996). Like renters, many project residents depend on absentee landlords to prepare or repair their dwellings. When affordable housing is not available to them, women displaced from public housing units become long-term residents in "temporary" postdisaster accommodations (Morrow 1997).

The nation's supply of *affordable housing* is declining despite the need (Nunez 1996; DeParle 1996). Low-income women and their children are likely to reside in substandard structures built where land is cheap and often hazard-prone; their shelter in trailers and on floodplains provides them little protection. Low-income women in minority populations are disproportionately subjected to routine toxic exposure and the risk of catastrophic toxic events in contaminated neighborhoods (Brown and Ferguson 1995; Taylor 1997).

Homeless families headed by women are the fastest growing sector of the homeless population and now constitute approximately 40 percent of this highly vulnerable population (Nunez 1996: 5; Glasser 1994). Increasing numbers of American women cope with the relentless "daily disaster" of homelessness, among them women leaving violent relationships and runaway teenaged girls on the street (Kozol 1988). Their daily rounds in and out of shelters, hotels, or borrowed space render them socially invisible, difficult to locate and assist, and well outside the normative household disaster planners target for information and resources.

Women in domestic violence shelters are also socially invisible yet highly vulnerable. Shelters offer safe space of last resort to women forced from their homes by violence; to maintain this lifeline, residents, volunteers, and staff may need physical assistance preparing and repairing their facility and locating alternate evacuation space unknown to abusers (Enarson 1999). Women living with physical or mental disabilities, or serious illness, in *group homes* or other public settings may need help tailored to their abilities and needs as they prepare and repair their living spaces.

These patterns and trends make housing in the disaster context a gendered issue in the United States, with particular significance for women raising families alone, those on low-incomes or in poverty, marginally housed women in public housing or domestic violence shelters, older women living alone, and homeless women. What can we add from the concrete experiences of U.S. women living through specific disasters?

HOUSING EXPERIENCES OF WOMEN IN TWO U.S. DISASTERS

Taking up the challenge of feminist standpoint theory to understand and critique ruling relations and power structures from women's everyday domestic experiences (Smith 1987), some researchers have recently investigated women's disaster experiences in the developed world, during Miami's Hurricane Andrew (Alway, Belgrave, and Smith 1998; Morrow and Enarson 1996; Enarson and Morrow 1997, 1998a; Morrow 1997); in flooded areas of North Dakota (Fothergill 1998), Wales and Scotland (Fordham 1998; Fordham and Ketteridge 1998), Australia (Finlay 1998), and Canada (Enarson and Scanlon 1999); and in the aftermath of fire (Cox 1998; Hoffman 1998) and earthquake (Phillips 1990). Though not directly investigating gender and post-disaster housing, these studies suggest that women are highly impacted by issues arising during emergency preparation, evacuation, emergency shelter, temporary accommodation, repair, and reconstruction.

This paper reports on original data from an earlier study conducted with Betty Hearn Morrow following Hurricane Andrew in Miami and from my on-going investigation of women's disaster experiences during the 1997 Red River Valley flood in the Upper Midwest (North Dakota and Minnesota). In these studies, too, housing loss and recovery were critical issues facing women.

RESEARCH STRATEGY

The field studies were conducted to document and analyze the experiences of women in a recent U.S. hurricane and flood, among them women's housing needs and interests. The studies employed qualitative methods appropriate to this goal, primarily open-ended interviewing and focus group sessions. Guiding research questions elicited information about women's vulnerabilities and losses and about their resources and responses in each phase of the disaster cycle. Interviews and focus groups were conducted with the use of informed consent forms and background data sheets; all discussions were tape-recorded, translated from Spanish to English if necessary, and later transcribed for computer-assisted qualitative analysis.

Because their ideas, feelings, and observations are often marginalized, narrative accounts were solicited from women particularly vulnerable to disasters. In addition to professional women in service-providing agencies, emergency response organizations, and local government, interviews or focus groups sessions were conducted with migrant farm workers, refugees, seniors, women in public housing and in domestic violence shelters, home-based workers, single women, rural women, low-income single mothers, racial-ethnic minority women, and small business owners. In most cases, potential focus group participants were identified and contacted by knowledgeable key informants (e.g., shelter manager, agency director, community leader). This strategy resulted in a non-probability, purposive sample of women representing the broad range of community difference across the divides of race, ethnicity, age, citizenship status, and social class.

Research conducted in Miami in 1992-1994 included interviews with 25 service providers (e.g., the YWCA, South Dade Immigration Services, Legal Services of Miami); five focus groups involving 25 women; observations in tent cities, service centers, and provider organizations; and extended participant-observation of an emergent community group. In "Grand Forks" (used here to include Grand Forks, North Dakota, and East Grand Forks, Minnesota), I conducted interviews with 95 impacted women, service providers, and disaster responders during three field visits at 6, 12, and 18 months after the April 1997 flood.

Other data sources included agency documents, local research reports, and media accounts; numerous informal conversations with residents during field visits; personal letters and other documents in the University of North Dakota's Special Collections Library; and oral histories conducted under the auspices of the University of North Dakota Museum of Art.

FINDINGS

The following section reports sequentially on key patterns or issues which emerged from women's accounts through the disaster cycle of household preparation, evacuation, emergency shelter, temporary accommodation, rebuilding, and resettlement in permanent housing. I emphasize that the findings are not conclusive but suggestive, raising a host of questions for further investigation, among them how gender interacts with race, class, and age to bring these dynamics into play, and what gender-specific issues might emerge in a similar study of male residents.

1. *Conflict with men was reported over priorities during household preparation and evacuation.* When couples in the Red River Valley differed over how much and how soon to prepare their homes for flood, and whether and when to evacuate, women took action earlier and wanted more help from male partners and kin. In contrast, a study of middle-class couples in Miami found most men highly involved in physically preparing their own and others' homes, perhaps finding hurricane warnings more credible then flood level predictions (Always, Belgrave and Smith 1998). Facing more remote threats, men were less likely than women to seek information or protect household items in a study of aftershock communication after the Loma Prieta earthquake (O'Brien and Atchison 1998). As the Red River waters rose dangerously high, most child-free and able-bodied residents, male and female, volunteered at "Sandbag Central"

to help dike endangered homes, schools, businesses, and other public structures. But women and men were often divided over the need for mitigation at home. Interpreting women's desire for action not as mitigation but as "panic," husbands in some cases actively resisted women's efforts to gather sandbagging materials for the home, pack belongings for evacuation, or move furniture and other possessions to safer ground. Their partners later spoke bitterly about this male resistance to protecting their homes and property, resenting both the material losses and the emotional cost. As one woman explained:

> When the women showed this concern (to buy flood insurance, to move things upstairs), their significant others . . . in many cases discounted their turbulence, little was done, and much was lost . . . . [My husband] disconnected himself from my efforts. In the early stages, he used little words that discounted what I felt. In the later stages, I knew I had to move regardless of how he felt and I moved like a woman possessed. I didn't force him to help me, but I missed his companionship when I felt our home was at stake. This created a chasm between us which we recently have begun to bridge.

2. *Highly vulnerable women sometimes lacked needed assistance preparing their homes.* As Hurricane Andrew approached, women in public housing units in Miami reported that managers ignored their requests for plywood and nails to cover apartment windows: "Everything was right there. All they had to do was open it up and give us some nails—we could have did it ourselves. They didn't want to do it. They didn't tell us anything." As a result, living units were damaged or destroyed, resulting in increased losses of personal belongings. Eighteen months later, women and children reported numerous respiratory problems caused by mildew and mold in apartments still under repair. Similarly, in some rural homesteads along the Red River Valley, a strong regional ethic of self-reliance may have inhibited widows living

alone on deteriorating family farms from asking for help, leaving them in substandard housing "with their basements collapsing" after the flood.

3. *Women were less likely than men to resist or delay evacuation.* In the Grand Forks area, many families experienced emergency evacuation in darkness as dikes broke overnight, and virtually all residents were evacuated when city services ceased. Women tended to evacuate earlier than men, due both to safety concerns about youngsters and because the men in their families resisted evacuation, increasing women's caregiving responsibilities. Gender bias in evacuation can also be explicit, as occurred across the U.S. border in the rural municipality of Richot in Manitoba. There, only women providing direct services to the remaining male responders (e.g., waitresses) were exempt from mandatory evacuation orders as the Red River floodwaters moved north (Enarson and Scanlon 1999). Australian researchers found stress levels to be higher among evacuees from Cyclone Tracy, among them virtually all the women and children of Darwin (Milne 1979).

In one professional family, the wife was seriously ill at the time of the flood crest but more concerned about her husband's recent heart problems:

> After about 1½ hours of sleep Friday night, I turned the radio back on and they were saying that the whole town should evacuate—our area was specifically named. I woke [my husband and grown son] about 5:00 a.m. Both said they would not go . . . . It took me until the afternoon on Saturday to convince [him] that we should leave. All medical services were down, and I didn't want to have to worry about getting him to medical help if he should need it in an area where none was available. [My son] refused to go.

4. *Lack of housing and safe space put some women at higher risk of violence.* Increasing incidents of domestic violence were reported after Miami's hurricane and the Red River Valley flood (Enarson

forthcoming). Designated evacuation space or relief centers may not be safe spaces for women in violent relationships, as this shelter worker explained:

> [T]hey're in that shelter because they're in danger. And the Red Cross shelters, those types of shelters, are not safe for them. Their other courses of action tend to be neighbors, friends, family members who are logical places for the perpetrator of that violence upon them to look for them . . . And so I think this really shows that we need to have a plan of action ahead of time . . . . Because they're there for a reason.

When floodwaters destroyed the community shelter for homeless and abused women, Grand Forks residents were made more aware of the needs of battered women for emergency shelter and affordable transitional housing. The flooded shelter in Grand Forks had not been replaced one year later, and crisis workers had physically relocated the crisis intervention center to five different locations.

Housing shortages brought former boyfriends and recently divorced spouses back into many women's lives during evacuation, shelter, and temporary housing; some spoke of increased conflicts with children, threatened violence, substance abuse, and emotional strain. In Miami, lack of accommodation for out-of-town construction workers and their families was the proximate cause of abuse of a young woman who lived in a tent for six months while her partner repaired homes.

5. *Women's domestic and kin work intensified when living conditions were disrupted.* Women in both studies spoke frequently of what "putting the house to rights" entailed in the aftermath of a hurricane or flood. Lack of facilities, equipment, supplies, space, and time clearly expanded women's postdisaster domestic labor, magnifying the demands of the "second shift" most employed women face. This was especially true of low-income women

unable to purchase such replacement services as child or elder care, restaurant meals, domestic help, or dry cleaning.

The inability to perform basic household tasks was emotionally stressful for women who saw themselves as family providers:

> When I couldn't fix a meal because I didn't have water, when I had basement water in my kitchen—that's what I felt like I was responsible for, washing their clothes and—it *majorly* disrupted *my* life, where my husband could go off and go to his job and bring a pay check home, and "Everything's just fine." And I'm like, "Everything's not!" I couldn't shop at the stores I wanted to shop at, I couldn't do anything.

Insecure housing during the evacuation and resettling period also greatly expanded women's traditional socioemotional and kin work. They reported having primary responsibility for assessing the extended family's housing needs and resources and arranging for appropriate temporary living space. Overcrowded living conditions in damaged houses, relatives' homes, or government-provided trailers intensified women's emotion work as caregivers in much the same way that non-functional kitchens intensified their physical labor. Respondents and service providers in both Grand Forks and Miami attributed increased family stress, leading in some cases to conflict and violence, to overcrowding in tents, trailers, hotels, the homes of relatives, or their own damaged houses or cars.

Households often expanded in size as women able to do so offered space and personal services (cooking, laundry, child care, emotional support) to kin, co-workers, friends, and evacuated families not known to them personally. Many women recalled the struggle to keep up with their paid jobs, clean up their damaged property and workplaces, and create a "home" away from home for their own families or those they hosted:

> I know of a lady who had 17 families living with her— families! And the last one left two days ago [six months

after the flood]. We're talking long-term. Families still have families with them, because they don't want to move—the denial—they don't want to move into a trailer. They want a home situation as much as they possibly can.

6. *Government-provided temporary housing communities were not designed around the needs of women and children.* During their long stays in temporary trailers, women's day-to-day efforts to cook, clean, and care for their families, often in combination with paid jobs and unpaid community work, were complicated by the physical limitations of temporary accommodations, e.g., lack of privacy, few play spaces for children or activities for teens, insufficient laundry facilities, and social isolation. A study from Perth, Scotland, found that even basic household appliances like washing machines were not widely available, and time-consuming and expensive daily trips to buy food were necessary in temporary accommodation (Fordham and Ketteridge 1988: 88; see also Fordham 1998). That temporary housing during evacuation impacts women's lives more than men's was also apparent among families evacuated from the Red River flood in Canada (Enarson and Scanlon 1999). In Miami's trailer camps, women were often isolated, fearful for their personal safety, lacked needed mental and reproductive health services and reliable transportation, and were unable to access needed community services. There was no child care, elder care, or family respite care consistently provided in public spaces either in Miami or in Grand Forks to support women with dependents in their efforts to repair homes, search for new housing, or access relief services. A community center offered Grand Forks trailer residents needed recreational services, computer facilities, after-school care, and other services, but mothers spoke often about overcrowding and the lack of safe, outdoor play space for children. Outreach workers identified limited public bus transportation as an issue for women in temporary housing who lacked cars but were still responsible for searching for permanent housing, getting to jobs, and transporting children to child care and home schools.

7. *Women were slow to locate affordable housing and leave temporary accommodations.* Women's economic status and family roles were formidable barriers in the race for affordable housing, making women more dependent than men on private or public temporary accommodations. In Miami, women were the majority of those long-time residents of "temporary" housing, especially minority women heading multi-generational families. One year after the flood, a housing specialist in Grand Forks estimated that 30 to 40 percent of government-provided trailer residents were women, often single mothers with large families, on public assistance, or marginally employed. Disaster relief workers, Unmet Needs Committee members, and others engaged in Grand Forks' recovery process concurred that low-income women rearing families on their own were especially disadvantaged in the post-flood housing market, echoing the stories told by single mothers of their many moves in and out of trailers and around the community. One housing specialist explained:

> We have a lot of lower-income families, like single mothers with three children, you know, that can barely make it the way it is, let alone with paying rent, because they only pay utilities on these places . . . . I have a list of all rentals in Grand Forks and it's just—they're still real high. Even for sleeping rooms, they're like $200 a month . . . . We have one lady out here that has nine kids and she's going to need a four-bedroom. And the last apartment I saw was over a thousand a month for rent.

Lack of affordable permanent housing was a major setback for low-income single mothers, pushing some back into dependency and depression. They often spoke of behavioral problems with children in crowded living quarters, health problems, loss of home-based income, and unwelcome engagement with former spouses in need of housing. Treated earlier for depression, this mother of four repeatedly stressed the need for secure space for her active youngsters and two teenagers:

I had things set. I had a house leased until my eldest daughter graduated from high school. We had four bedrooms, a big enough house for my family, big yard. I was going to start college in June . . . . I was single, I was starting college, I was feeling good. I had my head together. When we get another house that we have space in, we'll feel better, but I'm starting to get the feeling that that's not going to happen and I'm starting to get real upset again, thinking I'm stuck—into an apartment and then we'll have to move again, and move again, and move again.

Among the predominantly Scandinavian residents of the Red River Valley, Latina women were highly visible in the search for relief goods and housing. After losing her home and its contents, one single mother of three drove non-stop to Texas for emotional and material support from her extended family. She focused on racial bias in describing her subsequent search for permanent housing and the conflicts which developed between her teenaged children and her landlord:

I had a hard time getting that apartment but I actually begged him—actually, I kneeled down and I said "Please, me and my kids need a place . . . . I have to go into storage to get clothing for me and my kids. I need a home." And he's over here, "Well, let me think about it for two weeks, because Mexicans used to live in my place and destroyed my apartments before the flood." That's what I was told by him. So that's where I thought racial had something to do with it.

8. *Gender was a factor in decisions about home repair and rebuilding.* Couples in both studies struggled to resolve conflicting priorities when making decisions about whether, when, and where to relocate, and about repair and rebuilding priorities. In Miami, an advocate for low-income refugee women recalled mediating many conflicts between couples when women more than men wanted

to use relief funds to make immediate home repairs and replace needed household supplies. As the account below suggests, home repairs were delayed for other Miami women when male partners more readily took on waged clean-up jobs than helped out with necessary but unwaged home repairs:

> [We] three women spent 39 days without electricity—washing clothes in the bathtub, heating water on the campfire for the children's baths, washing dishes in a bucket. We cooked Mexican food over a makeshift kitchen in the yard, preparing corn tortillas on a cast iron griddle . . . . Disaster or no disaster, the men demanded hearty meals of traditional foods and refused to eat at the military kitchens . . . . The men began to hire themselves out, repairing others' homes as the job market for workers boomed, but our home lay in disarray (Colina 1998).

Tenants in South Dade County were expected to continue rent payments, but landlords in low-income areas often failed to make needed repairs. As women are more likely to rent than to own homes, this impacted women directly, especially those most vulnerable to exploitation. This advocate for Haitian immigrants in Miami explained:

> Well, even if you got a [FEMA temporary housing] check, where are you going to go? Now a lot of them, what they did—they make deals with the landlord. OK, we stay, we pay you rent, you fix. So the landlords are getting the money but they're not fixing. [This young single mother had] no electricity, no lights, and she had her 14-day-old baby, and she was paying $260 rent every month.

In Grand Forks, service providers noted that poor health and special needs kept many elderly widows from returning promptly after their evacuation. Because they were not in town to arrange for prompt clean-up and repairs before construction work slowed for the winter, repairs were delayed on their homes and they returned to depressing living conditions in damaged homes and deserted neighborhoods. On the other hand, returning too soon created problems for some women. A public health educator observed that the husbands and fathers she worked with were sometimes overeager to begin repairing their homes; this led some men to bring women and children back to wood-frame homes not yet thoroughly dry and safe for occupancy.

9. *Housing loss had direct economic consequences for some women.* Women generally did not benefit from casual work on construction and clean-up crews in either Miami or Grand Forks. There were many reports of women's secondary unemployment as a direct result of housing damage, among them domestic workers in Miami. Often primary hurricane victims themselves in hard-hit South Dade County, many lost work when their middle-class employers lost their homes or temporarily relocated during reconstruction. Contractor fraud was reported by some respondents in Miami during the rebuilding phase, particularly targeting older, non-English-speaking women.

Home-based work losses were reported by self-employed women in both cities. Grand Forks flood victims minimized housing damage ("just six feet in my basement"), but basements often provided needed living space. Basements were also used for storing equipment and supplies used by low-income women in home day care, hair dressing, bookkeeping, and other forms of home work. For example, each of the Grand Forks family day care providers interviewed reported significant economic losses; estimates of how much their earnings contributed to family income ranged from 30 to 100 percent. Home-based child care was a vital but invisible part of the Grand Forks economy until floodwaters washed away basement services and kept thousands of employed mothers at home. A childhood educator observed:

> What happened was that most of the facilities in which children were cared for were flooded. There were very few that weren't flooded, because most of them were in

basements. That's where we keep kids! . . . So everything shut down. And even the ones that didn't get damaged, they didn't have water—it was impossible to provide care. So what happened was the astounding realization that when businesses needed parents back in the work force, they didn't have anywhere to leave their kids. So all of a sudden it became an important issue. It was one of the key issues in getting people back to work.

10. *Emotional impacts of housing loss were gendered.* Returning to damaged or destroyed housing may be especially difficult emotionally for those who built or remodeled their own homes, more often men than women. A member of the disaster outreach team touring Grand Forks met this distressed wife in an affluent flooded neighborhood:

> We had a lady call us and say "Just come, I'll show you." We go down there and the guy got out of the car and he stopped at the end of the driveway and he sobbed and he sobbed. And she goes, "This is what he does every time. We can't even talk. He's a wreck and I have to hold everything together."

Women often articulated especially strong ties to place, reflecting the gendered division of labor and the material grounding of women's lives in the domestic realm. Women, in turn, may experience the loss of relational space more acutely. In both studies, women recalled their destroyed or damaged homes as places of personal growth where babies were born, family rituals enacted, gardens tended, and emotional and physical lives constructed under their care. The loss of household possessions was the loss of family history and personal identity: "Every box of my life was floating around," one Grand Forks woman remembered feeling as she surveyed her flooded basement (Fothergill 1998). Less visible than male-dominated clean-up in the public realm, women's work in and around the damaged household enhances the emotional and material recovery of the family, for example when Grand Forks mothers retrieved and cleaned family memorabilia discarded on curbside berms. Participants at an Australian symposioum on women and disaster noted that male clean-up crews tended to throw away damaged personal items, which conflicted with women's desires to clean and preserve emotionally significant household items. Such conflict may contribute to post-disaster stress (Dobson 1994; Fuller 1994; Honeycombe 1994).

11. *Some women took on nontraditional roles in the housing crisis.* Though rarely employed in construction trades, women in a number of families reported practicing or developing new construction skills as they worked alongside husbands to repair their homes, especially in low-income households. As this woman reported:

> I can do wire now! Changed all my outlets and I can put up lights. I'm real scared of wiring even though I've done that. And I really got to be a good plasterer because I didn't like the way they did it so I redid it at nights myself.

In Grand Forks and Miami families, supervising or negotiating conditions with contractors, repair crews, and insurance agents often became women's work. Women reportedly took on most of the bureaucratic work of rebuilding (e.g., applying for building permits and arranging for volunteer assistance) as they had taken on the paperwork of emergency relief earlier on. The migrant community agency in Miami that built replacement housing after the hurricane reported that women were among those residents most actively involved in hands-on construction work. In the construction of Habitat for Humanity homes in Grand Forks, women were engaged in critical roles as board members, construction managers, and volunteers.

12. *Women organized politically to influence housing policy during the rebuilding phase,* though social action was difficult in post-disaster conditions. Often lacking cars, burdened by the needs of dependents, and facing the challenges of home repair, it was difficult for women in both communities to make their housing

needs visible in the public rebuilding process. As this outreach worker observed in Grand Forks: "We have a lot of public forums where people are allowed to come and—but I don't think that works for [women]. You don't take your kids, or you can't get there, for starters. It just doesn't work."

Women did successfully organize around housing and other issues in Miami, where the multicultural women's coalition, Women Will Rebuild (Enarson and Morrow 1998b), established a working committee to investigate women's housing conditions and needs [see also Leavitt's (1990) description of women's activism after civil disorder and Turner's (1997) analysis of Anglo women mobilizing around home clean-up and sanitation issues after the 1900 Galveston hurricane]. A founding member of Women Will Rebuild in Miami described the housing conditions which moved her to action:

> What I was seeing when I went to the trailer parks . . . over and over again the people who were living in unbelievable circumstances were women. They were living in those ghastly trailers. There was no playground, there wasn't a swing, there wasn't anything. The kids' main toys were razor-sharp pieces of metal from the blown-away trailers. They were being incredibly persecuted by the white mobile park owners who were getting zillions from the feds and who never had "funny people" in their place before. And it was hell down there. Grandmothers were taking care of a trailer full of kids. Mothers were out working. There was one huge park with no phones because the owner wouldn't let them in. So try to imagine all those children with no access to a 911 number. These were the kinds of stresses I was seeing. I was listening to those fancy people sitting over in the Gables who had no sense of what was going on down on the ground.

Latina women in Grand Forks reported racial bias in apartment rentals (and in the distribution of relief goods), lack of rental housing affordable to low-income Latina families, and lack of recovery assistance for migrant workers absent during the flood but impacted indirectly by housing shortages when they returned for the growing season. A focus group of seven Latinas criticized city officials' approval of expensive new townhouses, asking:

> So who's going to benefit? There's homeless people still . . . . We're thinking of forming a group. It's still in the making, but we want to get together—all Hispanic women—so we can have a voice. We still need to get some basics.

IMPLICATIONS FOR ACTION

The patterns and issues reported here from two field studies are suggestive but far from conclusive. Disaster responders, elected officials, government leaders, community activists, and vulnerable women in at-risk communities all need more concrete knowledge about women and disaster housing. Practitioners need more concrete information on specific housing issues likely to impact women in order to more effectively anticipate problems and match resources and needs.

This analysis focused on utilizing gender-specific knowledge to reduce community vulnerability. Women's housing needs are frequently subsumed under generalized categories (e.g., low-income households, racial-ethnic groups, and the elderly), although the root causes of their housing crisis and their need for services may well differ, for example in the case of female and male homelessness before and after disasters.

In this regard, funding gender-sensitive research on local vulnerability patterns is a significant mitigation strategy. Emergency management organizations should also consider gender audits of housing policies and practices to assess whose needs are addressed, what groups are targeted, what assumptions are made, what resources are made available, what benefits are likely, and how gender relations are impacted (Kabeer 1994: 302).

Grassroots women's organizations can and should be fully engaged as co-researchers in participatory research projects, drawing on their local knowledge about women's living conditions to design studies providing local practitioners with useful information and insight. Qualitative methods such as focus groups, semi-structured interviewing, and oral history will be useful strategies for bringing the diverse voices of ordinary women to community emergency planning. Evaluation researchers can identify "best practice" models in which women's housing needs in disaster contexts are successfully addressed. As Blaikie and his colleagues note (1994: 227), sex-specific data on the "hazardousness of home and workplace" will provide important information on the root causes of community vulnerability. More longitudinal research projects are also needed to track women's housing recovery in diverse racial, economic, and age groups.

Hazards assessment at the local level should incorporate a gendered analysis of housing vulnerability and accurately reflect the needs of all at-risk populations. Vulnerability maps should incorporate such indicators as the location and size of public housing units, residential patterns and trends among single parents and elderly women, home work patterns, migrant housing and labor market patterns, average numbers of women residing in emergency domestic violence shelter, spaces utilized by homeless women, local housing costs, and sex-specific income and employment data. If not yet available at the local and regional levels (and gender-specific data are rare in the tool kit of most emergency planners), this information should be developed through collaborative research projects involving academic researchers, community members, and disaster planners.

Meeting practical needs and long-term interests

Figure 3. Strategies for Meeting Women's Practical Needs in Disaster Housing

1. Identify insecurely housed women at the local level for priority assistance with preparedness, evacuation, repair, and re-housing, including women in domestic violence shelters, low-income women heading households, senior and disabled women, public housing residents, and home-working women.

---

2. Include locations of group homes, homeless shelters, public housing, non-confidential domestic violence shelters, extended care facilities, and migrant labor camps in community hazards maps.

3. Organize and administer emergency and temporary housing projects to meet women's needs for personal safety, child care, access to relevant employers, public transportation, reproductive health care, and gender-sensitive mental health services; employ a gender-fair checklist to plan and evaluate housing projects.

4. Develop educational materials for use by women's grassroots organizations to educate senior women, non-English-speakers, low-income single mothers, undocumented women, and other vulnerable women about safe clean-up, home repair, fraud, exploitation, redevelopment policies, and other housing issues.

5. Develop gender-specific emergency communications, e.g., publications responding to male resistance to home preparedness and evacuation, providing contact information for caregiver support, etc.

6. Provide and subsidize drop-in child care and adult respite care in temporary housing sites and central community facilities during evacuation, clean-up, and rebuilding; provide on-site child care at meetings of temporary residents' councils, community committees, and government bodies deliberating post-disaster housing decisions.

7. Monitor progress of repairs in public housing, migrant housing, women's shelters and other sites housing vulnerable women; liaise with knowledgeable community groups, e.g., through an appointed municipal ombudsperson.

8. Develop a community roster of women in the construction professions and trades and offer nontraditional skills training for women during repair and reconstruction; strive for gender-balanced contracting during clean up and rebuilding.

9. Mandate consultation with low-income women, women heading households, and other insecurely housed residents in the design and location of new housing units.

10. Implement gender audits assessing and monitoring impacts of new housing initiatives or land use policies on women operating home businesses, low-income single mothers, women with mobility barriers, and other vulnerable women.

Figure 3 offers ten strategies for addressing the material housing needs of different groups of women through the disaster cycle. Researchers and responders have offered a variety of models for mitigating housing losses, stressing the need to address the chronic housing needs of the "persistently vulnerable" (Bolin and Stanford 1998: 33), map the housing vulnerabilities of migrants, transients, complex households, the disabled, and other groups and broaden the planning base to utilize the local knowledge of community-based organizations (among others, see BAREPP 1992; Bolin and Stanford 1998; Morrow 1999; Phillips 1996;). The strategies offered here build on this framework but identify women as a housing-vulnerable group with specific needs and resources.

Meeting women's practical housing needs—for example, of senior women living alone for home repairs or of single mothers in trailer camps for adequate transportation—is vital but does not challenge deeply-rooted patterns of gender, race, and class power producing women's housing insecurity. To reduce social inequalities placing women at risk, *disaster housing policies and practices must also support women's autonomy.* Reconstruction programs should support women's right to secure housing; accommodate women's responsibilities in the home, work force, and community; and facilitate women's access to nontraditional skills, tools, and responsibilities.

Affordable, safe, and appropriate housing for women is both an immediate post-impact need and in the long-range interest of gender equality and community solidarity before and after damaging extreme events. Secure housing which meets the needs of women at all income levels, in all cultural communities, across the life cycle, and with varying physical abilities is an essential precondition for women's autonomy.

Engendering reconstruction is also in the long-term interest of women as well as men. Post-disaster redevelopment forces the issue of how communities are constructed socially as well as materially, affording a window of opportunity for revisioning housing and community life. Feminist urban planners, geographers, architects, and activists have offered models for woman-friendly redevelopment including such features as affordable and accessible housing for women through the life cycle, shared open space, on-site child care and other social and human services, decentralized employment and city services, safe public lighting, and affordable public transit (e.g., Hayden 1981; Eichler 1995). Disaster professionals working with communities to rebuild should include this perspective and these professionals in their consultations.

Finally, *women need decision-making voice in constructing sustainable built environments.* Local mitigation initiatives must engage women's groups and advocates representing migrant and homeless families, minority families in at-risk neighborhoods, battered women, the frail elderly, women in public housing, and other insecurely housed women. Women's long-range housing interests are rarely part of public discourse in the highly politicized process of postdisaster housing redevelopment. But effective planning for sustainable and disaster-resilient human settlements cannot engage only the energies and ideas of men; women, too, must be fully engaged as full and equal partners. Rebuilding without taking the material conditions of women's lives into account not only fails to mitigate the impact of future disasters but reconstructs significant housing vulnerabilities.

CONCLUSION

Understanding that disasters are as much social constructions as the individuals, households, organizations, and communities they touch, disaster researchers have searched for underlying fault lines and fractures placing communities at risk—including gender inequalities. Women's practical needs and long-range interests in secure housing were investigated in this context, suggesting root vulnerabilities in developed societies and addressing the practical question, "So what?"

The absolute need for shelter, land, and secure housing is manifestly greater in the world's most impoverished nations and where women lack land and inheritance rights. Secure housing under those conditions is a vital need for women before, during, and after disasters. But demographic trends and global development patterns suggest that housing is and will increasingly be salient for women in the world's wealthiest nations as well. Persistently high poverty rates, women's longevity, the global trend toward single mothering, cutbacks in social subsidies for affordable housing, and increases in family homelessness and homelessness caused by violence against women undermine the housing security of women across the nation long before the threat of flood or hurricane.

Preliminary and suggestive in nature, findings from the gender-focused field studies reviewed here also suggest a range of housing issues that arise for at-risk women impacted by disaster in wealthy developed nations like the United States. Both overlapping and distinct from those experienced by women in developing countries, these include: shortage of housing affordable to women, especially to low-income women supporting families; gender-based barriers to household preparation and repair; stressful living conditions for women caregivers in temporary accommodations; economic losses to home-based businesses; increased risks for women in domestic violence shelters or otherwise homeless; and neglect of women's long-term housing interests as communities rebuild. A better understanding of these complex and inter-related housing issues can guide community planning and may help untangle the causes of women's apparently higher levels of post-disaster stress (e.g., Ollenburger and Tobin 1998).

Finally, a number of action steps for planners and practitioners were suggested to help integrate gender-specific housing issues into community-based mitigation and response planning. Why should practitioners take this up? In the final analysis, focusing on women's housing needs is a needed tool, providing a framework for planners and residents to work together in practical ways to anticipate and plan for disasters. Disaster practice based on concrete knowledge of how and where women live and the housing issues they face in emergencies is an essential step toward building more disaster-resilient households and communities.

8

ELDERLY FEMALE-HEADED HOUSEHOLDS

IN THE DISASTER LOAN PROCESS

Cheryl D. Childers

INTRODUCTION

Age is a characteristic shown to influence ability to recover from disaster. In over 30 years of study on elderly in disaster, though, researchers have disagreed on the nature of that influence, or even its direction; either elderly persons are more affected or are less affected than younger people (Phillips 1993: 3). The discussion of gender and disaster, on the other hand, has been largely ignored by disaster researchers until the last decade or so (Fothergill 1996). Since the mid-1990s, however, researchers are beginning to understand the specific problems that women face during disasters (see Enarson and Morrow 1998; Morrow and Enarson 1996; Phillips 1996a). This paper fills a critical void, in that it provides the results of a multivariate analysis examining the intersection of age and gender. I focus on a category of disaster-victim households about which very little is known: elderly women living alone. Do these households differ from other types of households in terms of their vulnerability to recover from disaster and/or how the federal relief organization responds to them?

LITERATURE REVIEW

Friedsam (1961, 1962) and Hutton (1976) suggested that elderly people were more vulnerable than others to disaster because they may be less able to evacuate due to poor health, lack of transportation, or isolation from family or relatives. In retesting Friedsam's hypothesis of relative deprivation, however, Hutton (1976) found elderly people to be as likely as others to evacuate if they received warning. If not warned, though, elderly persons die at a disproportionate rate because of physical limitations.

Bell (1978) has insisted that elderly people are not affected any more than other disaster victims. Bolin (1982) found, however, that elderly individuals tend to have less insurance coverage. Because of fixed incomes, they may also live in poorly constructed housing, which is more likely to be heavily damaged in a disaster. Elderly victims are also less likely than younger victims to use formal aid (Bolin 1982). Older people might reject aid because they perceive it as a blow to their independence or as a form of charity (Bell 1978; Huerta and Horton 1978). Another explanation might be that they may become weary of dealing with formal agencies, in part because of complicated claim forms or feeling lost in the bureaucracy (Huerta and Horton 1978). They may also lack information or understanding on how to access the system. Consequently, elderly victims are more likely than younger victims to use kin networks rather than formal aid agencies (Bell 1978; Bolin and Klenow 1982; Huerta and Horton 1978). When elderly do apply for formal aid, though, their fixed incomes make it less likely that they will qualify for low-interest loans or be able to find permanent housing quickly (Bolin 1982; Phillips 1995).

Gender differentiation and stratification disadvantage women in a variety of ways, which ultimately affects their ability to recover from disaster (Fothergill 1996). In the United States, women tend to be concentrated in low-wage positions; their annual earnings are on average about 72% of males (U.S. Dept. of Labor 2000). According to the U.S. Census Bureau (2001), women are disproportionately poor. More specifically, female-headed households are four times as likely as male-headed households to be in poverty. The relationship between poverty and disaster vulnerability has been well established (Bolin and Bolton 1986; Bolin and Stanford 1991; Morrow-Jones and Morrow-Jones 1991; Phillips 1996b; Tierney 1989). Female-headed households, therefore, are likely to be much slower to recover from disaster than other households.

Females are also more vulnerable to disaster impact and recovery because of socially-defined gender roles. Women in lower-income countries are more likely to die in disasters, for example, because of caregiving responsibilities, whether to children or to the elderly (Chowdhury et al. 1993; Miyano et al. 1991; Parasurtaman 1995); because they do not have decision-making power over whether to leave for safety (Haider et al. 1991); and/or because they are physically isolated and do not get word of the danger (Ikeda 1995). In addition, Morrow and Enarson (1996) suggested that aid programs which are geared toward a nuclear-family model do not work well for some women. When males, designated as "head-of-household," receive the family's aid money and sometimes use it for other purposes, the family can be left without means to recover.

While we are beginning to understand the elderly in disaster and are developing a base of knowledge on women in disaster, very little is known about elderly women in disaster. This study is among the first of its kind in examining elderly women, specifically women living alone, who applied for federal aid after a disaster. How do they compare with younger people and also with elderly single male-headed households? Which characteristics emerge as most important in their experiences with the federal disaster relief organization? The findings should have implications for trying to expand theories connecting gender, age, and socioeconomic status to explain elderly women's disaster experiences

METHODS

Context

During the evenings of May 8 and 9, 1995, a series of severe storms rolled through the New Orleans, Louisiana area. In just over 12 hours, approximately 20 inches of rain fell on the south bank of Lake

Pontchartrain, killing six people and leaving thousands homeless. The amount of water overwhelmed the drainage system of the city and its closest suburbs, resulting in a circular area of flooding about 45 miles around New Orleans. That same storm dumped seven inches of rain on the northern shore of Lake Pontchartrain, flooding the southern portion of the bordering parishes. The next evening, another storm dumped an additional 17 inches of rain on the northern shores of the lake. The flooding qualified as a 100-year flood. On May 10, President Clinton declared the area a major disaster, setting in motion the release of resources coordinated through FEMA to aid flood victims.

This project used data gathered by FEMA's National Teleregistration Center (NTC), the nationwide telephone registering system that disaster victims call when applying for federal assistance. When victims call the NTC, interviewers ask a scripted list of questions concerning demographic information, the damage they sustained, and their needs. Inspectors later verify the damage, along with the victims' eligibility. All contact with the victim is recorded in the database, up to and including the final resolution of the claim.

All 3,037 disaster-victim households applying for federal assistance from two of the more devastated parishes became the target population for this study.

Research hypotheses

Several hypotheses about elderly single-female households generated from the literature review were tested:

1. they are more likely than other types of households to be under-represented in the population of victim households applying for federal aid;

2. they are more likely than other types of households to be low income;

3. they are less likely than other types of households to have insurance; and

4. they are less likely than other types of households to receive low-interest loans.

Variables and measurement

Victim type. Three categories of victim household types were identified: (1) "Elderly Single-Female Households," where the registrant was female, aged 65 or older, and had no financial dependents living in the same household; (2) "Elderly Households—Other," registrants over the age of 65 who had financial dependents living in their household; and (3) "Non-Elderly Households." One other category was identified for in-depth analysis of elderly households: "Elderly Single-Male Household," where the registrant was male, aged 65 or older, and had no financial dependents living in the same household.

Income. The gross yearly household income reported to FEMA was recoded into the following categories: (1) "< ½ Median," containing those households which reported earning lass than half of the median income for the state of approximately $22,000; (2) "½ Median to Median," containing those households which reported earning between half the state median and the median income; and (3) "> Median," containing those households which reported earning above the state median income.

Source of income. FEMA collects employer name or source of income for each household applying for assistance. The answers were recoded into the following categories: (1) "Public/Private Assistance," containing households who reported Social Security, disability, supplemental income (SSI), and/or savings/family/friends; (2) "Pension," containing households who reported just Social Security, pension, and/or retirement plan; and (3) "Wage/Salary," containing households who reported an employer or were self-employed.

Type of insurance. Two types of insurance were identified: (1) "Basic," which included Homeowner/Condo/Renters insurance; and (2) "Extended," which included Homeowner/Condo/Renter insurance with sewer backup and/or flood insurance.

Type of aid. FEMA coordinates a variety of types of disaster assistance: (1) housing assistance, which can be either (a) emergency minimal repairs or (b) emergency rent assistance for victims whose homes are severely damaged or destroyed or who are waiting for insurance payments to begin repairs or rebuilding efforts; (2) low-interest household loans from the Small Business Administration (SBA); and (3) Individual and Family Grant (IFG) program, which offered at that time grants up to $12,600 for uninsured expenses, if all other sources of assistance have been exhausted. For the purposes of this paper, analysis was confined to low-interest loans because this is the type of assistance which comprises the majority of aid distributed by the government.

Race. No comparison of various racial/ethnic groups could be made. FEMA does not collect racial/ethnic information on disaster victims. In addition, efforts to circumvent the problem by matching households with census block groups failed because FEMA did not include specific street addresses in the data available for analysis.

RESULTS

My first hypothesis, that elderly single-female households would be under-represented in the target population, was rejected. In fact, they were over-represented. While accounting for approximately 5% of the total households in the census profile of the two parishes, elderly single-female households represented over 12% of the total households applying for federal aid (see Table 5).

Table 5.
Distribution of Applicant Households

	Frequency	Percent
Elderly Single-Female	369	12.2%
Elderly Households—Other	283	9.3%
Non-Elderly—All	2385	78.5%
Total	3037	100.0%

A couple of explanations might account for the differences. Elderly women living alone may have had fewer internal resources with which to recover and thus turned to the governmental organization for help. The findings might also be somewhat reflective of the scope of the flooding, which was in large part a result of the topographical arrangement of the affected area. New Orleans and its surrounding suburbs are at or below sea-level. Consequently, the disaster affected a broad range of the population. Informal support networks that ordinarily might have been used by households may have also been affected by the disaster (Neal, Perry, and Hawkins 1982; Neal et al. 1988; Phillips 1993).

Huerta and Horton (1978) surmised that elderly people might tire of the bureaucratic process. Older persons may also require support service, such as transportation, when leaving their homes (Poulshock and Cohen 1975). Since 1995, FEMA has simplified its application process. Victims no longer have to travel to an application center and wait in line to fill out myriad forms. Disaster victims can apply for all relevant assistance programs through one phone call. This simplification might make a difference for elderly victims, who may have limited mobility or need transportation.

The lower incomes of elderly single-female households was strongly supported by the data. As Table 6 shows, just over 70% of the elderly single-female households reported earnings below $11,000. The median income for elderly single-female households was about 50% of other elderly households and only 44% of non-elderly households. Thus, elderly women living alone were about 2.5 times as likely as other elderly households to have yearly incomes below $11,000.

Table 6.
Income Category by Type of Victim Household

Relationship to State Median (S.M.)	Elderly Single-Female (n=369)	Elderly— Others (n=280)	Non-Elderly (n=2377)
< ½ S.M. (<$11,000)	70.5%	29.3%	31.6%½
S.M. to S.M. ($11,000-$21,999)	25.5%	42.1%	25.2%
> S.M.	4.0%	28.6%	43.3%
λ = .15	Mdn=$8,000	Mdn=$16,000	Mdn=$18,000

To examine the connection between gender and socioeconomic status, a more in-depth comparison between households headed by elderly women and men was made. Elderly single-victim households applying for federal aid (N=466) were overwhelmingly female (79%). Elderly single-male households reported higher incomes. In fact, they were over four times as likely (18.6%) than elderly single-female households (4.0%) to report earnings above the state median income. In addition, while over 90% of all households with elderly registrants reported fixed incomes, incomes were much lower for the women-alone households.

Part of the explanation may be that of those elderly households reporting no pension or retirement income, single-female households were twice as likely (16.8%) as single-male households (8.2%) to be on public/private assistance. Single-male households, on the other hand, were about 1.5 times as likely (7.2%) as single-female households (4.6%) to have a job. The $8,000 median income of elderly single-female households was approximately 73% that of single-male household incomes.

This gender gap in the income of elderly households is strikingly similar to the gender wage gap in the United States. As we know, most fixed incomes earned by the elderly, whether through retirement plans or social security, are based on level of income while in the labor force, number of years in the labor force, or on a percentage of their spouse's income. These findings suggest that economic disadvantages faced by women during their younger years affect their ability later in life to access resources with which to recover from disaster.

The third hypothesis, that elderly single-female households would have less insurance than other types of households, was rejected. There is no appreciable relationship between type of household and level of insurance. Between one-third and almost one-half of all victim households applying for federal aid reported having no insurance. For those with insurance, however, elderly single-female households (13.9%) were slightly less likely to have extended insurance that covered flooding than other elderly households (20.1%) or non-elderly households (24.3%).

Insurance status was somewhat reflective of family size and income. Households with younger registrants tended to have larger families, as well as higher incomes. They may, therefore, be able to afford the higher costs of extended coverage. These findings concur with Bolin (1982), Morrow-Jones and Morrow-Jones (1991), and others regarding inadequate insurance among lower-income households.

The last hypothesis leads to the most important findings. Elderly single-female households were, in fact, least likely to receive low-interest loans. Of the 1,772 low-interest loan applications processed, SBA approved only 243 (13.0%) of them. As Table 7 shows, the approval rate for all types of households was small. Elderly single-female households, however, were much less likely to be approved for a loan. In fact, they were five times less likely than other elderly households to be approved. Income appears to be a deciding factor. Elderly women living alone were over twice as likely (66.4%) than other elderly households (31.8%) or non-elderly households (33.0%) to be denied because of failing the income test.

Table 7.
SBA Application Resolution
by Type of Victim Household

	Elderly Single-Female (n=289)	Elderly— Others (n=140)	Non-Elderly (n=1343)
Approved	2.8%	14.3%	16.0%
Denied	97.2%	85.7%	84.0%

A re-examination also showed that elderly single-female households (2.8%) were still about 2.5 times less likely than elderly single-male households (7.2%) to be approved for a low-interest loan. They were 1.5 times as likely as elderly single-male households to be denied the loan because of failing the income test. For elderly households that passed the income test, single-male and single-female households were equally likely (4.1%) to be denied a low-interest loan because of perceived inability to repay the loan.

The findings agree with Bolin (1982, 1986) and Phillips (1995), who suggest that the elderly are not as likely as younger people to qualify for low-interest loans. In this study, elderly single-female households were five times less likely than other elderly households, and almost six times less likely than younger people, to be approved for a loan. At the same time, elderly single-male households were only slightly less likely than households with younger registrants to qualify for a low-interest loan. Because qualification for the loans is in large part based on level of income, these findings should not be surprising.

Households which are denied a low-interest loan are referred to the IFG program, which provides the least amount of assistance of all the programs because of its capped dollar amount of aid. In this study, over 90% of elderly single-female households ultimately were referred to the IFG program. Elderly women living alone were over 1.5 times as likely (50.1%) as all other types of households to use the program. The data clearly indicate the extent to which elderly women living alone are disadvantaged in times of disaster. These findings are consistent with much previous research, which has found that low-income households have the least amount of choice in the type of disaster assistance they receive and have the greatest difficulty recovering (Bolin and Bolton 1986; Bolin and Stanford 1991; Clark and Short 1993; Kreps 1984; Morrow-Jones and Morrow-Jones 1991; Peacock, Morrow, and Gladwin 1997; Phillips 1996b).

DISCUSSION AND CONCLUSION

This study has been a preliminary attempt to understand how gender, age, and income interact to affect elderly women's experiences with federal disaster aid. Not surprisingly, the findings suggest that income is a major contributing factor. In other words, gender effects are largely a reflection of lifetime differences in work careers and income. Once again, gender inequality plays itself out in the social and economic structures of our society.

Overall, the results show that elderly single-female households were disproportionately low income, particularly in comparison to elderly single-male households. Researchers have agreed that low-income households have a much harder time recovering after disaster. As the United States becomes an increasingly aged population, it becomes an increasingly female population. Elderly single-female households in 2001 outnumbered elderly single-male households more than 3:1, and the gap is projected to widen (U.S. Census Bureau 2001). Consequently, low-income elderly single-female households will become increasingly vulnerable to the effects of disasters. If for no other reason than their sheer numbers, this sector of the population must be dealt with if we are to have disaster-resistant communities.

Because income is so often a function of gender, the findings concur with Fothergill (1996), who suggested that theories of gender stratification need to be incorporated into disaster research. As she stated: "It is necessary to move beyond the descriptive, to ask why, and to begin placing the disaster findings within larger, structural contexts" (Fothergill 1996: 49). From a sociological perspective, income acts as an aid or barrier to accumulation of resources needed to gain political and economic power, which are necessary for individuals or households to make decisions and control their lives (Weber 1921/1968). Theories of gender stratification would ultimately help disaster researchers understand the social arrangements—such as the gendered division of labor—within society and the economic, political, and social consequences to women. Only by understanding the cultural and/or sociopolitical contexts within which the interactions take place can we begin to address the root causes of female poverty among the elderly.

In the meantime, special initiatives and programs which target elderly women living alone should be incorporated into every disaster mitigation program. With FEMA's commitment to providing grants for mitigation, communities should be able to better protect a most vulnerable population. Possibilities are including elderly women in the decision-making process; using American Association of Retired Persons (AARP), along with other organizations which cater to the elderly, to create a network of citizens on which elderly women living alone can rely; flexible qualifications in the loan application process for low-income households; community grants which would enable low-income elderly women to purchase insurance for the hazard most likely to affect them; community grants to retrofit homes of elderly women to better withstand disaster and/or ensure that they find permanent housing quickly after the disaster. Using Bolin's (1982) suggestion of "recovery capacity profiles," decision makers can identify particular concerns of elderly women living alone and develop specific resources within the community to address these needs.

9

PROFESSIONALIZATION AND GENDER IN LOCAL EMERGENCY MANAGEMENT

Jennifer Wilson and Arthur Oyola-Yemaiel

INTRODUCTION

There is no doubt that women are in short supply as emergency managers at the local level. In many parts in our society women still do not hold positions of leadership, authority or management. Emergency response agencies are no exception. Indeed, contemporary county offices of emergency management evolved from the traditional local offices of civil defense which were predominately occupied and operated by men. Thus, there is a long history of emergency management being considered a male domain. Although the number of women involved in the process of local emergency management is increasing, there has been little research on women's and men's different experiences in this environment. This exploratory study examines women in local emergency management by looking at how gendered expectations, roles, and relationships might affect local offices of emergency management.

A number of U.S. disaster researchers have conducted important studies of the field of emergency management focusing on such issues as legitimacy of local Offices of Emergency Management (OEMs) and models of directors' management styles (Dynes and Quarantelli 1975); a comparative study over a ten year period of changes in local emergency management agency operations (Quarantelli 1985); varying types of local emergency management agencies (Wenger et al. 1987); and a comparison of strategies and structures of successful and less-successful local emergency managers (Drabek 1987). Each of these studies makes a significant contribution to the social science investigation of emergency management by characterizing the field's structure and function, shedding light on the evolution of the field and its consequent effect on disaster mitigation and recovery.

None of these studies address the issue of gender difference among emergency managers probably because so few females held such positions at the time of these studies. In Drabek's (1987) study only one OEM director was female leading him to conclude,

> ... there were no gender differences among the comparison groups. While the number of females holding emergency management positions has increased greatly during the past decade, the total number selected for this study was too small to analyze separately .... As the proportion of local emergency management agency directors who are female increases over the next decade, it will be important to assess potential variations in the types of managerial strategies that are used.

However, there has been a recent increase of interest in gendered social science analysis of disasters. Disaster researchers have begun to pay more attention to the heretofore absent perspective of women in the social experience of disaster. Neal and Phillips (1990) examined female-dominated local citizen groups which emerged in response to a disaster threat. Phillips (1990) explored the effect of gender differences in emergency response. Lastly, Enarson and Morrow (1998a) compiled a comprehensive volume of gender in disasters which incorporates the missing element of gender into the disaster research discourse. Chapters discuss women's specific vulnerabilities to disasters as well as women's experiences in disaster planning and as disaster survivors, responders, volunteers and emergency managers. These significant works have increased the base of knowledge of the relationship between gender and disaster.

This paper uses examples from several open-ended interviews with women emergency managers to illustrate how little is known about the relevance of gender in local emergency management and to ascertain some of the significant issues facing women in this field. All informants are current or former emergency managers in Florida (U.S.) county offices of emergency management. The majority of our respondents are rather young (mid-20s to mid-30s) and have been in the field from one to five years. Although race and class differences can be as important as gender differences in forming our "social locations" (Lorber 1998), none of our respondents are women of color. Therefore, we are only able to address the circumstances of white women emergency managers here.

WOMEN IN GENDERED ORGANIZATIONS

As a preface to examining the specific case of women in emergency management, it is useful to review the organizational "gendering" process in general. "Gendered" organizational structures and practices have been well described in social science research (e.g. Acker 1991; Ferree and Martin 1995; Rantalaiho and Heiskanen 1997; Witz and Savage 1992). According to Rantalaiho and Heiskanen (1997), gender is organized simultaneously in social structures, cultural meanings and personal identities. The basic rules of the present male-dominated "gender system" are based on "difference" and "hierarchy" where women should be clearly distinct from men in both ideas and practices. One way to achieve this is structural by creating a public sphere for men and a private sphere for women, or segregating women and men to each their "own" jobs and tasks in working life (Lorber 1994). In this process both genders develop their own special skills which then seem to be part of their "nature." Furthermore, men take precedence or rate higher than women especially with reference to power and prestige (Rantalaiho and Heiskanen 1997).

Acker (1991) studied the "gendering processes" that reproduce gendered social structures in both public and private organizations. These processes include the creation of symbols and forms of consciousness, social interactions enacting gendered relations, and the internal mental work of individuals in their construction of gendered understandings. Building on Acker's work, Reskin and Padavic (1994) list three gendering processes in working life: the sexual division of labor, the devaluation of women's work and the construction of gender on the job. They are able to show how these processes mold women's position relative to men. Thus, gender relations are not just one thing or one process, but many simultaneous processes.

The common hierarchical difference between men and women—with men in the dominant position—is quite strong in working life. Gendered hierarchies are not always explicit at the workplace level but are more often tacit (Rantalaiho and Heiskanen 1997). Open and conscious discrimination of women is becoming more rare in the West. In fact, people in organizations quite often are not conscious that their practices are gendered because they take them for granted (Goffman 1967). Gender is constructed at the workplace in the daily work process and it is involved in solutions about how to organize the work. Some jobs and tasks almost unnoticeably become defined as feminine and others as masculine (Lorber 1994).

TRADITIONAL BARRIERS TO WOMEN'S PARTICIPATION IN EMERGENCY MANAGEMENT

Emergency management agencies have been traditionally formed by male-oriented occupations of the military and civil defense resulting in a male workforce and work culture (Barnecut 1998; Gibbs 1990;, Phillips 1990; Robertson 1998; Wraith 1997). These were men's jobs in a man's world. Robertson (1998) claims that women are so underrepresented in Australian emergency management because they find the male-oriented culture of such organizations in which women are not readily accepted or respected as equal partners unappealing. Thus, for a long time women have been virtually non-existent in structurally significant emergency management roles. Formal training for emergency management was previously only available through the military. As long as the military was gender segregated, women were denied access to participation and, thus, access to prerequisite training. In this case, women were doubly segregated—directly by gender discrimination itself, and indirectly by the lack of formal training and experience. Women who do choose to join and remain in emergency management need training courses as a means through which they can be included in the networking and information exchange of the emergency management community (Robertson 1998).

Local emergency management offices often reflect a paramilitary, controlled management approach (Dynes 1983). Thus, the work culture may assume "command and control" authority relations that promote a strict or rigid approach to disaster management (Neal and Phillips 1995). This type of working environment may be a deterrent to many women who do not come from a military background and/or who do not feel comfortable with this style of decision-making and communication.

When women have participated in emergency management organizations, the work culture has reflected an implicit gender division of labor (Barnecut 1998; Enarson 1997; Robertson 1998). Women may be deterred from moving into positions and developing their careers in the high priority areas that are considered "more masculine" such as radiological or other hazardous materials, terrorism, communication, transportation and mass evacuation.

This pattern of underutilizing women's capacities in emergency management is not limited to the U.S. Noels' (1998) study of the Caribbean Region disaster management networks revealed that women are represented sparsely on national and local emergency committees and their "potential as a resource for organized action at all levels of the managerial process" has been ignored. This is also illustrated through the participation of women in the first "Hemispheric Congress on Disaster Reduction and Sustainable Development" held in Miami, Florida in the fall of 1996. The Congress brought together 215 key stakeholders from public, private and international organizations from North, South and Central America, Europe and the Caribbean, to discuss and formulate a series of policy initiatives supporting disaster reduction and sustainable development as part of the UN Decade for Disaster Reduction. Only fifty-eight participants (27%) were women, twenty-four (11%) were North American or European, and thirty-four (16%) were women representing government and private emergency management agencies from the rest of the hemisphere.

PROFESSIONALIZATION OF EMERGENCY MANAGEMENT

New opportunities for women?

Drabek (1994) claims that the field of emergency management is "professionalizing." The entire nation has experienced a major redirection in disaster preparedness since the 1960s that reflects the rapid emergence of a new professional. Indeed, the decade of the 1980s saw a surge of interest among both academics and practitioners in formalizing emergency management as a profession to cope with the increasing demand in technological advances needed to mitigate and respond to disasters (Wilson 2001).

In the past, emergency managers have had little formal emergency management training. The new era of professionalism is indicated in part by new educational and training opportunities such as intensive courses at the Federal Emergency Management Agency's Emergency Management Institute. In addition, emergency management certification is now available and a growing number of degree-based university programs such as the Institute of Emergency Administration and Planning at the University of North Texas have been developed. Former director, David Neal (1998), stated that during the first few years of the program (1985-1989) women made up about 20 percent of enrolled students with the number rising close to 40 percent by winter 1998. In contrast, according to Wraith (1997), only about 5% of participants in Australia's Emergency Management Institute courses are women. Although the situation at the University of North Texas is encouraging, it is too early to tell to what extent these training and educational programs will draw more women into the field.

In this era of increasing professionalization, it is important to understand women's primary paths of entry into emergency management and how these are likely to change (Enarson 1997). The evaluation of women's career paths in emergency management and their performance in actual disaster-related activities, whether technological, educational, managerial or otherwise, will contribute not only to equalize gender differences but will improve social resilience to technological and natural disasters.

More and more our society is affected by unforeseen events and more people are affected every year. There is concern among the public and the government that structural mechanisms to cope with such events need to be developed. According to one informant,

> . . . only recently has emergency management become an important entity. For a long time the OEM was considered a small off-shoot . . . of the fire department. But, as disasters increase in size, more people realize the importance of the office and a lot more positions are being created and a lot more opportunities are available now. In general, I think that the whole field of emergency management is opening up which creates opportunities for anybody.

However, there is no doubt that women remain in short supply within emergency management organizations at the local level. Although there is little research concerning the utilization of available individuals in a disaster situation, it is evident that status ascription such as age, sex, race, and/or ethnicity affects disaster planning and emergency response through discrimination/power barriers (Phillips 1990). My respondents recalled specific instances of difficulty working with male organizational representatives in the community, some subtle, some very direct. One respondent described a man who was reluctant to cooperate with her and would often say that he wished they could go back to the "old days"—when her job was done by a man.

Women's qualifications for emergency management participation

Women's traditional roles often prepare them to be primary contributors to disaster management. In this day and age, women continue to do most of the household and family caregiving work so that an unequal division of domestic responsibility persists even when women participate in the formal labor force in post-industrial societies. The "second shift" occurs when working women return home after a full day in the paid labor force to begin their "second" full day of cleaning house, cooking meals, and caring for children (Hochschild 1983). Running a household with children in today's fast paced world has become a challenging activity. Motherhood is as an excellent school for management, demanding many of the same skills: organization, pacing, teaching, guiding, leading, monitoring, handling disturbances, and imparting information (Helgesen 1990). Experience in balancing work and family develops skills to deal with conflicting demands.

Similarly, women's experiences as community workers, informal neighborhood leaders, and social activists equip them to respond to community crisis. Enarson and Morrow (1998b) found that women's formal and informal networks were central to both household and community recovery after Hurricane Andrew in 1992.

In addition, women have been part of the paid labor force for a long time especially when their family's economic need makes it necessary for women to seek outside income (Dunn 1997). Now, women not only work in traditionally held positions such as nursing and teaching, but are increasingly gaining entry into higher paid, more prestigious public and private occupations and professions including management level positions. According to Colwil (1997), women form one third of the management work force in the United States. However, such progress does not seem to have filtered into local emergency management in which we find a much lower percentage of women in high-ranking positions.

Thus, although women play crucial private and public roles managing households and caregiving and as part of the paid labor force, their voices have been largely absent in organizational and community policy-making, including decisions about disaster response and recovery (Enarson and Morrow 1998a). This, is in spite of the fact that the technological and managerial skills women use in their daily lives can be used in disaster management and their contribution can greatly help a community's response effort. And, as Robertson (1998) says, efficient and effective disaster management systems depend on the knowledge and skills of all those who can make a positive contribution.

Women in local emergency management

Today, barriers to women's participation in emergency management are changing, at least partially explained by equal opportunity laws which make it illegal to discriminate against women either in educational opportunities or hiring practices. Although women are now more able to enter the field, the process of full integration appears to be slow and uneven. Even as women play increasingly important roles in emergency management organizations they are still minimally represented in high-ranking positions. Attitudes may be changing even more slowly. One respondent said,

> . . . a lot of younger people have been coming into the field of emergency management although traditionally this office has been primarily made up of retired military personnel especially under the realm of the fire department which has been traditionally male-dominated. It is obvious that there is still some leftovers of this heritage at state, regional, etc. conferences and meetings because I am either the only woman or one of two or three women in attendance at these functions with 50 or so men . . . .
> I don't think there are actually many female directors. Probably some of the other women in emergency management come from a fire department background.

Our informants believe that a division of labor exists within the field where "most . . . women . . . are in special needs and mass care or human services" coordinating positions rather than being represented throughout the entire spectrum of emergency management functions. Indeed, the state of Florida is comprised of 67 counties that maintain an office of emergency management, but as of June, 1998, only ten county OEM directors were female (15%) and nine assistant directors were female (13.5%).

A study by Phillips (1990) identified the characteristics that both men and women deem necessary for women to possess when they participate in leadership roles in emergency response organizations. Respondents indicate that female emergency managers should "be aggressive" which social scientists have shown to be more frequently a product of male socialization. A female emergency manager illustrates the complexity of this issue in this statement:

> It is hard especially for women and assertiveness because women have been told that in order for them to be more accepted in a man's world they have to be more assertive but not aggressive because if you are aggressive then you are seen as pushy. But for women even if a person is assertive they are viewed as aggressive. If I or other women are in a room full of men who are talking and talking and making decisions but I have some important things to say also then it is sometimes very intimidating to say, "Whoa, wait, what about this . . .' I think it takes a person who has trained herself to be assertive and be able to interrupt other people and speak out rather than not say anything—in this field if you are not like that then you might as well not have been in the meeting because they don't let you talk.

Phillips (1990) advises that in order to challenge negative stereotypes women need to be assertive, obtain female mentors, use networking skills, and be careful of gendered speech patterns. However, the above respondent's quote implies that not only do women have to modify their social behavior but also they must first internalize new ideas of appropriate behavior in order to operate effectively within the emergency management structure. In other words, women must modify their learned female characteristics considerably to match men's work role characteristics. This illustrates Goffman's (1959) thesis that individuals (in this case, women) need to construct a particular image or persona that matches the expectations of the group in order to be accepted and to acquire social mobility.

This in turn places women who aspire to achieve managerial positions or other "men's jobs" in a critical spot. On one hand, women must behave, look and think like men effectively becoming "masculinized." On the other hand, women must create a paradigmatic shift that changes the social structure to allow them to remain the way they are—as women—and still be an integral part of the labor force. It will be a challenge for local emergency management organizations and the field at large to preclude women from having to recreate themselves as men, but accept women for who they are with the skills they possess and integrate them into the structure as vital parts of emergency management.

Possible constraints for women in emergency management

Other issues arise that particularly affect women as they enter the field of emergency management. For example, how are emergency management organizations impacted by work and family conflicts as increasing numbers of women come on board (Enarson 1997)? For instance, each staff member at local OEMs are required to be "on call" 24 hours a day, one week per month. All of my female informants are single with no children. But, how might this job requirement affect the chances that a married woman with young children is able to do the job? Male responders have traditionally relied on the taken-for-granted presence of women at home to resolve conflicting demands on their time and energy while they are at work (Scanlon 1996).

Furthermore, we should study the effect of the complex intersection of gender and age on female emergency managers. One informant said that she believed some difficulties/barriers that women face in this field have to do with ageism: " . . . if you are young . . . then this is paired up with the gender thing . . . then it is a double whammy." Another informant mentioned the high level of stress of the job "especially being a woman and being young." Although these women feel discrimination now while they are young, will this change as they get older? It may be that as they get older, gain expertise and prove themselves worthy, they will receive more respect. On the other hand, discrimination may continue or increase as they age, similar to other careers like television broadcasting. In short, we do not know how the aging process will affect the careers of women emergency managers.

We have not had much opportunity to discover how women progress, or not, in their local emergency management careers. Few women currently in the field have been there long. Only time and longitudinal research will reveal the career paths and successes of women emergency managers.

CONCLUSION

It is evident that women have contributed in unprecedented ways in times of disaster. They are leaders in emergent organizations during and after disaster, especially those responding to structural response deficiencies resulting from restricted visions of response and recovery needs (Neal and Phillips 1990; Wilson and Oyola-Yemaiel 1998). Yet, women's activities in disaster contexts including their roles and experiences in emergency management are still largely understudied. Specifically, Enarson (1997) claims that very few researchers or emergency managers have examined the conditions under which gender makes a difference in emergency management practice or policy. Women have been incorporated into the field, bypassing the military route through formal education and professionalization. But still we do not know whether women operate the OEM differently than men. Are there structural and cultural differences in the organization? How do gender differences effect interagency coordination? How do these differences influence disaster mitigation, preparedness, response, and recovery activities? There is reason to expect that better understanding of the impacts of gender differences among emergency managers, as well as women's ways of exercising leadership, is likely to increase the effectiveness of emergency management (Enarson 1997).

The number of women involved in the formal structure of emergency management is increasing. Therefore, it is pertinent to examine issues such as: women's experiences in emergency management agencies; women's contributions to the emergency management process; the barriers that women face in performing their jobs and in building their careers; and, the effects that changes in the field are having on women's place within it. At the moment we have many questions with too few answers. Future research should explore the intersection of race/ethnicity and class among professional women emergency managers. In sum, further analysis of gendered expectations, roles, and interactions within agency dynamics has the potential to significantly increase the effectiveness of disaster preparedness, mitigation, response and recovery at the local level.

10

BUT SHE IS A WOMAN AND
THIS IS A MAN'S JOB

Lessons for participatory research and participatory recovery

Richard L. Krajeski and Kristina J. Peterson

INTRODUCTION

"If 'Anne' thinks she is going to get the position of director of the Interfaith Recovery just because she has been doing it for the last six weeks, she is mistaken. She is not a professional and she does not have the education. As a board member I can't support her." This was spoken not at a board meeting but along the banks of a river. Dick was fishing for salmon (and having no luck). Kris was doing a different kind of fishing—and they were biting. The 'bait' had been taken and the fight was to begin . . . . "They have just left us black folks out," said 'Beatrice' about the white interfaith recovery organization. 'Beatrice' and women from the black community told Kris, "Can you help us?" Kris who carries a community organizing tackle box with everything in it, said . . .

The leadership roles of women in formal disaster response organizations like the Federal Emergency Management Agency (FEMA), American Red Cross (ARC), United Way, and the religious community are not well documented or understood. Even less is known or appreciated about the leadership of local, non-professional, and historically-vulnerable women in disasters. How do recovery efforts enable or disable these grass-roots women as they seek to serve their communities? What are the implications for the overall recovery when recovery organizations remove local residents from rebuilding communities?

Disasters provide a unique opportunity for understanding and promoting local capacity-building. Some disaster response agencies are beginning to understand that "there are women out there" who bring valuable resources, skills, insights, and knowledge to the recovery process. Our experience compels us to agree that women are ideal for the demanding and complex tasks of recovery. In this paper, we explore the assets local women bring to disaster recovery and the ways in which they can be further enabled despite norms that marginalize women, particularly women of color.

'Anne' did not have the education the board member was looking for. There were some other contenders with Master's degrees. But in our professional opinion, 'Anne' was the woman for the job; in our minds she did have the 'education' and skills necessary to direct a complex long-term disaster recovery:

> Well, I have teenagers. I worked in a doctor's office—I set up meetings and conferences for him. I am very active in my church. I know these people, they are my neighbors and friends. I almost lost my home, too.

She brought to the recovery what we believe are the necessary ingredients for doing the job well: deep caring for the people; the trust of a community that did not take well to strangers or "officials;" the street (in this case dirt road) smarts to run the system; and, finally, incredible intuition. She knew how to learn and that she needed to learn. She had two advocates. All that was left to do was to "land the board."

'Beatrice' had little or no "education," but she could run the system, knew the "art of the possible" and no one was going to stop her. These were her people! 'Beatrice' had the organization (but you could not find it on paper), a little money, the trust of the community, and an advocate with a lot of knowledge.

THE SOURCES OF OUR PERSPECTIVES AND INSIGHTS

While women lead more formal organizations and agencies like the American Red Cross and the United Way, much remains to be learned about the local level. At present, we see little evidence that national disaster response organizations are doing little more than paying lip service to women's needs and abilities in disaster recovery, preparedness and mitigation. Our disaster advocacy recovery work spans 29 years (Kris) and 19 years (Dick) across many different regions and hazards. We see some common denominators in the contributions of women, obstacles to their participation, and interventions needed that enable local women to exercise leadership. We focus on the grass-roots level, the source of our forty-years of combined experientially-based remarks which arise from interactions with community based organizations (CBOs) like the Big Lake Recovery Center, Alaska; the Cape Mendencino Earthquake Recovery Group, California; and TRAC (Terrebone Readiness Action Committee) in Louisiana.

In our experience, we would estimate that women comprise about half of the directors of local community-based recovery groups and that the vast majority of the care managers and outreach workers are women. The larger and more formal the recovery organization is in terms of funding, geographic area, and scope, the less likely it is to have a woman as the director. Only a small percentage of the women who lead these CBOs have college degrees: the majority hold a high school diploma or less. Few in our experience are trained in the social sciences, psychology, or business. However, our experience leads us to believe that "formal knowledge"—at the expense of other skills and attitudes—can be detrimental to local disaster recovery organizations.

Indeed, we have seen women lead some of the nation's most effective recovery organizations, but have even more frequently seen their contributions thwarted.

SKILLS AND INSIGHTS WOMEN BRING TO DISASTER RECOVERY

To a significant degree, "natural" or human-caused disasters are, for vulnerable people, "everyday life writ large." Everyday life, for the most economically marginalized, represents a string of disasters that women prepare for, respond to, recover from, and mitigate against— including sexism, racism, ageism, ableism, economic deprivation, and health crises. Disaster response is their everyday vocational reality, and they respond creatively. Most importantly, they survive.

Most of the women we have worked with come from working-class backgrounds, and all have been homemakers. Not just working-class, they come from modest to poor circumstances. Their homemaking experience, often overlooked or trivialized by the larger society, give these women the skills, values, insights, and attributes necessary for long-term, community-based, and effective organizing.

> 'Carol' was a very shy housewife with almost no experience outside the home and school her children attended. Her pastor thought, "It might be good for her to get out a little and help with the recovery." Well, 'Carol' did, and she became one of the most effective mental health outreach workers of the recovery. She knew her people, and they knew her.

Household and family caregiving, often with limited resources and combined with employment, means that these women must be frugal and effective time-managers as well as creative and collaborative networkers. Experience within families enhances their sensitivity to human needs and feelings and also means that they must make difficult decisions, know how to say no, and do more with less. They seem to understand the holistic, systemic, and community-wide nature of disasters, sensing the root causes of vulnerability. They show a keen interest in local capacity-building, and often develop creative, ecologically-sound programs.

Women bring additional skills that enhance abilities to direct recovery efforts. The most basic and, we believe, the most important survival resource women (or men) bring to a recovery effort is local knowledge. Knowledge of the people, the issues, and the historical and political contexts gives these women advantages over even the best-trained, outside professional. Combined with local trust and respect, their knowledge outweighs all other resources. We have seen that women are usually the first to begin to offer aid to survivors and start the early organizing process. They usually simply DO IT, by collecting resources, starting informal recovery centers, and providing food, shelter, emotional support, and childcare. Their localized knowledge is key because they know where things are, whom to go to, and how to gauge the effectiveness of the effort. They know when someone is "burning out" and who can go the distance, as well as which agencies are most flexible in a chaotic environment and which politicians are most responsive to their needs.

However, they may not see themselves as a key recovery resource:

> "I've never done anything like this before. Where do I go for help?" 'Diane' asked Kris. "I can help you." "But you are leaving soon," said 'Diane'. "Well, there is the phone and fax and if necessary I can come back for a while."

'Diane' had a formal education, not in anything closely related to disaster recovery, but she knew people. Her training was in the creative arts. She was a single parent and looking for a job. She knew the media and the political system of her area, and, like 'Anne,' 'Beatrice,' and 'Carol,' she cared, knew how to learn, and enjoyed the trust of other locals. As a consequence, she has run what must be the longest (six years) and most successful community-based recovery we have seen. This organization has repaired and rebuilt homes and developed a strong preparedness program and a mitigation project. All from a woman who "did not know how to do this."

Women who rise to leadership offer creative rather than traditional solutions which established organizations may resist. Grass-roots women seem less confined to "we have always done it this way" and more willing to take risks, to innovate, and to share power. Based on our observations, these women are more cooperative and collaborative than men are in similar positions, but they are not pushovers. They tend to be client—and community-centered rather than agency-centered and thus may seem unwilling (to outsiders) to "play the bureaucratic game." Nonetheless, their knowledge, experience, and skills should not be overlooked.

Many women, in our experience, seem to have an intuitive knowledge of the chaotic nature of disasters and seem more comfortable with the ambiguities of recovery. They see possibilities whereas others may see problems or see problems where others may see nothing. They are more likely to see the needs of children and the elderly and appear to be more comfortable with feelings—their own and others. Women seem to understand the "symbolic" nature of recovery and the importance of community ritual and symbols. They are the keepers of traditions and celebrations, and thus the providers of meaning and hope. They not only survive, they sustain themselves, their families, and—given the opportunity—their communities.

OBSTACLES TO WOMEN'S LEADERSHIP

> "She can't do it." "She doesn't know how." "She is too
> busy." "They will eat her up!"
> "I can't do it." "I don't know how." "I am too busy."
> "They will eat me up!"

As things begin to "calm down" and get "more organized," and as agencies, organizations, and governments—local, regional, and/or national—enter the picture, the role of local women may diminish or even disappear. Some women may choose or need to go back to their regular caregiving. But in our experience they are often involuntarily replaced with men. Those who come together to organize the recovery—be they from the government, business, non-governmental organizations, or the religious community—are mostly men. Local women are usually not included in these meetings.

Local survivors and caregivers are generally not invited to these meetings. These meetings are, more and more, made up of combinations of local and national agency and organizations staff. Church World Service (CWS) is dedicated to enabling local survivors and caregivers the opportunities to control and direct their own recovery. CWS regularly advocates with and for women, minorities, and other marginalized people and seeks to help them organize effective, long-term recovery groups. The growth in the number of women clergy and women heads of community-based organizations (CBOs) is having some positive impact on the make-up of organizing groups and the boards of directors of local recovery groups. Women on a board of directors are no guarantee that there will be sensitivity to the abilities of local non-professional women.

Professional recovery experts may view the local women as the "victims" who need assistance. Such a belief sidelines the critical resources local women bring to the recovery process. Organizing groups tend to look for people with social service, business, or psychological degrees and experience. Outside organizations tend to prefer professionals or to not recognize the skills of non-professional women. Organizing groups generally do not value local knowledge, respect, and trust as resources; nor do they understand that "homemaking" skills and experience provide strong backgrounds for directing a community-based disaster recovery.

When local non-professional women do become the directors of the recovery group they are often "over-controlled" by their board, and they will often be patronized and even resented by other "professional" agency staff of both sexes. Yet, their voices need to be heard in order for the reasons we have outlined above. Next, we offer some ideas on how to make that happen.

ENABLING WOMEN'S LEADERSHIP IN DISASTER RECOVERY

"We really think 'Anne' is the right person for the job and here is why . . . ," we said to each board member we could meet with.

"I think, 'Beatrice', I can help you find some funding and I think we can get you a VISTA [Volunteers in Service To America] position so you will have at least some income as you work on the recovery for the next year or so.

"Well, 'Carol,' you should be able to get a JTPA [Jobs Training Partnership Act] job position under the interfaith recovery. Here is how you do it—first . . ."

Women who are involved in long-term disaster recovery need advocates. On several occasions we have forcefully advocated for women leaders when organizations formalized. Typically, a board of directors wants someone with academic degrees and experience who knows the system, sometimes meaning the formal and informal "good-old-boy" system and sometimes meaning the federal aid delivery system. It is not unusual that a board excludes persons from the impacted community. Sometimes, in our haste to put formally educated "movers and shakers" on boards, we overlook the reason why these boards exist—to aid local victims. Excluding those with localized expertise is patronizing at best and undoubtedly slows recovery, confuses victims about new procedures and personnel, and moves victims from active leadership to passive recipient status.

We need to remember that working-class families and homeowners intuitively understand their marginalized position. One consequence of being pushed repeatedly to the side is that a person doesn't feel confident or may need to be taught particular skills. Some women will benefit from some advice about how to be taken seriously in the formal agency and government world. Moving about in the formal work environment of bankers, politicians, and career recovery professionals can be intimidating. Usually, however, a little coaching about effective strategies to present issues, ideas, and concerns can go a long way. With a little success, confidence grows and a grass-roots leader can become a pivotal resource.

CONCLUSION

Our experience has taught us that women—professionals and non-professionals, formally and informally—play critically important roles in all aspects of disaster preparedness, response, and mitigation with all types of organizations and groups. We are particularly convinced that non-professional, historically vulnerable, and marginalized women play important informal and formal organizing and leadership roles. We believe we have identified some of the obstacles that get in the way of women and some ways to overcome these obstacles, but the women described here—as well as those of us who try to enable them—need more and better information. Taking a cue from our own experience, we encourage *participatory research* that will develop a better understanding of the roles, obstacles, and strategies for women in disaster recovery leadership. We offer our four decades of insights to encourage researchers to methodically and rigorously develop usable models for women's leadership at the grass-roots level in disaster situations.

'Anne,' 'Beatrice,' 'Carol,' and 'Diane' proved they had what it takes to direct a major complex long-term disaster recovery effort. Many of the women we have had the honor to work with have gone on to make major contributions to disaster preparedness, recovery, and mitigation at the national level. We believe that our encouragement, coaching, and advocacy helped—but we know that THEY DID IT.

With an enabling perspective, organizations can hasten recovery and restore individual lives as well as communities. Toward that goal, we offer the following suggestions for *participatory recovery*:

- Upon arrival in a community, identify local, grass-roots leaders and ask their opinion. Validate their participation and efforts. Keep index cards on each person, because the person that is too busy right now might be free later—or be able to find someone from their community network.
- Identify obstacles that might prevent such leaders from participating, such as childcare, income, skills, or confidence. Find a mentor for them, or funding such as VISTA or JTPA.
- Include local leaders on boards or other positions of influence and leadership. If their voices remain quiet, solicit their opinions to make them feel included. Verbally reward good ideas to build confidence. Educate other board members about the value of local knowledge and community-based leadership.

- Emphasize diversity by including women of all locally-present racial and ethnic groups as well as single parents, elderly women, and women with disabilities. Work toward eliminating the phrase, "They fell through the cracks." Sometimes the most marginalized groups provide keen insights into the source of the cracks and how to prevent or fix them.
- Understand that experience can be as valuable as formal education. In combination with localized knowledge, and community relationships built on trust and established networks, recovery can speed up or be improved.
- Exercise patience if you are an outsider, bearing in mind that local persons have been besieged with not only the disaster also but federal forms, rules and regulations, and media. It takes time to build trust.

BIBLIOGRAPHY

Abbott, Pamela and Roger Sapsford. 1987. *Women and Social Class.* London: Tavistock Publications.

Abraham, Margaret. 1996. "Ethnicity, Gender, and Marital Violence." *Gender and Society.* 9(4):450-468.

Acker, Joan. 1991. "Hierarchies, Jobs, Bodies: A Theory of Gendered Organizations." Pp. 162-179 in *The Social Construction of Gender*, edited by Judith Lorber and Susan Farell. Newberry Park, CA.: Sage Publications.

Adams, M.L. 1994. "There's No Place Like Home: On the Place of Identity in Feminist Politics." Pp. 345-352 in *The Woman Question*, edited by M. Evans. Newbury Park, CA: Sage.

Agarwal, Bina. 1990. "Social Security and the Family: Coping with Seasonality and Salamity in Rural India." *Journal of Peasant Studies* 17(3): 341-412.

Agarwal, Bina. 1992. "The Gender and Environment Debate: Lessons from India." *Feminist Studies* 18(1): 119-158.

Agarwal, Bina. 1997. "Environmental Action, Gender Equity and Women's Participation." *Development and Change* 28: 1-44.

Ahlburg, Dennis and Carol DeVita. 1992. "New Realities of the American Family." *Population Bulletin* 47(2). Washington, D.C.: Population Reference Bureau.

Ahmad, Tahmina. 1994. "Women and Water." Pp. 31-52 in *Rivers of Life*, edited by Kelly Haggart. London: Panos Institute; and Dhaka: Bangladesh Centre for Advanced Studies.

Ahmed, Imtiaz, Editor. 1999a. *Living With Floods: An Exercise in Alternatives*. Dhaka: University Press.

Ahmed, Syed I. 1999b. "The Dhakaites: Battling the Deluge." Pp. 25-28 in *Living With Floods: An Exercise in Alternatives*, edited by Imtiaz Ahmed. Dhaka: University Press.

Akhter, Farida. 1992. "Women Are Not Only Victims." Pp. 59-66 in *From Crisis to Development: Coping With Disasters in Bangladesh*, edited by Hameeda Hossain, Cole P. Dodge, and F. H. Abed. Dhaka: University Press.

Alexander, David. 2000. *Confronting Catastrophe*. New York: Oxford.

Ali, Mehtabunisia. 1987. "Women in Famine." Pp. 113-134 in *Famine as a Geographical Phenomenon*, edited by Bruce Currey and Graeme Hugo. Dordrecht: D. Reidel.

Alway, Joan, Linda Liska Belgrave, and Kenneth Smith. 1998. "Back to Normal: Gender and Disaster." *Symbolic Interaction* 21: 175-195.

American Psychiatric Association. 1987. *Diagnostic and Statistical Manual of Mental Disorders: DSM-III-R*. Washington, D.C.

Anam, Shaheen. 1999. "Women Coping With Floods." Pp. 29-31 in *Living With Floods: An Exercise in Alternatives*, edited by Itmiaz Ahmed. Dhaka: University Press.

Aysan, Y. and P. Oliver. 1987. *Housing and Culture after Earthquakes*. Oxford: Oxford Polytechnic.

Baisden, Barbara. 1979. "Crisis Intervention in Smaller Communities." Pp. 325-332 in *The Small City and Regional Community: Proceedings of the 1979 Conference*, edited by E. J. Miller & R. P. Wolensky. Stevens Point: University of Wisconsin.

Bari, Sona. 1992. "How Women Cope." Pp. 55-58 in *From Crisis to Development: Coping With Disasters in Bangladesh*, edited by Hameeda Hossain, Cole P. Dodge, and F. H. Abed. Dhaka: University Press.

Bari, Farzana. 1998. "Gender, Disaster and Empowerment: A Case Study from Pakistan." Pp. 125-131 in *The Gendered Terrain of Disaster: Through Women's Eyes*, edited by Elaine Enarson and Betty Morrow. Westport, CT: Greenwood.

Barnecut, Carrie. 1998. "Disaster Prone: Reflections of a Female Permanent Disaster Volunteer." Pp. 151-160 in *The Gendered Terrain of Disaster: Through Women's Eyes*, edited by Elaine Enarson and Betty Hearn Morrow. Westport, CN: Greenwood Press.

Barton, Christopher and Stuart Nishenko. 1997. "Natural Disasters: Forecasting Economic and Life Losses." *USGS Fact Sheet* <www.marine.usgs.gov/fact-sheets/nat_disasters/>:1+.

Bates, Frederick. 1982. *Recovery, Change, and Development: A Longitudinal Study of the 1972 Guatemalan Earthquake*. Athens: University of Georgia Press.

BAREPP (Bay Area Regional Earthquake Preparedness Project). 1992. *Findings and Recommendations: Symposium on Policy Issues in the Provision of Post-Earthquake Shelter and Housing*. Buffalo, NY: State University of New York at Buffalo, National Center for Earthquake Engineering Research.

Begum, Recede. 1993. "Women in Environmental Disasters: The 1991 Cyclone in Bangladesh." *Focus on Gender* 1: 34-39.

Benin, L. 1981. "An Examination of Health Data Following Two Major Earthquakes in Russia." *Disasters* 5: 142-146.

Belknap, Joanne. 1995. "Law Enforcement Officers' Attitudes about the Appropriate Responses to Woman Battering." *International Review of Victimology*. 4(1):47-62.

Belknap, Joanne. 1996. *The Invisible Woman: Gender, Crime, and Justice*. Belmont, CA: Wadsworth.

Bell, Bill D. 1978. "Disaster Impact and Response: Overcoming the Thousand Natural Shocks." *The Gerontologist* 18(6): 531-540.

Benin, L. 1981. "An Examination of Health data Following Two Major Earthquakes in Russia." *Disasters* 5(2): 142-146.

Bhatt, Mihir. 1995. *Gender and Disaster: Perspectives on Women As Victims of Disasters*. Discussion Paper, Disaster Mitigation Institute, Gulbia Tekra, Ahmedabad, India.

Bingham, A. 1989. "Floods of Aid for Bangladesh." *New Scientist* 16(93):42-46.

Blaikie, Piers, Terry Cannon, Ian Davis, and Ben Wisner. 1994. *At Risk: Natural Hazards, People's Vulnerability, and Disasters*. London: Routledge

Bolin, Robert. 1982. *Long-Term Family Recovery from Natural Disaster.* Boulder, CO: Institute of Behavioral Science, University of Colorado.

Bolin, Robert. 1986. "Disaster Impact and Recovery: A Comparison of Black and White Victims." *International Journal of Mass Emergencies and Disasters* 4(1): 35-50.

Bolin, Robert. 1993. *Household and Community Recovery after Earthquakes.* Boulder, CO: Monograph No. 56, Institute of Behavioral Science.

Bolin, Robert and Patricia Bolton. 1986. *Race, Religion, and Ethnicity in Disaster Recovery.* Boulder, CO: Institute of Behavioral Science, University of Colorado.

Bolin, Robert, Martina Jackson, and Allison Crist. 1998. "Gender Inequality, Vulnerability, and Disaster: Issues in Theory and Research." Pp. 27-44 in *The Gendered Terrain of Disaster: Through Women's Eyes*, edited by Elaine Enarson and Betty Morrow. Westport, CT: Greenwood.

Bolin, Robert C. and Daniel J. Klenow. 1982-1983. "Response of the Elderly to Disaster: An Age Stratified Analysis." *International Journal of Aging and Human Development* 16: 283-296.

Bolin, Robert C. and Lois Stanford. 1991. "Shelter, Housing, and Recovery: A Comparison of U.S. Disasters." *Disasters* 15: 25-34.

Bolin, Robert C. and Lois Stanford. 1998. "The Northridge Earthquake: Community-based Approaches to Unmet Recovery Needs." *Disasters* 22: 21-38.

Bondi, Liz. 1993. "Locating Identity Politics." Pp. 84-101 in *Place and the Politics of Identity*, edited by Michael Keith and Steve Pile. London: Routledge.

Boris, Eileen and Elisabeth Prügl (eds.). 1996. *Homeworkers in Global Perspective.* New York: Routledge.

Bourdieu, Pierre. 1986. *Distinction: A Social Critique of the Judgement of Taste.* London: Routledge and Kegan Paul.

Brown, Phil and Faith Ferguson. 1995. "'Making a Big Stink': Women's Work, Women's Relationships, and Toxic Waste Activism." *Gender and Society* 9: 145-172.

Bryson, B. 1994. "Riding out the Worst of Times: Des Moines, Iowa." *National Geographic*, 185: 82-87.

Burnam, A.M., K.B. Wells, B. Leake, and J. Landsverk. 1988. "Development of a Brief Screening Instrument for Detecting Depressive Disorders." *Medical Care* 26: 775-789.

Canino, G., M. Bravo, M. Robio-Stipec, and M. Woodbury. 1990. "The Impact of Disaster on Mental Health: Prospect and Retrospect Analysis." *Journal of Mental Health* 19: 51-69.

Carty, Linda. 1996. "Seeing Through the Eye of Difference: A Reflection on Three Research Journeys." Pp. 123-142 in *Feminism and Social Change: Bridging Theory and Practice*, edited by Heidi Gottfried. Chicago: University of Illinois Press.

Chant, Sylvia. 1996. *Gender, Urban Development and Housing*. New York: United Nations Development Program.

Chenoweth, Lesley. 1996. "Violence and Women With Disabilities." *Violence Against Women*. 2(4):391-411.

Chowdhury, A., R. Mushtaque, Abbas U. Bhuyia, A. Yusuf, and Rita Sen. 1993. "The Bangladesh Cyclone of 1991: Why So Many People Died." *Disasters* 17(4):291-304.

Chowdhury, A. M., Abbas U. Bhuyia, A. Y. Choudhury, and Rita Sen. 1993. "The Bangladesh Cyclone of 1991: Why So Many People Died?" *Disasters* 17(4):291-304.

Chowdhury, Mahjabeen. 2001. "Women's Technological Innovations and Adaptions for Disaster Mitigation: A Case Study of Charlands in Bangladesh." Presented at the Expert Group Meeting on Environmental Management and the Mitigation of Natural Disasters: A Gender Perspective, United Nations. Ankara, Turkey.

Chowdhury, Mushtaque, Yusuf Choudhury, Abbas I. K. Bhuyia, Zakir Hussain, Omar Rahman, Roger Glass, and Michael Bennish. 1992. "Cyclone Aftermath: Research and Directions for the Future." Pp. 101-33 in *From Crisis to Development: Coping With Floods in Bangladesh*, edited by Hameeda Hossain, Cole P. Dodge, and F. H. Abed. Dhaka: University Press.

Clark, Lee, and James F. Short, Jr. 1993. "Social Organization and Risk: Some Current Controversies." *Annual Review of Sociology* 19: 375-399.

Clark, Terry and Seymour Lipset. 1998. "Are Classes Dying?" In *Classic and Contemporary Readings in Sociology*, edited by Ian Marsh. Harlow, Essex: Longman.

Colina, Diana Gail. 1998. "Reflections from a Teacher and Survivor." Pp. 181-183 *in The Gendered Terrain of Disaster: Through Women's Eyes*, edited by Elaine Enarson and Betty Hearn Morrow. Westport, CT: Praeger.

Collins, Patricia Hill. 1993. "Toward a New Vision: Race, Class, and Gender as Categories of Analysis and Connection." *Race, Sex, & Class* 1(1):25-45.

Colwil, Nina L. 1997. "Women in Management: Power and Powerlessness." Pp. 186-197 in *Workplace/Women's Place*, edited by Dana Dunn. Los Angeles: Roxbury.

Connell, Robert. 1995. *Masculinities*. New South Wales: Allen and Unwin.

Cox, Helen. 1998. "Women in Bushfire Country." Pp. 133-142 in *The Gendered Terrain of Disaster: Through Women's Eyes*, edited by Elaine Enarson and Betty Hearn Morrow. Westport, CT: Praeger.

Crawford, Glinda. 1997. "Moving to Higher Ground: Seeking Wisdom from the Earth, River and Critters in the Wake of the 1997 Flood." Grand Forks, ND: unpublished manuscript, Special Collections Library, University of North Dakota.

Currie, Dawn and Anoja Wickramasinghe. 1997. "Engendering Development Theory From the Standpoint of Women." *Gender, Technology and Development* 1 (2): 247-276.

Cutrona, C., D. Russell, and J. Rose. 1986. "Social Support and Adaptation to Stress by the Elderly." *Journal of Psychology and Aging* 1: 47-54.

Cutter, Susan. 1995. "The Forgotten Casualties: Women, Children, and Environmental Change." *Global Environmental Change* 5(3): 181-194.

Cutter, Susan L., John Tiefenbacher, and William D. Solecki. 1992. "En-Gendered Fears: Femininity and Technological Risk Perception." *Industrial Crisis Quarterly* 6:5-22.

Davis, Angela. 1982. *Women, Race and Class*. London: The Women's Press.

Davis, Ian. 1978. *Shelter After Disaster*. Oxford: Oxford Polytechnic Press.

Davis, Karen. 1998. "Impact of the 1997 Red River Valley Flood on Marital Relationships." Masters Thesis, University of North Dakota.

DeParle, Jason. 1996. "Slamming the Door." *The New York Times Magazine*, October 20: 52.

DeVault, Marjorie L. 1999. *Liberating Method: Feminism and Social Research*. Philadelphia: Temple University.

DiStefano, Christine. 1990. "Dilemmas of Difference: Feminism, Modernity and Postmodernism." Pp. 63-82 in *Feminism/ Postmodernism*, edited by Linda J. Nicholson. New York: Routledge.

Dobash, R. Emerson and Russell Dobash. 1979. *Violence Against Wives*. New York: The Free Press.

Dobash, Russel P., R. Emerson Dobash, Margo Wilson, and Martin Daly. 1992. "The Myth of Sexual Symmetry in Marital Violence." *Social Problems* 39(1):71-91.

Dobash, Russell P., R. Emerson Dobash, Kate Cavanagh, and Ruth Lewis. 1998. "Separate and Intersecting Realities." *Violence Against Women*. 4(4):382-414.

Dobson, Narelle. 1993. "From Under the Mud-Pack: Women and the Charleville Floods." Symposium: Women in Emergencies and Disasters. Queensland Bureau of Emergency Services. Brisbane, Queensland.

Dobson, Narelle. 1994. "From Under the Mud-Pack: Women and the Charleville Floods." *Australian Journal of Emergency Management* 9: 11-13.

Drabek, Thomas E. 1987. *The Professional Emergency Manager: Structures and Strategies for Success*. Boulder: Institute of Behavioral Science, University of Colorado.

Drabek, Thomas E. 1994. "Disaster in Aisle 13 Revisited." Pp. 21-36 in *Disasters, Collective Behavior, and Social Organization*, edited by Russell R. Dynes and Kathleen J. Tierney. Newark, Delaware: University of Delaware Press.

Dreze, Jean and Amartya Sen. 1989. *Hunger and Public Policy*. Oxford: Clarendon Press.

Dufka, Corrine. 1988. "The Mexico City Earthquake Disaster." *Social Casework: The Journal of Contemporary Social Work* 69: 162-170.

Dunn, Dana, editor. 1997. *Workplace/Women's Place*. Los Angeles: Roxbury.

Durkin, M. S., N. Khan, and L. L. Davidson. 1993. "The Effects of a Natural Disaster on Child Behavior: Evidence for Post-Traumatic Stress." *American Journal of Public Health* 83:1549-53.

Dutton, Donald G. 1988. *The Domestic Assault of Women*. Boston: Allyn and Bacon, Inc.

Dutton, Mary Ann. 1996. "Battered Women's Strategic Response to Violence: The Role of Context." Pp. 105-124 in *Future Interventions with Battered Women and their Families*, edited by J. Edleson and Z. Eisikovits. Thousand Oaks: Sage Publications.

Dynes, Russell R. 1983. "Problems in Emergency Planning." *Energy* 8:653-660.

Dynes, Russell R. and E. L. Quarantelli. 1975. *The Role of Local Civil Defense in Disaster Planning*. Columbus, Ohio: Disaster Research Center, The Ohio State University.

Eade, Diane and Suzanne Williams (Eds.). 1995. *The Oxfam Handbook of Development and Relief*. Oxford: Oxfam UK.

Eichler, Margrit. 1995. *Change of Plans: Towards a Non-Sexist Sustainable City*. Toronto: Garamond Press.

Eldar, Reuben. 1992. "The Needs of Elderly Persons in Natural Disasters: Observations and Recommendations." *Disasters* 16: 355-357.

Enarson, Elaine. 1997. "His and Hers Disaster: New Questions for Disaster Social Science." Paper presented to the First Annual Add-On Disaster Researcher Meeting held in conjunction with the 21st Annual Natural Hazards Workshop, Denver, Colorado, July.

Enarson, Elaine. 1997. "Responding to Domestic Violence in Disaster: Guidelines for Women's Services and Disaster Practitioners." Internet paper: http://www.emforum.org/ vlibrary/980603.htm

Enarson, Elaine. 1998. "Through Women's Eyes: A Gendered Research Agenda for Disaster Social Science." *Disasters* 22: 157-173.

Enarson, Elaine. 1998a. "Battered Women in Disaster: A Case Study of Gendered Vulnerability." Paper presented at the American Sociological Association, San Francisco, August 1998.

Enarson, Elaine. 1998b. "Why Gender? Why Women?: An Introduction to Women and Disaster." Pp. 1-8 in *The Gendered Terrain of Disaster: Through Women's Eyes*, edited by Elaine Enarson and Betty Hearn Morrow. Westport, CT: Praeger.

Enarson, Elaine. 1999a. "Violence Against Women in Disasters: A Study of Domestic Violence Programs in the U.S. and Canada." *Violence Against Women* 5(7): 742-768.

Enarson, Elaine. 1999b. "Women and Housing Issues in Two U.S. Disasters: Case Studies from Hurricane Andrew and the Red River Valley Flood." *International Journal of Mass Emergencies and Disasters* 17(1): 39-64.

Enarson, Elaine. 2000. "We Will Make Meaning Out of This: Women's Cultural Responses to the Red River Valley Flood." *International Journal of Mass Emergencies and Disasters* 18(1): 39-62.

Enarson, Elaine. 2001. "What Women Do: Gendered Labor in the Red River Valley Flood." *Environmental Hazards* 3(1): 1-18.

Enarson, Elaine and Maureen Fordham. 2001. "Lines That Divide, Ties that Bind: Race, Class and Gender in Women's Flood Recovery Work in the U.S. and U.K." *Australian Journal of Emergency Management* 15(4): 43-53.

Enarson, Elaine and Betty Hearn Morrow. 1997. "A Gendered Perspective: The Voices of Women." Pp. 116-140 in *Hurricane Andrew: Ethnicity, Gender, and the Sociology of Disasters*, edited by Walter G.Peacock, Betty H. Morrow, and Hugh Gladwin. New York: Routledge.

Enarson, Elaine and Betty Hearn Morrow (eds.). 1998. *The Gendered Terrain of Disaster: Through Women's Eyes*. Westport, CT: Praeger

Enarson, Elaine and Betty Hearn Morrow. 1998. "Women Will Rebuild Miami: A Case Study of Feminist Response to Disaster." Pp. 185-200 in *The Gendered Terrain of Disaster: Through Women's Eyes*, edited by Elaine Enarson and Betty Hearn Morrow. Westport, CT: Praeger.

Enarson, Elaine and Joe Scanlon. 1999. "Gender Patterns in a Flood Evacuation: A Case Study of Couples in Canada's Red River Valley." *Applied Behavioral Science Review* 7/2.

Evans, Mary. 1997. *Introducing Contemporary Feminist Thought*. Cambridge: Polity Press.

Erez, Edna and Joanne Belknap. 1998. "In Their Own Words: Battered Women's Assessment of the Criminal Processing System's Responses." *Violence and Victims* 13(3):3-20.

Erikson, Kai. 1994. *A New Species of Trouble: Explorations in Disaster, Trauma, and Community*. New York: W. W. Norton.

Erlandson, David A., Edward L. Harris, Barbara L. Skipper and Steve D. Allen. 1993. *Doing Naturalistic Inquiry: A Guide to Methods*. Thousand Oaks, CA: Sage.

Ferguson, Peter and Bridget Byrne. 1994. *Gender and Humanitarian Assistance, a Select Bibliography*. Compiled by BRIDGE at the Institute of Development Studies for the Office of Women in Development of the U.S. Agency for International Development.

Fernando, S. and Fernando. 1996. Women Facing Disasters, Securing Life. Colombo, Sri Lanka: Duryog Nivaran/ITDG.

Ferraro, Kathleen J. and John M. Johnson 1983. "How Women Experience Battering: The Process of Victimization." *Social Problems* 30(3):325-337.

Ferree, Myra and Patricia Yancey Martin, editors. 1995. *Feminist Organizations: Harvest of the New Women's Movement*. Philadelphia, PA: Temple University Press.

Fieth, Rosemary. 1995. "Saving Lives after Disaster Strikes." *Stop Disasters* 24.

Finlay, Christine. 1998. "Floods, They're a Damned Nuisance": Women's Flood Experiences in Rural Australia." Pp. 143-149 in The Gendered Terrain of Disaster: Through Women's Eyes, edited by Elaine Enarson and Betty Hearn Morrow. Westport, CT: Praeger.

Fordham, Maureen. 1998. "Making Women Visible in Disasters: Problematising the Private Domain." *Disasters* 22: 126-143.

Fordham, Maureen. 1999. "The Intersection of Gender and Social Class in Disaster: Balancing Resilience and Vulnerability." *International Journal of Mass Emergencies and Disasters* 17(1): 15-38.

Fordham, Maureen and Lisa Clarke. 1996. *Evacuation. Technical Annex 14 for the EUROflood Project. Report to the European Union.* Enfield, Middlesex: Middlesex University Flood Hazard Research Centre.

Fordham, Maureen and Anne-Michelle Ketteridge. 1995. *Flood Disasters: Dividing the Community.* Enfield: Middlesex University Flood Hazard Research Centre.

Fordham, Maureen and Anne-Michelle Ketteridge. 1998. "Men Must Work and Women Must Weep: Examining Gender Stereotypes." Pp. 81-94 in *The Gendered Terrain of Disaster: Through Women's Eyes*, edited by Elaine Enarson and Betty Hearn Morrow. Westport, CT: Praeger.

Fothergill, Alice. 1996. "Gender, Risk and Disaster." *International Journal of Mass Emergencies and Disasters* 14: 33-56.

Fothergill, Alice. 1998. "From Sandbagging to Childcare: Women's Traditional and Nontraditional Work in a Crisis." Paper presented to the American Sociological Association, San Francisco.

Fothergill, Alice. 1999a. "Women's Roles in a Disaster." *Applied Behavioral Science Review* 7(2): 125-144.

Fothergill, Alice. 1999b. "An Exploratory Study of Woman Battering in the Grand Forks Flood Disaster: Implications for Community Responses and Policies." *International Journal of Mass Emergencies and Disasters* 17(1): 79-98.

Fothergill, Alice, Enrique Maestas, and JoAnne Darlington. 1999. "Race, Ethnicity and Disasters in the United States: A Review of the Literature." *Disasters* 23(2):156-73.

Fraser, Nancy. 1995. "From Redistribution to Recognition? Dilemmas of Justice in a 'Post-Socialist' Age." *New Left Review* 212: 68-93.

Fraser, Nancy 1997. *Justice Interruptus: Critical Reflections On The "Postsocialist" Condition.* New York: Routledge.

Friedsam, Hiram J. 1961. "Reactions of Older Persons to Disaster-Caused Losses: An Hypothesis of Relative Deprivation." *Gerontologist* 30(3): 34-37.

Friedsam, Hiram J. 1962. "Older Persons in Disaster." Pp. 151-184 in G.W. Baker and D.W. Chapman (eds.), Man and Society in Disaster. New York: Basic Books.

Fritz, Charles E. and Eli S. Marks. 1954. "The NORC Studies of Human Behavior in Disaster." *The Journal of Social Issues* 10(3): 26-41.

Fuller, Helene. 1994. "Development of Women's Policies for Emergencies and Disasters." *Australian Journal of Disaster Management* 9: 24-27.

Geipel, Robert. 1991. *Long-Term Consequences of Disasters: The Reconstruction of Friuli, Italy, in its International Context, 1976-1988.* New York: Springer-Verlag.

Gell, Fiona. 1999. "Gender Concerns in Emergencies." Pp. 37-46. in *Gender Works* by Fenella Porter, Ines Smyth, and Caroline Sweetman, editors. London: Oxfam UK.

Gelles, Richard J. 1997. *Intimate Violence in Families.* Thousand Oaks: Sage Publications.

Gibbs, Susan. 1990. "Women's Role in the Red Cross/Red Crescent." *HDI Studies on Development #1.* Geneva: Henry Dunant Institute.

Glasser, Irene. 1994. *Homelessness in Global Perspective.* New York: G. K. Hall.

Glassick, Nancy. 1999. *http://www.nwsa.org.* Accessed March 1999.

Goffman, Erving. 1959. *The Presentation of Self in Everyday Life.* New York: Doubleday Anchor.

Goffman, Erving. 1967. *Interaction Ritual: Essays on Face-to-Face Behavior.* New York: Pantheon Books.

Goldstein, Herman. 1977. *Policing a Free Society.* Cambridge, Mass.: Ballinger Publishing Co.

Gorelick, Sherry. 1996. "Contradictions of Feminist Methodology." Pp. 23-45 in *Feminism and Social Change: Bridging Theory and Practice* by Heidi Gottfried, editor. Chicago: University of Illinois Press.

Gould, Carol C. 1997. *Key Concepts in Critical Theory: Gender.* New Jersey: Humanities Press.

Green, Bonnie. 1993. "Mental Health and Disaster: Research Review." *Report for the National Institute for Mental Health.*

Guarnizo, Caroline Clarke. 1993. "Integrating Disaster and Development Assistance After Natural Disasters: NGO Response in the Third World." *International Journal of Mass Emergencies and Disasters* 11(1):111-22.

Haider, Raana, A. Atiq Rahman, and Saleemul Huq (eds.). 1991. *Cyclone '91: An Environmental and Perceptional Study.* Dhaka, Bangladesh: Bangladesh Centre for Advanced Studies.

Hanchett, Suzanne. 1997. "Women's Empowerment and the Development Research Agenda: A Personal Account From the Bangladesh Flood Action Plan." *Feminist Issues* 15(1,2):42-72.

Haque, Emdad and Mohammad Zaman. 1994. "Vulnerability and Responses to Riverine Hazards in Bangladesh: A Critique of Flood Control and Mitigation Approaches." Pp. 65-79 in *Disasters, Development and Environment,* edited by Ann Varley. New York: Wiley.

Harvey, David. 1993. "Class Relations, Social Justice and the Politics of Difference." Pp. 41-66 in *Place and the Politics of Identity,* edited by Michael Keith and Steve Pile. London: Routledge.

Hashemi, Syed H. and Imtiaz Ahmed. 1999. "The Post-Flood Period: Still Too Early to Celebrate." Pp. 145-50 in *Living With Floods: An Exercise in Alternatives,* edited by Imtiaz Ahmed. Dhaka: University Press Ltd.

Hayden, Dolores. 1981. *The Grand Domestic Revolution: A History of Feminist Designs for American Homes, Neighborhoods, and Cities.* Cambridge, MA: The MIT Press.

Hays, R. D. and C. D. Hays. 1992. "RAND 36-Item Health Survey 1.0." *RAND Health Sciences Program.* Santa Monica, CA: RAND.

Helgesen, Sally. 1990. *The Female Advantage: Women's Ways of Leadership.* New York: Doubleday.

Hena, Hasna. 1992. "Why Women Appear Vulnerable." Pp. 67-73 in *From Crisis to Development: Coping With Disasters in Bangladesh,* edited by Hameeda Hossain, Cole P. Dodge, and F. H. Abed. Dhaka: University Press Ltd.

Hewitt, Kenneth. 1995. "Excluded Perspectives in the Social Construction of Disaster." *International Journal of Mass Emergencies and Disasters* 13: 317-339.

Hewitt, Kenneth (ed.). 1983. *Interpretations of Calamity.* London: Allen and Unwin.

Hewitt, Kenneth. 1997. *Regions Of Risk: A Geographical Introduction to Disasters.* Harlow, Essex: Addison Wesley Longman.

Hobsbawn, Eric. 1996. "Identity Politics and the Left." *New Left Review* 217: 38-47.

Hochschild, Arlie Russell. 1989. *The Second Shift.* New York: Avon.

Hochschild, Arlie with Anne Machung. 1989. *The Second Shift: Working Parents and the Revolution at Home.* New York: Viking Penguin.

Hoffman, Susanna. 1998. "Eve and Adam among the Embers: Gender Patterns after the Oakland Berkeley Firestorm." Pp. 55-61 in *The Gendered Terrain of Disaster: Through Women's Eyes*, edited by Elaine Enarson and Betty Hearn Morrow. Westport, CT: Praeger.

Honeycombe, Beth. 1993. "Special Needs of Women in Emergency Situations." Presented at the Symposium: Women in Emergencies and Disasters. Queensland Bureau of Emergency Services. Brisbane, Queensland.

hooks, bell. 1982. *Ain't I a Woman?* London: Pluto Press.

hooks, bell. 1994. "Postmodern Blackness." Pp. 421-427 in *Colonial Discourse and Post-Colonial Theory: A Reader*, edited by P. Williams and L. Chrisman. New York: Harvester Wheatsheaf.

Hossain, Hameeda, Cole P. Dodge, and F. H. Abed, Editors. 1992. *From Crisis to Development: Coping With Disasters In Bangladesh.* Dhaka: University Press.

Hout, M. C. Brooks, and J. Manza. 1998. "The Persistence of Classes in Post-Industrial Societies." In *Classic and Contemporary Readings in Sociology*, edited by I. Marsh. Harlow, Essex: Longman.

Huerta, F. and R. Horton. 1978. "Coping Behavior of Elderly Flood Victims." *The Gerontologist* 18: 541-546.

Hull, Gloria T., Patricia Bell Scott and Barbara Smith, eds. 1982. *All the Women are White, All the Blacks are Men, But Some of Us Are Brave: Black Women's Studies.* NY: The Feminist Press.

Hutton, Janice R. 1976. "The Differential Distribution of Death in Disaster: A Test of Theoretical Propositions." *Mass Emergencies* 1(4): 261-266.

Ikeda, Keiko. 1995. "Gender Differences in Human Loss and Vulnerability in Natural Disasters: A Case Study from Bangladesh." *Indian Journal of Gender Studies* 2: 171-193.

Ikeda, Keiko. 1995. "Gender Differences in Human Loss and Vulnerability in Natural Disasters: A Case Study from Bangladesh." *Indian Journal of Gender Studies* 2(2):171-193.

Jiggins, J. 1986. "Women and Seasonality: Coping with Crisis and Calamity." *IDS Bulletin* 17: 9-18.

Johnson, Norris. 1987a. "Panic at 'The Who' Concert 'Stampede': An Empirical Assessment." *Social Problems* 34: 362-373.

Johnson, Norris. 1987b. "Panic and the Breakdown of Social Order: Popular Myth, Social Theory, Empirical Evidence." *Sociological Focus* 20: 171-183.

Kabeer, Naila. 1994. *Reversed Realities: Gender Hierarchies in Development Thought.* London: Verso.

Kabeer, Naila. 2001. "Conflicts Over Credit: Re-Evaluating the Empowerment Potential of Loans to Women in Rural Bangladesh." *World Development* 29(1):63-84.

Kabir, Royeka. 1995. "Bangladesh: Surviving the Cyclone is not Enough." *Stop Disasters* 24: 5-6.

Kachic, Albert S. 1998. "The Flood Forecasts and Warning Programme in Bangladesh." Pp. 67-76 in *Bangladesh Floods: Views From Home and Abroad*, edited by Mir Ali, Mozzammel Hoque, Rezaur Rahman, and Salim Rashid. Dhaka: University Press.

Kafi, Sharif. 1992. *Disasters and Destitute Women: Twelve Case Studies.* Dhaka: Bangladesh Development Partnership Centre.

Kantor, Glenda K. and Murray A. Straus. 1987. "The 'Drunken Bum' Theory of Wife Beating." *Social Problems.* 34(3):213-230.

Kerner, Donna and K. Cook. 1991. "Gender, Hunger and Crisis in Tanzania." Pp. 257-272 in *The Political Economy of African Famine*, edited by R. E. Downs, Donna Kerner, and Stephen Reyna. Philadelphia: Gordon and Breach Science Publishers.

Ketteridge, Anne-Michelle and Maureen Fordham. 1996. "Policy Alternatives: Evacuation." Pp. 10.1-10.26 in *Improving Flood Hazard Management across Europe*. Report to the European Union, edited by Edmund Penning-Rowsell. Enfield, Middlesex: Middlesex University Flood Hazard Research Centre.

Ketteridge, Anne-Michelle and Maureen Fordham. 1998. "Flood Evacuation in Two Communities in Scotland: Lessons from European Research." *International Journal of Mass Emergencies and Disasters*. 16(2):119-143.

Ketteridge, Anne-Michelle, Maureen Fordham, and Lisa Clarke. 1996. *Evacuation. Technical Annex 14 for the EUROflood Project. Report to the European Union*. Enfield, Middlesex: Middlesex University Flood Hazard Research Centre.

Khan, Amjad H. 1998. "International Water Management Issue: South Asian Perspective." Pp. 219-26 in *Bangladesh Floods: Views From Home and Abroad*, edited by Mir Ali, Mozzammel Hoque, Rezaur Rahman, and Salim Rashid. Dhaka: University Press.

Khan, M. M. I. 1991. "The Impact of Local Elites on Disaster Preparedness Planning: The Location of Flood Shelters in Northern Bangladesh." *Disasters* 15(4):340-354.

Khondker, Habibul H. 1996. "Women and Floods in Bangladesh." *International Journal of Mass Emergencies and Disasters* 14(3):281-92.

Khondker, Habibul.H. 1996. "Women and Floods in Bangladesh." *International Journal of Mass Emergencies and Disasters* 14: 281-292.

Koranci, Noray. 1995. "Turkey: What Makes Women Act." *Stop Disasters* 24.

Kozol, Jonathan. 1988. *Rachel and Her Children: Homeless Families in America*. New York: Fawcett Columbine.

Krauss, Celene. 1993. "Women and Toxic Waste Protests: Race, Class and Gender as Resources of Resistance." *Qualitative Sociology* 16(3): 247-262.

Krause, N. 1987. "Exploring the Impact of a Natural Disaster on the Health and Psychological Well-being of Older Adults." *Journal of Human Stress* Summer: 61-69.

Kreps, Gary A. 1984. "Sociological Inquiry and Disaster Research." *Annual Review of Sociology* 10: 309-330.

Krishnaraj, Maithreyi. 1997. "Gender Issues in Disaster Management: The Latur Earthquake." *Gender, Technology and Development* 1: 395-411.

Larabee, Ann. 2000. *Decade of Disaster.* Chicago: University of Illinois Press.

League of Red Cross and Red Crescent Societies. 1991. *Working With Women in Emergency Relief and Rehabilitation Programmes.* Field Studies Paper No. 2. Geneva: IFRCRC.

Leavitt, Jacqueline. 1992. "Women under Fire: Public Housing Activism in Los Angeles." *Frontier* 13: 109-130.

Lincoln, Yvonne S. and Egon Guba. 1985. *Naturalistic Inquiry.* Newbury Park, CA: Sage.

Lindsey, Linda. 1997. *Gender Roles.* Upper Saddle River, NJ: Prentice Hall.

Lipman-Blumen, Jean. 1984. *Gender Roles and Power.* Englewood Cliffs, NJ: Prentice-Hall.

Levinson, David. 1981. "Physical Punishment of Children and Wifebeating in Cross-Cultural Perspective." *Child Abuse & Neglect: The International Journal* 5:193-196.

Lorber, Judith. 1994. *Paradoxes of Gender.* New Haven: Yale University Press.

Lorber, Judith. 1998. *Gender Inequality: Feminist Theories and Politics.* Los Angeles: Roxbury.

Lorde, Audre. 1981. "An Open Letter to Mary Daly." Pp. 94-97 in *This Bridge Called My Back*, edited by C. Moraga. Boston: Persephone Press.

Lorde, Audre. 1984. *Sister Outsider.* New York: The Crossing Press.

Madakasira, S. and K. F. O'Brien. 1987. "Acute Posttraumatic Stress Disorder in Victims of a Natural Disaster." *The Journal of Nervous and Mental Disease* 175: 286-290.

Mahony, Pat and Christine Zmroczek. 1997. *Class Matters: 'Working-Class' Women's Perspectives on Social Class.* London: Taylor and Francis.

Maskrey, Andrew. 1989. *Disaster Mitigation: A Community Based Approach.* Development Guidelines No. 3. Oxford: Oxfam

Massey, Doreen. 1994. *Space, Place and Gender.* Cambridge: Polity.

Maybin, Eileen. 1994. "Rebuilding Shattered Lives." *Focus on Gender* 2: 34-36.

McDowell, Linda. 1986. "Beyond Patriarchy: A Class-Based Explanation of Women's Subordination" *Antipode* 18: 311-321.

McFarlane, A.C. 1988. "The Phenomenology of Posttraumatic Stress Disorders Following a Natural Disaster." *The Journal of Nervous and Mental Disease* 175: 22-29.

Melick, M.E. and J. N. Logue. 1985-1986. "The Effect of Disaster on the Health and Well-being of Older Women." *International Journal on Aging and Human Development* 21: 27-38.

Meyers, Diane Tietjens, editor. 1997. *Feminist Social Thought.* NY: Routledge.

Mileti, Dennis S. 1999. *Disasters by Design.* Washington D.C.: Joseph Henry Press.

Miliband, Ray. 1987. "Class Analysis." Pp. 325-346 in *Social Theory Today*, edited by Anthony Giddens and Jonathan Turner. Stanford CA: Stanford University Press.

Miller, Susan L. 1989. "Unintended Side Effects of Pro-arrest Policies and their Race and Class Implications for Battered Women." *Criminal Justice Policy Review* 3:299-317.

Milne, Gordon. 1979. "Cyclone Tracy: Psychological and Social Consequences." Pp.116-123 in *Planning for People in Natural Disasters*, edited by Joan Innes Reid. Townsville, Queensland: James Cook University of North Queensland.

Miyano, Michio, Lu Heng Jian, and Toshio Mochizuki. 1991. "Human Casualty Due to the Nankai Earthquake Tsunami, 1946." IUGG/IOC International Tsunami Symposium.

Molyneux, Maxine. 1985. "Mobilisation Without Emancipation? Women's Interests, the State and Revolution in Nicaragua." *Feminist Studies* 11: 227-54.

Momsen, Janet Henshall. 1991. *Women and Development in the Third World.* New York: Routledge.

Morrow, Betty Hearn. 1997. "Stretching the Bonds: The Families of Andrew." Pp. 141-170 in *Hurricane Andrew: Ethnicity, Gender and the Sociology of Disasters*, edited by Walter Gillis Peacock, Betty Hearn Morrow, and Hugh Gladwin. London: Routledge.

Morrow, Betty Hearn. 1999. "Identifying and Mapping Community Vulnerability." *Disasters* 23: 1-18.

Morrow, Betty Hearn and Elaine Enarson. 1994. "Making the Case for Gendered Disaster Research." Bielefeld, Germany: Paper presented at the World Congress of Sociology.

Morrow, Betty Hearn and Elaine Enarson. 1996. "Hurricane Andrew Through Women's Eyes: Issues and Recommendations." *International Journal of Mass Emergencies and Disasters* 14: 5-22.

Morrow, Betty Hearn and Brenda Phillips. 1999. "What's Gender Got to Do With It?" *International Journal of Mass Emergencies and Disasters* 17(1): 5-11.

Morrow-Jones, Hazel A. and Charles R. Morrow-Jones. 1991. "Mobility Due to Natural Disaster: Theoretical Considerations and Preliminary Analysis." *Disasters* 15(2): 126-132.

Moser, Carolyn. 1987. "Mobilization and Women's Work: Struggles for Infrastructure in Guayaquil, Ecuador." In *Women, Human Settlements and Housing*, edited by Carolyn Moser and Linda Peake. London: Tavistok.

Moser, Carolyn and Linda Peake (eds.). 1987. *Women, Human Settlements and Housing*. London: Tavistock.

Myers, Mary. 1994. "'Women and Children First': How to Introduce a Gender Strategy into Disaster Preparedness." *Focus on Gender* 2: 14-16.

Naples, Nancy, editor. 1998. *Community Activism and Feminist Politics: Organizing Across Race, Class, and Gender*. NY: Routledge.

National Women's Studies Task Force Report. *http://www.nwsa.org* Accessed March 1999.

Nasreen, Mahbuba. 1999. "Coping With Floods: Structural Measures or Survival Strategies." Pp. 32-39 in *Living With Floods: An Exercise in Alternatives*, edited by Imtiaz Ahmed. Dhaka: University Press.

Neal, David. 1998. Personal Communication.

Neal, David M. and Brenda D. Phillips. 1990. "Female-Dominated Local Social Movement Organizations in Disaster-Threat Situations." Pp.

243-255 in *Women and Social Protest*, edited by Guida West and Rhoda Lois Blumberg. New York: Oxford University Press.

Neal, David and Brenda Phillips. 1995. "Effective Emergency Management: Reconsidering the Bureaucratic Approach." *Disasters* 19: 327-337.

Neal, David M., Joseph B. Perry, Jr., and Randolph Hawkins. 1982. "Getting Ready for Blizzards: Preparation Levels in the Winter of 1977-78." *Sociological Focus* 15(1): 67-76.

Neal, David M., Joseph B. Perry, Jr., Ken Green, and Randolph Hawkins. 1988. "Patterns of Giving and Receiving Help During Severe Weather Conditions: A Research Note." *Disasters* 12(4): 366-374.

Nicholson, Linda, editor. 1997. *The Second Wave: A Reader in Feminist Theory*. NY: Routledge.

Noel, Gloria. 1998. "The Role of Women in Health-Related Aspects of Emergency Management: A Caribbean Perspective." Pp. 213-223 in *The Gendered Terrain of Disaster: Through Women's Eyes*, edited by Elaine Enarson and Betty Hearn Morrow. Westport, CN: Greenwood Press.

Norris, F. H. and S. A. Murrell. 1988. "Prior Experience as a Moderator of Disaster Impact on Anxiety Symptoms in Older Adults." *American Journal of Community* Psychology 16: 665-683.

Nunez, Ralph da Costa. 1996. *The New Poverty: Homeless Families in America*. New York: Insight Books, Plenum Press.

O'Brien, Paul and Patricia Atchison. 1998. "Gender Differentiation and Aftershock Warning Response." Pp. 173-180 in *The Gendered Terrain of Disaster: Through Women's Eyes*, edited by Elaine Enarson and Betty Hearn Morrow. Westport, CT: Praeger.

Okun, Lewis. 1986. *Woman Abuse: Facts Replacing Myths*. Albany: State University of New York Press.

Oliver-Smith, Anthony. 1986. *The Martyred City: Death and Rebirth in the Andes*. Albuquerque: University of New Mexico Press.

Oliver-Smith, Anthony. 1990. "Post-Disaster Housing Reconstruction and Social Inequality: A Challenge to Policy and Practice." *Disasters* 14: 7-19.

Ollenburger, Jane and Graham Tobin. 1998. "Women and Postdisaster Stress." Pp. 95-107 in *The Gendered Terrain of Disaster: Through Women's Eyes*, edited by Elaine Enarson and Betty Hearn Morrow. Westport, CT: Praeger.

Ollenburger, Jane C. and H. A. Moore. 1993. *A Sociology of Women: The Intersection of Patriarchy, Capitalism and Colonization*. Englewood Cliffs, N.J: Prentice Hall.

Ollenburger, Jane C. and Graham A. Tobin. 1995. "Stress Responses to the Flood Hazard in Two Rural Communities." Pp. 119-127 in *The Small City and Regional Community: Social Science and the Community*, edited by E. J. Miller and R. P. Wolensky. Stevens Point: University of Wisconsin.

OPCS. 1992. *1991 Census: Great Britain*. London: Office of Population and Statistics.

Palinkas, Lawrence, Michael Downs, John Petterson, and John Russel. 1993. "Social, Cultural, and Psychological Impacts of the Exxon Valdez Oil Spill." *Human Organization* 52(1): 1-13.

Palmer, Paula, Juanita Sanchez, Gloria Mayorga. 1993. *Taking Care of Sibo's Gifts: An Environmental Treatise From Costa Rica's Kekoldi Indigenous Reserve*. San Jose, Costa Rica: Editorama.

Parasuraman, S. 1995. "The Impact of the 1993 Latur-Osmanabad (Maharashtra) Earthquake on Lives, Livelihoods and Property." *Disasters* 19(2):156-169.

Paul, Bimal K. 1997. "Flood Research in Bangladesh in Retrospect and Prospect: A Review." *Geoforum* 28(2):121-31.

Paul, Bimal K. 1999. "Women's Awareness of and Attitudes Towards the Flood Action Plan (FAP) of Bangladesh." *Environmental Management* 23(1):103-14.

Peacock, Walter Gillis, Betty Hearn Morrow and Hugh Gladwin (eds.). 1997. *Hurricane Andrew: Ethnicity, Gender and the Sociology of Disasters*. London: Routledge.

Peacock, Walter, C. Killian, and F. Bates. 1987. "The Effects of Disaster Damage and Housing Aid on Household Recovery Following the 1976 Guatemalan Earthquake." *International Journal of Mass Emergencies and Disasters* 5: 68-88.

Peacock, Walter Gillis and Kathleen Ragsdale. 1997. "Social Systems, Ecological Networks and Disasters: Toward A Socio-Political Ecology of Disasters." Pp. 20-35 in *Hurricane Andrew: Ethnicity, Gender and the Sociology of Disasters*. London: Routledge.

Pearl, Daniel and Michael M. Phillips. 2001. "Small Change." *Wall Street Journal* Nov. 27:1A+.

Penning-Rowsell, Edmund (ed.). 1996. *Improving Flood Hazard Management across Europe. Report to the European Union.* Enfield, Middlesex: Middlesex University Flood Hazard Research Centre.

Penning-Rowsell, Edmund and Maureen Fordham. 1994. *Floods Across Europe: Flood Hazard Assessment, Modeling and Management.* London: Middlesex University Press.

Perry, Ronald W. and Mushkatel, A. H. 1984. *Disaster Management: Warning Response and Community Relocation.* Westport, CT: Quorum Books.

Phifer, James F. and F. H. Norris. 1989. "Psychological Symptoms in Older Adults Following Natural Disaster: Nature, Timing, Duration and Course." *Journal of Gerontology* 44: S207-S217.

Phillips, Anne. 1997. "From Inequality to Difference: A Severe Case of Displacement?" *New Left Review* 224: 143-153.

Phillips, Brenda. 1990. "Gender as a Variable in Emergency Response." Pp.84-90 in *The Loma Prieta Earthquake: Studies of Short-Term Impacts,* edited by Robert Bolin. Boulder, CO: Institute for Behavioral Science, University of Colorado.

Phillips, Brenda D. 1991. *Post-Disaster Sheltering and Housing of Hispanics, the Elderly and the Homeless.* Final Report to the National Science Foundation. Dallas, TX: Southern Methodist University.

Phillips, Brenda D. 1993. "Cultural Diversity in Disasters: Sheltering, Housing, and Long Term Recovery." *International Journal of Mass Emergencies and Disasters* 11: 99-110.

Phillips, Brenda D. 1993. "Disasters and the Elderly: Past, Present, and Future Research." Unpublished manuscript.

Phillips, Brenda D. 1995. "Shelter and Housing of Elderly SRO Disaster Victims: Organizational Response in the Loma Prieta Earthquake." Unpublished manuscript.

Phillips, Brenda D. 1996a. "Gender and Disasters." Unpublished manuscript.

Phillips, Brenda D. 1996b. "Sheltering and Housing Low Income and Minority Groups after the Loma Prieta Earthquake." In the U.S. Geological Survey Report on the Loma Prieta Earthquake.

Phillips, Brenda D. 1996. "Creating, Sustaining, and Losing Place: Homelessness in the Context of Disaster." *Humanity & Society* 20: 94-101.

Phillips, Brenda D. 1997. "Qualitative Methods and Disaster Research." *International Journal of Mass Emergencies and Disasters* 15(1): 179-195.

Phillips, Brenda and Dave Neal. 1996. "Enabling and Empowering Women for a Sustainable Future." Unpublished manuscript.

Pleck, Elizabeth. 1987. *Domestic Tyranny: The Making of American Social Policy Against Family Violence from Colonial Times to the Present*. New York: Oxford.

Poulshock, S. Walter and Elias S. Cohen. 1975. "The Elderly in the Aftermath of a Disaster." *The Gerontologist* 15(4): 357-361.

Prandy, Ken. 1990. "The Revised Cambridge Scale of Occupations." *Sociology* 24: 629-655.

Quarantelli, E. L. 1982. *Sheltering and Housing After Major Community Disasters: Case Studies and General Conclusions*. Columbus, OH: The Ohio State University, Disaster Research Center.

Quarantelli, E.L. 1985. "The Functioning of the Local Emergency Services Offices in Disasters." Final Report No. 32. Newark, Delaware: Disaster Research Center, University of Delaware.

Quarantelli, E.L. 1994. "Looting and Antisocial Behavior in Disasters," Paper #205, Disaster Research Center, University of Delaware.

Quarantelli, E.L. 1998. *What is a Disaster? Perspectives on the Question*. London: Routledge.

Radloff, L. S. 1977. "The CED-D Scale: A Self-report Depression Scale for Research in the General Population." *Applied Psychological Measurement* 1: 385.

Radner, Joan Newlon, editor. 1993. *Feminist Messages: Coding in Women's Folk Culture*. Chicago: University of Illinois Press.

Rahman, Saidur. 1992. "The First Five Days." Pp. 13-25 in *From Crisis to Development: Coping With Disasters in Bangladesh*, edited by Hameeda Hossain, Cole P. Dodge, and F. H. Abed. Dhaka: University Press.

Rajan, S. Ravi. 1999. "Bhopal: Vulnerability, Routinization, and the Chronic Disaster." Pp. 257-277 in *The Angry Earth* by Anthony Oliver-Smith and Susanna Hoffman, editors. NY: Routledge.

Rantalaiho, Liisa and Tuula Heiskanen, editors. 1997. *Gendered Practices in Working Life*. New York: St. Martin's Press.

Rashid, Sabina Faiz. 2000. "The Urban Poor in Dhaka City: Their Struggles and Coping Strategies During the Floods of 1998." *Disasters* 24(3):240-253.

Rashid, Sabina Faiz and Stephanie Michaud. 2000. "Female Adolescents and Their Sexuality: Notions of Honour, Shame, Purity and Pollution During the Floods." *Disasters* 24(1):54-70.

Reinharz, Shulamit. 1992. *Feminist Methods in Social Research*. New York: Oxford University Press.

Reskin, Barbara and Irene Padavic. 1994. *Women and Men at Work*. Thousand Oaks, CA: Pine Forge Press.

Rivers, J.P.W. 1982. "Women and Children Last: An Essay on Sex Discrimination in Disasters." *Disasters* 6: 256-267.

Rivers, J.P.W. 1982. "Women and Children Last: An Essay on Sex Discrimination in Disasters." *Disasters* 6: 256-267.

Robertson, Doone. 1998. "Women in Emergency Management: An Australian Perspective." Pp. 201-206 in *The Gendered Terrain of Disaster: Through Women's Eyes*, edited by Elaine Enarson and Betty Hearn Morrow. Westport, CN: Greenwood Press.

Robinson, John P. 1988. "Who's Doing the Housework." *American Demographics* 10: 24-28.

Rocheleau, Dianne, Barbara Thomas-Slayter and Esther Wangarai, editors. 1996. *Feminist Political Ecology: Global Issues and Local Experiences*. London: Routledge.

Rodda, Annabel. 1994. *Women and the Environment*. London: Zed Books.

Rose, Gillian. 1993. *Feminism and Geography*. Minneapolis: University of Minnesota Press.

Rossi, Alice, editor. 1973. *The Feminist Papers: From Adams to deBeauvoir*. Boston: Northeastern University Press.

Rowbotham, Sheila. 1973. "Woman's Consciousness, Man's World." Pp. 93-97 in *Feminisms: A Reader*, edited by Maggie Humm. New York: Harvester Wheatsheaf.

Rozario, Santi. 1977. "Disasters' and Bangladeshi Women." Pp. 255-268 in *Gender and Catastrophe*, edited by Ronit Lentin. London: Zed.

Russell, D.W. and C. E. Cutrona. 1991. "Social Support, Stress and Depressive Symptoms among the Elderly: Test Of A Process Model." *Journal of Psychology and Aging* 6: 190-201.

Saunders, Peter. 1990. *Social Classification and Stratification*. London: Routledge.

Scanlon, Joseph. 1996. "Human Behavior in Disaster: The Relevance of Gender." *Australian Journal of Emergency Management* 2-7.

Scanlon, Joseph. 1998. "The Perspective of Gender: A Missing Element in Disaster Response." Pp. 45-51 in *The Gendered Terrain of Disasters* edited by Elaine Enarsona nd Betty Morrow. Westport, CT: Greenwood.

Schechter, Susan. 1981. *Women and Male Violence: The Visions and Struggles of the Battered Women's Movement*. Boston: South End Press.

Schmittroth, Linda (ed.). 1995. *Statistical Record of Women Worldwide*. New York: International Thomson Publishing Company.

Schroeder, Richard A. 1987. "Gender Vulnerability to Drought: A Case Study of the Hausa Social Environment." Natural Hazards Research Working Paper #58. Boulder, CO: NHRAIC.

Schwartz, Martin. 1988. "Ain't Got No Class: Universal Risk Theories of Battering." *Contemporary Crises* 12:373-392.

Seager, Joni. 1996. "Hysterical Housevies and Other Mad Women: Grassroots Environmental Organizing in the United States." Pp. 271-283 in *Feminist Political Ecology.*, Dianne Rochaeleau et al, editors. London: Routledge.

Sen, Amartya. 1988. "Family and Food: Sex Bias in Poverty." Pp. 453-472 in *Rural Poverty in South Africa,* edited by T. N. Srinavaran and P. K. Bardham. New York: Columbia University Press.

Sen, Amartya K. 1990. "Gender and Cooperative Conflict." Pp. 123-149 in *Persistent Inequalities: Women and World Development*, edited by Irene Tinker. Oxford: Oxford University Press.

Serrat Viñas, Carolina. 1998. "Women's Disaster Vulnerability and Response to the Colima Earthquake." Pp. 161-172 in *The Gendered Terrain of Disaster*, edited by Elaine Enarson and Betty Hearn Morrow. Westport, CT: Praeger.

Shahjahan, M. 1998. "Flood Disaster Management in Deltaic Plain Integrated With Rural Development." Pp. 39-53 in *Bangladesh Floods: Views From Home and Abroad*, edited by Mir Ali, Mozzammel Hoque, Rezaur Rahman, and Salim Rashid. Dhaka: University Press.

Siddiqui, Hanif A. 2001. "Increasing Repression Against Women: A Serious Threat to Humanity." <independent-bangladesh. com/news/mar/30/30032001cp.htm#1>.

Skeggs, Beverley. 1997. *Formations of Class and Gender*. London: Sage.

Smith, Dorothy. 1987. *The Everyday World as Problematic: A Feminist Sociology*. Boston: Northeastern University Press.

Smith, Dorothy. 1996. "Contradictions for Feminist Social Scientists." Pp. 46-49 *in Feminism and Social Change*, edited by Heidi Gottfried. Chicago: University of Illinois Press.

Sobsey, R. 1994. *Violence in the Lives of People with Disabilities: The End of Silent Acceptance?* Baltimore, MD: Brookes.

Solomon, S. D., E. M. Smith, L. M. Robins, and R. L. Fischbach. 1987. "Social Involvement as a Mediator of Disaster-Induced Stress." *Journal of Applied Social Psychology* 8: 376-392.

Solomon, S., D. A. Regier, and J. D.Burke. 1989. "Role of Perceived Control in Coping with Disaster." *Journal of Clinical Psychology* 8: 376-392.

Spelman, Elisabeth V. 1988. Selection 16 from "Inessential Woman." Pp. 148-154 in *Gender: Key Concepts in Critical Theory*, edited by C. C. Gould. New Jersey: Humanities Press.

Staff Reporter. 2001. "Timely Warning Can Save Thousands of Lives From Cyclonic Disaster." Independent(Jan 9):<independent-bangladesh.com/news/jan/09-09012001mt.htm#7>.

Stake, Robert. 1994. "Case Studies," Chapter 14, pp. 236-247 in *Handbook of Qualitative Research*, edited by N. Denzin and Y. Lincoln. Thousand Oaks, CA: Sage Publications.

Steady, Filomena Chioma. 1993. "Gender, Shelter, and Sustainable Development." Pp. 301-317 in *Women and Children First: Environment, Poverty, and Sustainable Development*, edited by Filomena Chioma Steady. Rochester, Vermont: Schenkman Books.

Steady, Filomina Chioma. 1998. "Gender Equality and Ecosystem Balance." *Race, Gender and Class* 6(1): 13-32.

Steele, Fiona, Sajeda Ami, and Ruchira T. Naved. 2001. "Savings/Credit Group Formation and Change in Contraception." *Demography* 38(2):267-82.

Steinglass, P. and E. Gerrity. 1990. "Natural Disasters and Post-Traumatic Stress Disorder: Short-Term versus Long-Term Recovery in Two Disaster Affected Communities." *Journal of Applied Psychology* 20: 1746-1765.

Stewart, A.L. and J. E. Ware (eds.). 1992. *Measuring Functioning and Well Being: The Medical Outcome Study Approach*. Durham, NC: Duke University Press.

Stone-Meiatore, Shari. 2000. "Chandra Mohanty and the Revaluing of Experience." Pp. 110-127 in *Decentering the Center*, Uma Narayan and Sandra Harding, editors. Bloomington, IN: Indiana University Press.

Stop Disasters. 1995. "Building a Culture of Prevention." *Stop Disasters*, No. 24. Published by United Nations International Decade for Natural Disaster Reduction.

Sweetman, Caroline (ed.). 1996. *Women and Urban Settlements*. Oxford: Oxfam.

Taylor, Dorceta. 1997. "Women of Color, Environmental Justice, and Ecofeminism." Pp. 38-81 in *Ecofeminism: Women, Culture, Nature*, edited by Karen Warren. Bloomington: Indiana University Press.

Threlfall, Monica. 1996. *Mapping the Women's Movement*. London: Verso.

Thompson, Paul M. and Parvin Sultana. 1996. "Distributional and Social Impacts of Flood Control in Bangladesh." *The Geographical Journal* 162(1):1+.

Thomson, Rosemarie G. 1994. "Redrawing the Boundaries of Feminist Disability Studies." *Feminist Studies*. 20: 583-595.

Tierney, Kathleen J. 1989. "Improving Theory and Research on Hazard Mitigation: Political Economy and Organizational Perspectives." *International Journal of Mass Emergencies and Disasters* 7(3): 367-396.

Tinker, Irene (ed.). 1990. *Persistent Inequalities: Women and World Development*. New York: Oxford University Press.

Tobin, Graham A. and B. E. Montz. 1994. *The Great Midwestern Floods of 1993*. Fort Worth, TX: Saunders Press.

Tobin, Graham A. and Ollenburger, Jane C. 1994. "An Examination of Stress in a Flood-prone Environment." Papers and Proceedings of Applied Geography Conferences 17: 74-81.

Tobin, Graham A. and Jane C. Ollenburger. 1996. "Predicting Levels of Postdisaster Stress in Adults Following the 1993 Floods in the Upper Midwest." *Environment and Behavior* 28: 340-357.

Tokle, Manisha. 1994. "Some Problems Women are Facing." Pp. 37-38 in *Women and Emergencies*, edited by Bridget Walker. Oxford, UK: Oxfam.

Tong, Rosemarie. 1984. *Women, Sex, and the Law*. Totawa, NJ: Rowman & Allanheld.

Tong, Rosemarie. 1998. *Feminist Thought*, second edition. Boulder, CO; Westview.

Turner, Elizabeth Hayes. 1997. "After the Storm: Women, Public Policy, and Power." Pp. 187-228 in *Women, Culture, and Community: Religion and Reform in Galveston*, 1880-1920. New York: Oxford.

United Nations Centre for Human Settlements (Habitat). 1990. *Towards a Strategy for the Full Participation of Women in All Phases of the United Nations Global Strategy for Shelter to the Year 2000*. Nairobi, Kenya.

U.S. Bureau of the Census. 1997. *Statistical Abstract of the United States, 1996*. Washington DC: Government Printing Office.

U.S. Bureau of the Census. 1997. "Historical Poverty Tables—Families, (Table) 4. Poverty Status, by Type of Family, Presence of Related Children, Race and Hispanic Origin: 1959-1997;" <http://blue.

census.gov/hhes/poverty/histopov/hstpov4.html; accessed: 8 January 1998.

U.S. Bureau of the Census. 2001. *Statistical Abstract of the United States, 2001*. Washington, DC: Government Printing Office.

U.S. Department of Labor. 2000. Women's Earnings as Percent of Men's, 1979-1999. [Online]. Available *http://www.dol. gov/dol/wb/public/wb_pubs/achart.htm*.

Usher, Ann. 1994. "After the Forest Died: AIDS as Ecological Collapse in Thailand." Pp. 10-42 in *Close to Home*, edited by Vandana Shiva. London: Earthscan Publications Ltd.

Valdes, Helena Molin. 1995. "Expanding Women's Participation in Disaster Prevention and Mitigation: Some Approaches from Latin America and the Caribbean." *Stop Disasters* 24.

Van Willigen, Marieke. 2001. "Do Disasters Affect Individuals' Psychological Well-Being? An Over-Time Analysis of the Effect of Hurricane Floyd on Men and Women in Eastern North Carolina." *International Journal of Mass Emergencies and Disasters* 19(1):59-84.

Varley, Anne (ed.). 1994. *Disasters, Development and Environment*. Chichester: Wiley.

Vaughan, Megan. 1987. *The Story of an African Famine: Gender and Famine in Twentieth Century*. Malawi: Cambridge University Press.

Von Kotze, Astrid and Ailsa Holloway. 1996. *Reducing Risk: Participatory Learning Activities for Disaster Mitigation in Southern Africa*. Cape Town, South Africa: International Federation of Red Cross and Red Crescent Societies and Department of Adult Community Education, University of Natal.

Walby, Sylvia. 1990. *Theorizing Patriarchy*. Oxford: Blackwell.

Walker, Bridget (ed.). 1994. "Editorial." Pp. 2-6 in *Women and Emergencies*, edited by Bridget Walker. Oxford,UK: Oxfam.

Walker, Lenore E. 1979. *The Battered Woman*. New York: Harper & Row.

Wangari, Esther, Barbara Thomas-Slayter, and Diane Rocheleau. 1996. "Gendered Visions for Survival: Semi-arid Regions in Kenya." Pp. 127-154 in *Feminist Political Ecology*, by Esther Wangari et al, editors. London: Routledge.

Ware, J. E. and C. D. Sherbourne. 1992. "The MOS 36-Item Short Form Health Survey (SF-36): I. Conceptual Framework and Item Selection." *Medical Care* 30: 473-483.

Warren, Karen, editor. 1997. *Ecofeminism: Women, Culture, Nature.* Bloomington IN: Indiana University Press.

Weber, Max. 1921/1968. *Economy and Society*, 3 vols. Totowa, NJ: Bedminister Press.

Weestergaard, John and Henrietta Resler. 1976. Class in a Capitalist Society: A Study of Contemporary Britain. Harmondsworth, Middlesex: Penguin Books.

Wegner, M., L. Boone, and T. Cochrane (eds.). 1993. *Iowa's Lost Summer.* Ames: Iowa State University and the Des Moines Register and Tribune Co. 108.

Wenger, Dennis E., E. L. Quarantelli, and Russell R. Dynes. 1987. "Disaster Analysis: Emergency Management Offices and Arrangements." Final Report No. 34. Newark, Delaware: Disaster Research Center, University of Delaware.

Wiest, Raymond E., Jane Mocellin, and Thandiwe Motisis. 1992. *The Needs of Women and Children in Disasters and Emergencies.* Winnipeg: Disaster Research Unit, University of Manitoba.

Wiest, Raymond E. 1998. "A Comparative Perspective on Household, Gender, and Kinship in Relation to Disaster." Pp. 63-79 in *The Gendered Terrain of Disaster: Through Women's Eyes*, edited by Elaine Enarson and Betty Hearn Morrow. Connecticut: Praeger.

Wilson, Jennifer. 1999. "Professionalization and Gender in Local Emergency Management." *International Journal of Mass Emergencies and Disasters* 17(1):111-22.

Wilson, Jennifer. 2001. *The State of Emergency Management 2000: The Process of Emergency Management Professionalization in the United States and Florida.* Lakeland, FL: Dissertation.com.

Wilson, Jennifer, Brenda D. Phillips, and David M. Neal. 1998. "Domestic Violence after Disaster." Pp. 115-122 in *The Gendered Terrain of Disaster: Through Women's Eyes*, edited by E. Enarson and B.H.Morrow. Westport, Connecticut: Praeger.

Wilson, Jennifer and Arthur Oyola-Yemaiel. 1998. "Emergent Coordinative Groups and Women's Response Roles in the Central

Florida Tornado Disaster, February 23, 1998." Quick Response
Report #110. Boulder, CO: Natural Hazards Application and
Information Research Center. [Online] Available, *http://www.
colorado.edu/hazards/qr/qr110/qr110.html*

Witz, Anne and Mike Savage. 1992. "The Gender of Organizations."
Pp. 3-62 in *Gender and Bureaucracy*, edited by Mike Savage and
Anne Witz. Oxford: Blackwell.

Wood, D. P and M. L. Cowan. 1991. "Crisis Intervention following
Disasters: Are We Doing Enough? (A Second Look)." *American
Journal of Emergency Medicine* 9: 598-602.

Wraith, Ruth. 1997. "Women in Emergency Management: Where Are
They?" *Australian Journal of Emergency Management* 9-11.

Yin, Robert. 1984. *Case Study Research*. Beverly Hills: Sage Publications.

Young, Iris Marion. 1990. "The Ideal of Community and the Politics
of Difference." In *Feminism/Postmodernism*, edited by Linda J.
Nicholson. New York: Routledge.

Zilberg, N. J., D. S. Weiss, and M. J. Horowitz. 1982. "Impact of Event
Scale: A Cross-Validation Study and Some Empirical Evidence
Supporting a Conceptual Model of Stress Response Syndromes."
Journal of Consulting and Clinical Psychology 50: 407-414.

INDEX

Capitalized words indicate major chapter headings

G

W